# SEEING
# RED

Also by Dan Shaughnessy

*The Curse of the Bambino*

*Ever Green*

*One Strike Away*

# SEEING RED

## The **Red Auerbach** Story

## DAN SHAUGHNESSY

Adams Publishing

HOLBROOK, MASSACHUSETTS

Published by Adams Media Corporation
260 Center Street, Holbrook, MA 02343
by arrangement with Crown Publishers, Inc.

ISBN: 1-55850-548-2

Printed in the United States of America

J  I  H  G  F  E  D  C  B  A

Library of Congress Cataloging-in-Publication Data
Shaughnessy, Dan.
Seeing Red : the Red Auerbach story / Dan Shaughnessy.
          p.        cm.
Originally published:  New York : Crown, c1994.
Includes bibliographical references and index.
ISBN 1-55850-548-2 (pbk.)
1. Auerbach, Arnold, 1917–  . 2. Basketball coaches—United States—
Biography. 3. Basketball (Boston Celtics team) I. Title.
[GV884.A8S53   1995]
796.323'092—dc20
     [B]                    95-36951
                           CIP

Design by Leonard Henderson

*This book is available at quantity discounts for bulk purchases.
For information, call 1-800-872-5627.*

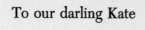

To our darling Kate

# CONTENTS

# LETTER FROM THE AUTHOR

I LIKE THE SMELL OF CIGAR SMOKE.

My father smoked cigars. In the years before I was born, he gave up cigarettes on doctor's orders and switched to Dutch Masters. He often smoked cigars in the car. On Saturday mornings we'd drive to the town dump together and Dad's cigar exhaust would cloud the front seat space. I loved it. Still do. I've never smoked anything in my life, but I've always liked secondhand smoke, particularly cigar fumes. This peculiar pleasure is handy if you're around Red Auerbach for any period of time. Smoke gets in your eyes.

I grew up in the tiny town of Groton, Massachusetts, in the late fifties and early sixties. Our house was only about a half mile from the local high school. Lying in bed on winter nights, I could see the gym lights across a line of snow-topped evergreen trees. My older brother was a high school basketball star and on the school nights when I couldn't go to the games, I'd lie in bed, look out the frosted window and imagine the sights and sounds inside the magic hardwood barn. In bitter New England January, the high school gym on Friday nights always was the warmest place in town. I was introduced to basketball in those small, loud gyms where the bounce of the ball echoed off the walls. You could see the players sweat, could smell the sticky stuff they sprayed on their hands.

This was a privileged time to be a young basketball fan, because our regional professional team, always the role model for youngsters taking up any sport, happened to be the greatest basketball team of all time. We grew up loving the game, and we wanted to be just like the Boston Celtics. The Celtics always won. They had the best players and they had the best coach.

Red Auerbach was the coach. He was the old, round, bald guy

who always was screaming at the referees, particularly Mendy Rudolph. He kept a program rolled up in his left hand. He stressed teamwork. His players sacrificed for the greater good of the team. The Celtics didn't have a scoring leader—their best player wasn't even much of a shooter. When victory was well in hand, the crusty coach lit his cigar.

He was the ultimate authority figure. He was the boss. His players did what their coach told them to do, and they won. Probably young basketball players in New England in the 1960s listened to their coaches more intently than players elsewhere. We had seen the master. We understood teamwork and winning.

No doubt we were spoiled by Auerbach's teams. One championship followed the next. There was no interruption. If you were a young New England basketball fan during the years 1957 to 1969, the NBA championship was taken as a birthright. The Celtics simply retired the trophy. You knew it was spring when snow melted, forsythia bloomed, the Red Sox stumbled through the Cactus Circuit and Red lit the cigar. It seemed that Auerbach's Celtics usually beat the Los Angeles Lakers with pathetic ease to win the finals. I was a teenager before I learned that the Celtics don't automatically win the NBA championship every spring.

Happily, writing about sports became my life's work, and in 1982 I started covering the Celtics as a full-time beat reporter for the *Boston Globe*. Often, in the newspaper business, one is disillusioned when first encountering heroes of one's youth. Not this time. Seeing Auerbach up close was even more fun than watching him from the grimy upper-deck heavens of the Boston Garden. Red and I had a few battles, but he was fair and anybody could see he'd earned his status as a legend-in-residence.

By the time I came around, Red was involved only in "big picture" decisions. He was no longer running the day-to-day operation of the ball club. You didn't have to make appointments to see him. I'd stop by his office late in the afternoon before a game and secretary Mary Faherty would send me in. Red would invite me to watch the conclusion of his favorite television show, "Hawaii Five-O." An hour later, my notebook would be pretty empty, and my clothes smelled like smoke, but I'd seen Jack Lord get his man.

The time with Red was fun. He was old-fashioned and uncomplicated. He saw everybody either as "with us or against us," and I'm not sure he ever knew where to put me. My colleague Will McDonough—a close friend of Red's—had given me an endorsement. This proved to be a blessing. Some of my odd questions, probes and critiques probably were forgiven because Willie told Red I was okay.

Editor Dick Marek first suggested this Auerbach biography in the winter of 1992–1993. I was dubious, because Red has written three autobiographies, a fundamentals book and a tome on business management. Auerbach's been telling a lot of the same stories over and over again for forty years. Like a veteran stand-up comic from the Catskills, he tells one story and it automatically leads to another. But as the demolition ball hangs over the old (1928) Boston Garden, and as the Celtics stagger through their longest championship drought since the pre–Bill Russell days, it's still fascinating to walk through Red's life one more time—viewing the incredible growth of the NBA along the way.

Red was a little suspicious when I first told him about this project. It is his way.

"I've known him since I was a little kid, and that's the way he takes things," said Celtic general manager Jan Volk. "His first reaction is 'no,' then 'maybe,' then a week later he comes at you with the same thing like it's his idea."

With or without Red's cooperation, the book was going to be written, but I was hoping to get as much access as possible. When I asked if he'd agree to be interviewed for the book, he thought about it for a moment, then said, "Oh, what the heck. Go ahead. I got nothing to hide."

A few weeks later, when I called to arrange an early interview, Red had second thoughts. "What's this book going to be about, anyway?" he asked.

I told him it would be like any biography. It was going to be about the life of a man. Suspicious Red snapped, "The only thing I don't want to get involved in is what that asshole did to Bobby Knight."

Auerbach was referring to John Feinstein's well-crafted bestseller

*A Season on the Brink*, a landmark book which did not portray University of Indiana basketball coach Knight as Knight would have liked. Knight is a close friend of Auerbach's.

As time went on, Auerbach was more receptive to the project. My wife and I went to his apartment in Washington in April 1993. During a lengthy interview in his home, I asked him if he ever thought about his own mortality. "I don't even talk about it," he said. "The thing I enjoy the most at this point is that I have my marbles, that I can still keep modern on my appreciation of the game and talent. I still see things that I talk over with [Celtic CEO] Dave [Gavitt] and [Celtic coach] Chris [Ford]. When it gets to the point when I lose that—and I'd be the first to admit it—I'll say I've lost it, and when it comes to that, then I'll totally retire."

Less than a month after that conversation, at the season-ending annual Celtic breakup dinner, Auerbach experienced chest pains and felt sweaty. After the dinner, he went home to his Prudential Center apartment, but the pain returned, and after calling his physician he took a cab to Massachusetts General Hospital. He spent the next eleven days at Mass General, where he underwent two angioplasties—procedures to clear clogged coronary arteries. On June 18, 1993, Auerbach underwent a six-hour, quintuple-bypass operation. He was weak for a long time after that—weak and somewhat frustrated. Convalescence is hell when you've been doing everything you want, when you want, for seventy-six years. Now he is back. No longer very involved in the decisions that govern the Celtics, he still watches the action from Loge 1, row seven, seat one at midcourt. Officially speaking, he is still president of the Boston Celtics. He is the lion in winter.

On the path to success, Auerbach has left a trail of angry opponents, referees, general managers, sportswriters and ballplayers' wives. He's never been particularly gracious in defeat or in victory. He can be sexist, crude and vengeful. He's a good friend and a bad enemy. He hasn't been actively running the Celtics in quite some time, but Boston fans, players and even front-office personnel still find comfort in his presence. Former Celtic great Dave Cowens once said he always felt things were going to be okay if he saw Red hanging around.

Auerbach comes from a fast-fading generation of accountability. He was raised in an era when men took responsibility for their actions. His life has been about competition and winning, and he's never content. There's always another game. That's what the victory cigar was about. The game at hand was over, and Auerbach was already thinking about the next one. While you read his story, Red is somewhere puffing on a stogie, plotting his next move, thinking about the next game.

My thanks go out to friend/agent Meg Blackstone, who put me together with Dick Marek, Steve Topping and the folks at Crown; NBA publicists Brian McIntyre, Terry Lyons and Pete Steber; Celtic publicists Jeff Twiss and Dave Zaccaro; Ed McKee, Sam Brogna, Clif Keane, Will McDonough, Bob Ryan, Peter May, Jackie MacMullan, Don Skwar, Sean Mullin, Jan Volk, Tod Rosensweig, Joe Fitzgerald, Ken Gloss, Roger Barry, Bill Tanton, Dave Smith, Vince Doria, Bob Pettit, Randy Auerbach, Nancy Collins, Dorothy Auerbach, Larry Bird, Dick Johnson, Wayne Patterson, Bob Cousy, former coaches John P. Fahey and Bill Mahoney, John Iannacci, John Horn, Steve Sheppard, Stephen Stills, Stan Grossfeld, Kevin Dupont, Lesley Visser, Bob Lobel, Alan Miller, Bobby Knight, Scott Thurston . . . and of course, Arnold "Red" Auerbach.

Authors need understanding families, and I'm lucky to have the support of all the Shaughnessys and Wits in Massachusetts, New Hampshire, Michigan, Arizona, Colorado, North Carolina and Kentucky. Sarah, Kate and Sam are beginning to understand why Dad is so busy most of the time. Most of all I am thankful for the support and encouragement of Marilou, who—legend has it—went to Michigan State when Magic was there and never saw him play.

# FOREWORD BY LARRY BIRD

I FIRST HEARD OF RED AUERBACH WHEN I SAW HIM ON THOSE King Edward cigar commercials. I never really saw him coach, but I had heard of him when I started to play basketball. The first time I saw him was in Atlanta, when I was playing on an All-Star team. I didn't know who it was, but then all of a sudden, it was like, "Boom, there's Red Auerbach." Later he and Dave Cowens came to Cincinnati to watch my Indiana State team play.

The only thing I really remember about that meeting was Red saying, "Well, when you guys get put out of the playoffs, you can come up to Boston and finish the year with us. We'll sign you and then you can play for us." He was trying to tell me that they were really doing me a favor by drafting me and by signing me. We were in our second round and he thought after we got beat, I could go with the Celtics. I thought it was kind of weird that he was talking about me becoming a Celtic when we weren't even done with our tournament yet.

When I went to Boston to sign my first professional contract, Red was into his thing. He and my agent, Bob Woolf, were going at each other. I was thinking, "Hey, if that's the way they want to act, let me get out of their way." I figured I'd just go back home and finish school and go fishing. I just didn't know how the NBA worked. They either wanted me or they didn't. I learned that Red's very good at acting like he's real mad at somebody, and once everything's settled, everything's fine. I'm good at that, too. Cuss somebody for two hours and then two hours later say, "We were just mad at each other."

Finally, I came to Boston to play for the Celtics. Red was involved. He would pull me aside and tell me what I should be doing and what I was doing wrong. I used to follow my shot all the time. I used to be a good offensive rebounder. But Red kept telling me, "Hey, every time you go toward that basket, your man's going the other way." And I was thinking that the guard was supposed to pick that guy up. Basketball [in the NBA] was completely different. From that point on, I never was a very good offensive rebounder. I think he was worried about my speed.

He'd tell me a lot of things. He really helped me out. I had certain moves when I was in college. He said I was going to have to adjust and learn to do other things, like go in the middle, and go to my left, and switch over, and go back to my right. He told me that if I kept doing the same things they'd get on to it and play me a certain way. He told me they'd catch up with me very quickly. He's pretty sharp.

Red is the best, and he's still one of the best at what he does. There's geniuses all over the world in certain fields, and there's no question he's a genius in our field.

He was there all those years I played. I can remember after a while guys saying, "Red's here again." He was there all the time, and he made himself seen. One thing I remember is that when we were in the playoffs on the road, if he didn't go with us and we lost the first game, he'd be there the second game. Everybody'd say, "Oh, Red's here, we better win today." He made you play harder and better. You knew he was watching the games, but if he wasn't there his presence wasn't felt. But when he was there, by God you knew something must be wrong, and you'd better win.

Everybody asks about the cigars. The one thing about the cigar was, Red could come into practice and you could never see him, but you always could smell that darn cigar. It was awful smelling. It was terrible. It would make you light-headed. You could tell he was there without even seeing him. He said he only smokes eight a day. I always thought he left off the zero. There's no way he smokes only eight of them a day.

He's the one that got me on Chinese food. Growing up I never even knew there were Chinese restaurants. Then I met Red. It was the first time I ever ate Chinese food, and now when I'm in Boston I eat it at least two times a week. I just love it.

No question ours was a professional relationship, but there was a little more added. Red knew how much I respected him and how much I wanted him around during the playoffs because I always felt he added something when he was there. I don't know about everybody else, but I know his presence always did something for me. When I saw him sitting there, it fired me up. Red gets fired up for games.

I think our relationship goes a little deeper than with most guys who played for him. In Boston, he would be the guy I would go to if I really got in trouble or if I really needed something. I wasn't intimidated by Red. I know he respected me as a player and as a person. If something really happened, he'd be the guy I'd go to of all the people there. Hands down.

He was always in the locker room after the games. Red's the only guy I ever saw walk around and shake everybody's hand after we lost. If he had something to say to you about how you played, he'd say it. He'd come around more when you lost than when you won. I've seen him give pep talks before games, especially around playoff times. It fired me up.

There's no way the NBA or the Celtics can ever be the same unless Red's there, because he's been there since the beginning. It's hard to say that somebody else could come in and be another Red Auerbach. A couple of years ago they had a vote about the best coach ever. It was said that Pat Riley was better than Red. To me, that's hard to believe. I like Pat Riley. I think he was the best coach I ever played against. But that's like saying Michael Jordan is better than Bill Russell or Wilt Chamberlain. Here's a man that's been there forty years, and who hasn't even been in coaching for almost thirty years. And to say that somebody else is better than him when you can't compare, it's just not right. Red must have really been something in his time.

A couple of years ago, I did a video with Red ("Winning Basketball"). The only reason I did that was because of who Red Auerbach was. It had nothing to do with money. I said, "Man, this is one chance to do something with him because one of these days, when he's gone, everybody's going to be going, 'God, who was that Red Auerbach?' Knowing that I made the tape with him was pretty neat."

I can remember him coming right across the floor after I got ejected in an exhibition game against Philadelphia in the Boston Garden. He went right after Moses Malone. It just showed the league that he isn't going to give up and that he's still The Man. At that time we had good teams, and he wasn't going to let anybody walk over us. When he saw something was going wrong, he was right there next to us. Philadelphia was our main rival then, and so he was right down there. We laughed when it was over with, but every guy on the team really appreciated it. When it was happening, by God, Red was there and we knew we had somebody behind us. And to think that it was just an exhibition game. We won the championship that year. It worked.

I have so much respect for him. Here I was, supposedly the star of the team, but when Red Auerbach walked in, you knew your place. He came to the games, and I'd get so fired up to see him sitting there. I know his old-time players have a lot of respect for him. Considering that he was a guy I never played for, it's amazing how much respect I have for him. When Red says something, you have to listen to him. Everything he says is so true. If Red wasn't into basketball, he'd be some big corporate executive somewhere. I have a tremendous amount of respect for him, probably more for him than anybody I've ever been around because of what he stands for and because I'm so involved in basketball. Red's still The Man. And if it wasn't for Red Auerbach, this league would be nothing.

# Introduction

# SEEING RED

---

*The cigar smoke in practice drove me crazy. The worst experience I ever had was when he drove me over to practice after I signed my first contract. I got off the plane from Milan and went to the Garden. I didn't even read any of the contract. Red just put it in front of me and said, "It's good, it's good. Sign the contract." He kept saying, "We've got to be at practice." That's why he wanted me to sign. Practice started in twenty minutes. He drove like a madman over from his office at the Garden. The cigar smoke was very thick and I started cracking my window because I didn't want to be rude and say, "That cigar stinks." I was so glad when we finally got there. Between smoke inhalation and the way we drove, I thought I might never make it.*

KEVIN MCHALE, *on his first day with the Boston Celtics*

BEFORE THE AGE OF ESPN, BLOOPER TAPES, DICK VITALE AND the All-Madden team—in a bygone era when a smoke was just a smoke, and you didn't need permission from the Health Police before you lit up—there was Red Auerbach and his victory cigar. The defending world champion Boston Celtics would crush yet another opponent, and when victory was secure, the Boston coach would pull a stogie out of his breast pocket, peel off the wrapper, sniff the length of the cigar, then stick it in his mouth and light it up. Subtle. Succinct. Definitive. The game was over. The game was won.

"When the league was picking on me, I tried to think of some-

1

thing that would aggravate the higher-ups," he said. "I wasn't having much luck until one day I lighted up a cigar during a game. Afterward I got a little note saying, 'It doesn't look good for you to be smoking cigars on the bench.' I haven't been without one since."

Sports in the nineties is polluted by end zone dances, taunts of "In your face," and the moronic, now-meaningless refrain of "We're Number One." Any achievement or victory, no matter how small, is celebrated by denigrating the opponent. Baseball players hit fastballs over the fence and take a minute and a half to circle the bases; it's important to show up the pitcher after you take him over the wall. Football's defensive linemen steamroll the enemy quarterback, then dance over his bones like television game show nitwits who've just won the jackpot. Running backs score touchdowns, then immediately remove their helmets to make sure everybody sees their face. Basketball Joneses dunk off the fast break, then hang on the rim for emphasis. It is a gesture that screams, "Look at me." Television is to blame for much of this. Make the 11 P.M. news clips and it strokes your ego and fattens your wallet. You are an entertainer, and you want people to know who you are and how good you are.

It's been almost thirty years since the smoke cleared from the end of the Celtic bench, but Auerbach's victory cigar remains one of the best traditions of American sports. Red Auerbach's lighting up is right there with "My Old Kentucky Home" at the Derby, green blazers at the Masters, and Touchdown Jesus at Notre Dame football games.

Auerbach is the only person in American professional sports who can never say, "That was before my time." In the winter of 1995–1996, the National Basketball Association will celebrate its fiftieth season. Auerbach was there at the creation. He is there today. He is to pro basketball what Vince Lombardi was to pro football and what Connie Mack was to major league baseball. But unlike Lombardi, Mack, John McGraw, Casey Stengel or Toe Blake, Auerbach's career spans the entire history of his league.

Arnold Auerbach was a twenty-nine-year-old head coach when the Basketball Association of America (the father of today's NBA) was formed in 1946. Nearly a half century later, seventy-seven-year-old Red sits as president of the Boston Celtics, the most successful franchise in the history of professional sports. He's seen two-handed set shots and three-point kings; Bob Ferry and Danny Ferry; Washington Caps and salary caps; folding franchises in Sheboygan and Dream Teams rolling the dice in Monte Carlo. He is the only individual in our four major pro sports who has been in a management capacity for the entire existence of a league. College football had Knute Rockne, the FBI had J. Edgar Hoover, Chicago had Richard Daley, and the NBA has Red Auerbach.

The NBA today is considered a model for all professional sports. It's a glossy, high-tech, marketing-savvy money-maker. Kids in malls no longer look for Yankee pinstripes or Dallas Cowboy silver and blue; they look for Charlotte Hornet teal. They want to be like Michael Jordan, Larry Johnson and Shaquille O'Neal. The NBA is the league of the nineties and probably the league of the twenty-first century. Between 1988 and 1989, four expansion franchises (Charlotte, Miami, Minnesota and Orlando) plopped down $32.5 million for the privilege of joining the NBA; five years later, it cost Toronto $125 million to join the NBA. From 1984 to 1993, the nine seasons of Michael Jordan's career, NBA revenues went from $200 million to $1 billion, and the league broke its attendance record seven times. NBA licensing revenues in 1992–1993 topped $2.1 billion. Player salaries averaged $275,000 in 1983; ten years later, the number was $1.2 million. The 1993 NBA finals were telecast to 109 nations, 56 of them on a live basis. When America sent a team of NBA stars to the 1992 Barcelona Olympics, the USA Dream Team was compared to and treated like a troupe of rock stars—universally adored and mobbed. In Mexico in 1993, hundreds of zealous fans almost overturned a limousine carrying Atlanta Hawk Dominique Wilkins. Charles Barkley sells noodles on Japanese television. The National Basketball Association someday soon will be the International Basketball Association, making it the first truly global pro sport.

"Sports really is the international language, and we think basketball is up there at the top of that list in terms of dialect," says NBA Commissioner David Stern.

It wasn't always this way. Auerbach knows. Red was there when the NBA was just a cut above pro wrestling—a carnival act, a sorry excuse to keep arenas lit during the dark days of winter. There were

NBA teams in Fort Wayne, Indiana, and Waterloo, Iowa. Owners had difficulty attracting fans and meeting payrolls. The game was played below the rim and there was no shot clock to limit boring stall tactics. Sneakers were black and players were white.

Auerbach rode the trains and the prop planes and helped deliver a new pro game to a population that had been satisfied with baseball, football, hockey and boxing. Auerbach coached an NBA team representing Tri-Cities—before it became Quad Cities. (Who can name the three cities that made up Tri-Cities? Moline, Illinois; Rock Island, Illinois; and Davenport, Iowa.) It took a long time for the NBA to become a "major" league. As recently as 1981, the league finals were broadcast on tape delay after the eleven o'clock news. Today the NBA draft is broadcast on live television, the All-Star Game is a weekend festival of self-congratulations and the finals are decidedly prime time. Poll-takers and advertisers know that America's youth looks up to pro basketball players, above all others. The sneaker deals players make today are bigger than the entire league payroll of 1946–1947.

In the late 1950s and early 1960s, Boston's coach carved out an image as a street-smart winner. In twenty seasons on the bench, he won 938 regular-season games. The NBA is almost a half century old, and still no coach has topped Auerbach's mark. The 938 number will soon fall, but it's safe to guess that no one will coach long enough, and well enough, to win nine NBA titles, eight in a row. A classic ref-baiter, Auerbach is believed to hold all records for fines and suspensions. Did any other coach ever score a one-punch knockout of a rival owner before a playoff game? The NBA became more sophisticated, but not Auerbach. In 1983, at the age of sixty-six, he challenged 6-11 Moses Malone to duke it out during a Boston Garden exhibition game. Luckily for Moses, it wasn't a playoff game.

As a coach and general manager, Auerbach from 1957 through 1969 guided, maneuvered and motivated his team to eight consecutive titles and eleven championships in thirteen seasons. There have been successes *and* flops since the string of championships was snapped in 1970, but Auerbach's place in sports history was etched into stone during those glory days of the Bill Russell Era. While still at the top, he walked away from the bench. He hasn't been a head coach since 1966, but if a hypothetical, global Dream Team needed a coach for one intergalactic game to save Planet Earth, seventy-seven-year-old Red Auerbach would no doubt still be the choice of the majority of basketball aficionados.

"I've read everything he's written," says Indiana coach Bobby Knight. "You talk about basketball and you talk about Clair Bee and Hank Iba and Pete Newell and Joe Lapchick. You talk about pro basketball, you talk about Red."

Beginning with their first championship in 1957, the Celtics and basketball became synonymous. Replay this scene from the television sitcom "Happy Days": The program was a portrait of white, middle-class America during the two-cars-in-every-garage, carefree days of the Eisenhower administration. In one of the episodes, written in the 1970s, a young girl wakes up in a roomful of basketball photographs and trophies. She finds out she is sleeping in the room of Richie Cunningham's ballplaying older brother. She tells Richie, "Gee, I thought I had died and heaven had been taken over by the Boston Celtics."

Quinn Buckner, former head coach of the Dallas Mavericks, was born in 1954, and has won every team championship the game has to offer. He's won an NCAA crown (Indiana), an Olympic gold medal (1976 USA) and an NBA championship (1984 Celtics). He grew up in Chicago and says, "I've always thought I was a Celtic, even when I was in college. That's the team I wanted to play for, and Red had a lot to do with that. I feel that the way the Celtics played epitomizes basketball. How could you not be aware of them growing up? The Celtic mystique is Red and how he treats people. He has forgotten more basketball than nine out of ten people involved in basketball today know. I know people think every now and then that Red can be a little crass, but at some point in your life you kind of have a right. He does know how to treat his players. I don't care who you talk about who's played there, everybody has a high opinion of Red Auerbach. They ought to name the NBA 'the Red Auerbach League.' That's what this is all about."

Jerry Krause, general manager of the Chicago Bulls, has been in the NBA for more than thirty years. He says, "When I came in the league with the Baltimore Bullets in 1962, I did not admire him. I thought, 'Here's a guy who pushes the Bill Russell button and they win.' I thought that he just had all these great players and he pushes the button and they win. I learned very quickly that that was not true. Red Auerbach is a genius. He's the best psychologist that I've ever known in sports. He's done something that no one in sports history has ever done. He made the trade for Russell—the greatest trade in the history of sports. Then he turned around and got Cowens and built it again. Then Bird, and the [Robert] Parish deal. Through the years, he stood the test of time. The only way I can describe Red Auerbach is he's a genius."

Jerry Colangelo, general manager of the Phoenix Suns since the first season of the franchise's existence (1968–1969), says, "When you talk about people who have contributed to the game, you can't go any further than Red Auerbach."

The game has changed tremendously since Auerbach took over the Washington Capitols in 1946, but Auerbach's ways never went completely out of style. When John Lucas took over as coach of the San Antonio Spurs in 1992–1993, folks were amazed because Lucas's coaching style allowed for input from all of his players. Lucas sometimes turned away from his players during a time-out and let them concoct a plan. It was considered revolutionary, but ex-Celtic Tom Heinsohn was quick to note, "That's what Red did. He made it a point to keep everybody involved."

Russell, in his 1979 book, *Second Wind,* wrote, "What really mattered was that we trusted him; we knew his actions were directed solely toward winning and not out of some petty grudge against one of us. We also respected his intelligence. Red is not someone you would wish to have leading a platoon against yours in a war game."

Atlanta Hawk coach Lenny Wilkens is the man who will break Auerbach's regular-season record of 938 victories. As coach of the Sonics, Blazers, Cavs and Hawks, Wilkens went into the 1994–1995 season with 926 wins, just 12 shy of Auerbach.

"I would say that if I took any ideas from anybody it would have been Red," says Wilkens. "Because I always liked the fact that he had great balance on his teams. Everybody made a contribution. There wasn't anybody on there that couldn't play, and I've always wanted my teams to be that way. From one through twelve, the guys have to be able to make a contribution. I've always had great respect for Red."

Auerbach left the bench after winning his eighth straight championship in 1966. Free of the duties of coaching, motivation and preparation, he put all of his energy into player procurement and solidified his reputation as the most shrewd and clever builder of teams. He rebuilt the Celtics twice, once in the seventies and again in the eighties; each time he took them from the bottom to the top and kept them at the highest level for several years. He did it with smarts and foresight that were years ahead of his competition. It turned out that the NBA's best coach was also its best general manager.

Pat Williams, general manager of the Orlando Magic, says, "What makes Red memorable is his coaching. What he has done since is like having Casey Stengel or Vince Lombardi stay years after as an executive. He's the most successful pro coach ever. As the general manager, he instantly became the most recognizable executive in sports history. You can almost believe he's bigger than the game."

Celtic owner Alan Cohen adds, "Red Auerbach understands the chemistry of a team and what makes a basketball team like no ten people in the world. He's still head and shoulders above everybody else in the NBA. Red can meet somebody and talk to him for a little while and he'll know what makes the guy run. He'll understand the sensitivity, the problems, and have a sense of the motivations and insecurities of the person so quickly it's unbelievable. He is a sharp student of personal machinery. He's probably the single most important factor in making this league until Larry [Bird] and Magic [Johnson] came along."

As a general manager, Auerbach is without question the best in the postwar era of American sports. Auerbach-the-GM has won sixteen championships, and he did it with three generations of athletes. The Russell-led Celtics won eleven titles in thirteen years. The Havlicek-Cowens-White Celtics won two in three years in the 1970s. And the Bird-Parish-McHale C's won three flags between 1981 and 1986. Baseball's John McGraw won only three championships. Football's George Halas and baseball's Connie Mack, like Auerbach, worked the sidelines and the smoke-filled rooms, but neither won with the consistency of Auerbach. Yankee GM George Weiss won eight World Series between 1947 and 1960, and Montreal Canadien GM Sam Pollock won nine Stanley Cups in fourteen seasons, ending in 1978. In both cases, there was only one rebuilding job. Auerbach built the greatest dynasty in pro sports, then he rebuilt it—twice.

This from David Halberstam, who wrote the definitive NBA history of the early 1980s (*The Breaks of the Game*): "Auerbach was so smart in an age when people weren't smart in professional sports in general, and in basketball in particular—when it was really embryonic, when everybody else was careless. Somebody who was a coach or a general manager tended to be somebody who was a good player, or a good guy. It was not yet a business, and it wasn't professional. He was smart and professional in thinking ahead and understanding the changing nature of the game. He had a good eye and he was in an underdeveloped world of professional sport. The other thing is that he goes at life on a wartime footing. Everything is a struggle. It's probably from that immigrant background and being Jewish or whatever. Everything is a struggle, no one is going to give you anything, so you have to fight for everything. So he won that way, and those combinations—that ferocity plus being intelligent—made him admirable if not likable."

*Boston Globe* sportswriter John Powers, who covered the team in the late seventies, remembers, "Red always cared more about what was written in Washington, because that's where all his buddies were. Steve Hershey of the *Washington Star* wrote something Red didn't like and the next time the Bullets played at the Garden, Hershey's seat was way up in the upper deck. I went to talk to Red about it. I said, 'Red, you can't do that.' He said to me, 'You're Irish. You should understand. You fuck me, I fuck you!' "

Bob Cousy, who has known Auerbach for more than forty years, says, "Arnold is not a lovable character. When you think about a Mommie Dearest, that's him. Like any household, if we go to a third party with a chip on our shoulder and reveal the intricacies of family life, you can make anybody look bad. If you apply that to Arnold, he is not only not lovable, but he's obnoxious. His ego always gets in the way.

"I think he's impeccably honest. He has the spirit of a wheeler-dealer, but he draws a line. I could never think of him getting caught with his hand in the cookie jar. He always watched the other guy's money. He used to bust our balls over the cab fares, but he was watching the other guy's money, and I respect that. He's dependable as hell in terms of commitments. In terms of what we consider important things, he's been there. He's never been a malingerer in terms of putting his time in with the Celtics. The effectiveness of the job is obvious.

"He hasn't had a great family life, but he's still married forty-five years later. So maybe we're allowing this outer shell, this demeanor that he puts on—which in my judgment is insecurity, pure and simple. This gruff, arrogant, obnoxious behavior . . . When you take him out of there, he's a pussycat."

In Boston, the sore loser and gloating winner is perceived as nothing less than an infallible civic treasure. Auerbach's a New York guy who's always lived in Washington, but his triumphs and immortality are rooted in New England, where he's on a par with any local hero of the last half century. Over Boston's last four decades, Auerbach's approval rating has ranked with the likes of Boston Pops conductor Arthur Fiedler, House Speaker Tip O'Neill and Richard Cardinal Cushing. In Boston's historic Faneuil Hall Marketplace, there are statues of three individuals: Sam Adams, James Michael Curley and Arnold J. Auerbach. Adams organized the American Revolution and signed the Declaration of Independence, Curley served as a congressman and mayor of Boston. He was the prototype Irish political rogue. Auerbach? What did he do? He never even paid taxes in Massachusetts. He simply was the Green Godfather of pro basketball's trademark winners, the Celtics.

The Red Auerbach story is a vehicle that allows us to track the long, potholed journey of professional basketball. Two decades before Michael Jordan became a billboard guy selling $170 sneakers, there was "Red on Roundball," short television segments in which Red, in black canvas sneakers, promoted the game to a skeptical constituency watching at home. Since joining the NBA at its inception, Auerbach's been a head coach, traveling secretary, contract negotiator, marketing director, television commentator, author, international tutor, ref-baiter, general manager, president, CEO and legend-in-residence. Along the way, he's offended a hearty share of NBA folks, from first commissioner Maurice Podoloff to today's leader, David Stern.

Will McDonough, a *Globe* columnist and longtime friend of Auerbach's, says, "He's a very, very bright guy, and he's very patient with what he does. He doesn't take the apple. He never took the apple when he coached. He doesn't panic about everything and he doesn't let what the public or the media has to say affect his decisions. He's the best guy I've ever seen with that. He's just so focused on what he does, and he has a great sense of what it takes to win. He's completely studied the game. He always wanted a certain type of guy. Unfortunately, with expansion and everything, in the last ten years he hasn't been able to do that."

Auerbach's been powerful and successful for so long that his enemies blame him for things over which he has no control. And he does little to discourage the notion that he's pulling the strings from behind the curtain. Leaguewide, there's always been a theory that Auerbach did his best to inconvenience opponents by providing them with shoddy locker rooms and horrid climate control in the bowels of the Boston Garden. When visiting teams arrive at Logan Airport and get caught in traffic coming through the Sumner tunnel, they blame Auerbach. New York Knick coach Pat Riley likes to say that room service never comes to Boston. Red loves it. He's like a crafty old pitcher who gets hitters out because they *think* he's doctoring the baseball. Suspicion takes the opponent out of the game. It's an edge, and Auerbach will do anything for an edge.

Longtime NBA coach Cotton Fitzsimmons says, "You can't be treated okay in the Boston Garden. There's no way. You watch it on television and you're expecting to see a palace and you see a dump. So how can you be treated okay in a dump? That's the way it is. And Red didn't want you treated okay. I accused him one day. We were in there playing and it was cold outside. We jumped all over the Celtics. This was at a time when they were struggling. In the second half, I noticed that the cold air was coming into the end next to our bench. Well, Red had opened the doors from the train station and let it all come flying in on our end. I finally got the officials to shut it, but it took a long time. I swear he opened it. He'd say, 'I'd never do anything like that.' Well, it must have been the ghost of Red Auerbach that turned the latch. He always said he had no control of those things in his building. If you have no control then you can never be blamed for anything, so that's what he would always say."

A child of Depression Brooklyn, Auerbach was born with the cynical city gene that gives one street smarts throughout life. He can be shy, he can be a softy and he can be emotional. He has several characteristics that defy his image, but there is one word that never will be associated with Arnold "Red" Auerbach: naive.

His daughter, Randy, vice president of creative affairs for Mel Brooks Films in Los Angeles, says, "He's two people. He's a father, family member, a quiet, withdrawn, introspective person . . . and then he's Red Auerbach."

Cousy, Auerbach's first rookie hotshot in 1950, says, "He's a Jekyll-and-Hyde personality. He literally runs away from confrontation. When he sits in his throne room and waits to be adored, that's one thing. I was there the night he hollered at Ted Kennedy. Joe Kennedy was running for Congress and it was during the playoffs and the offices were full of people. Ted was working the room. It took him about five or ten minutes and he's working his way toward Arnold, who was sitting in his chair. As he gets to the desk in front of Arnold, he sinks down on one knee and genuflects to the Pope and puts his hand out. We all started laughing. Arnold, who doesn't have a sense of humor, takes him literally. Evidently, Kennedy's office must have called and broke balls to get tickets and Arnold must have done his usual, 'Do you know how tough it is?'

"So he figures Kennedy is trying to make him look foolish and he starts in on him with, 'Do you know how much trouble it took me to get these tickets?' When he's in that milieu, he's in control. But you take him out of there, he sits there like a pussycat. When he wants to be, he can be a charming guy and actually very sophisticated in terms of his knowledge of wines and paintings and prices. But he does go through this transformation from his sports persona. He gets away from this dominant persona that he has when he sits in his office as Celtic GM Red Auerbach. Take him out of that milieu and he's an entirely different guy."

As two people, Auerbach's led two lives. His wife, Dorothy, and daughters, Nancy and Randy, always lived in Washington while he worked in Boston. Everybody in Boston and Basketball America saw Red Auerbach. His family saw the man who liked kids, letter openers, boxer dogs and movies. They saw a man who liked to cook and press his own pants.

"There's only one time I've seen Red when he wasn't in control," says longtime Auerbach ballplayer Frank Ramsey. "We always used to play one game every year at College Park, Maryland. We'd go out to Red's house for cold cuts, and Dottie always was in complete control. Red would be running around, getting us Cokes and cold cuts."

Arnold and Dorothy were married in 1941. She loved Washington and hated to fly. Early on, it was agreed that he would separate his work from his family life. Regardless of where he coached or how much money he made, Dorothy would raise their two daughters in Washington, D.C., near her family. When Arnold was home, he left basketball back in Boston. It was an unusual arrangement. Celtic fans still are stunned to learn that the great Red Auerbach never was a citizen of Boston. He was a shuttle commuter long before it became fashionable. Daughter Nancy guesses that her mother has been to Boston no more than five times during her dad's four and a half decades with the Celtics. After all, somebody had to stay back in D.C. and take care of the dogs. (There have been five Yankee boxer dogs since 1954: Maggie, Melvin, LeRoy, Alan and CP for Celtic Pride.)

Cousy, who has known the Auerbachs for forty-five years, says, "To this day, I don't know what his relationship was at home. It's weird. I used to kid Dorothy. I remember my wife and I having dinner with Arnold and Dorothy in the Catskills in the early sixties after I was through playing. I'd say, 'Okay, Dorothy. He's in Boston for eight months of the year. Then, I take him to Europe for six weeks. What do you think? Can you handle the son of a bitch for two months? Will the marriage hold up for two and a half months?' We'd all laugh. That's what everybody used to say.

"My general theory is that the animal isn't fit for cohabitation for long periods of time with anyone, opposite sex or otherwise. We ought to all be living alone. But Arnold, especially. I don't think the marriage with anyone, never mind Dorothy, could have survived twelve months a year with Arnold. It's peculiar, but that was it, that was the union they had. To my knowledge, I don't think there was ever any thought of separation. They enjoyed the relationship they had and it worked for both of them."

Randy Auerbach says, "Now that I can look back on it, I think ours was a very normal family life within an abnormal setting. Although he was traveling and away, my mother brought it in as part of the family, as opposed to the other-woman syndrome. It was a big to-do. On Sundays, we'd all sit on the sofa and watch the games. My grandparents would be there. My great-grandfather. Aunts and uncles. It was definitely a focal point of the weekend. I was born in April [NBA playoff time] and I asked my mother if he was home when I was born and she said, 'Well, we lost that year, so yes, he was home.' I can remember birthday parties focused around the television. We'd be in the backyard and we'd run in to see who was winning. It was just always so much a part of who we were.

"About once a week, I get asked the question about why our family never moved to Boston. It's difficult, because people don't understand. Now that I'm older, I see the complexities of it. My sister's asthma was a problem [according to Red, Nancy Auerbach found it easier to breathe in the D.C. climate] and my mother's father was a pediatrician. But now that I'm older I see that my father was so focused. It would probably have been a disaster had we been there, because you had certain needs—'take me here, buy me this, show me that, how come?' He was so focused and that's what made him successful, but there was a price that goes along with that. It was the family."

Red Auerbach was in New York the day the Nebraska Avenue house nearly burned down in 1957.

"I was five years old," remembers Randy. "My father was away, traveling with an All-Star team, and we were getting ready for the Catskills. My sister had an oxygen tank in the room because of her asthma. It caught a spark and she came running down to tell my mother. She couldn't put it out, and by that time there were flames. We called the fire department and the dog wouldn't let the fire department in. It was a three-alarm fire; it was huge. Finally, we went to my grandmother's house and my father finally reached us, yelling, 'Where were you? I've been trying to call you all day.' And we were just saying, 'We're at Mom's and the house burned down.'"

"I remember that call," says Nancy. "He was saying, 'What are you doing? What took you so damn long to answer the phone?' We said, 'Well, we're having a fire.' He said, 'What do you mean you're having a fire?'

"I think we understood why he was gone so much. It was his life. I don't think he would have been very happy doing it any other way. But when he was home, he was a softy. He insisted on only two things—honesty and loyalty. If you're honest with him, it doesn't matter what you did. As long as you were truthful."

The man who thinks of winning as the key to life raised two daughters who are decidedly noncompetitive.

"We're both like that," admits Randy, "to the point of saying, 'Oh no, you win. I don't care.' Because we grew up with it and I have none of that, and I think that affects me in business. I'm so non-aggressive."

His two daughters and his granddaughter call him "Goomp," a hangover from granddaughter Julie's baby-talk attempt to say "Grandpa." Dorothy is one of the few people in the world who calls him "Arnold." She also is the only person who can coach the ex-coach.

Though his immediate family is made up of only women, Auerbach can be quite uncomfortable when he is around persons of the female gender. His professional world always was a male world. Women were a distraction. Woman took the mind away from matters at hand. Around women, he can be alternately shy and crude. He doesn't seem to know what to say.

"He's very uncomfortable in the presence of women," says Celtic GM Jan Volk, who has been around Auerbach for thirty-four years. "He's intimidated. It's an interesting thing to see. This guy, who's so outgoing and strong and tough-minded, will absolutely melt. He'll have difficulty communicating."

Tod Rosensweig, a Celtic employee since 1974, adds, "He doesn't have the conventional social skills. When he first looked at my wife—

it was the first time he ever saw her—he looked at her and said, 'Imogene Coca.' He didn't say hello or anything like that. Just 'Imogene Coca.' Then he walked off."

"He is worse with women than anyone who ever lived," says Jeff Cohen, an assistant GM of the Celtics during the 1970s and today athletic director at Brandeis University. "The wives all used to hate him, and he just couldn't deal with them."

"He wasn't good for the wives," says Bob Brannum, an ex-Celtic who ran Auerbach's basketball camp for twenty-two years. "My wife always was scared to death of him. I told him one day that my wife was coming down to the camp with some people she needed to impress. She's a real estate agent and these were important bankers. When she got there, Red went over and gave her a hug and told these people what a great person she was. Then he gives me a wink and says, 'How's that, baby?'"

Marie Cousy, wife of Bob Cousy, says, "We used to say that if he flicked cigar ashes on your jacket shoulder, that meant he liked you. We ignored him. One time, a whole bunch of us went to New York. Each one of us would go home and tell our husband that all the other wives were going. We'd all say the same thing. So we all go to New York, even though we weren't allowed to go anywhere. So we're all in New York and we're all in the elevator and the door opens and Red comes in and we just turned our backs. He never said a word to us."

"He's terrible with small talk," says Bob Cousy. "That's one of the reasons he had problems with wives. He just can't stand there and make small talk. He always said one of the things that destroyed teams quickest was the females—allowing them to get into the minds of the players would somehow create controversy. I think for a while he tried to institute a system where he could seat the wives apart at games."

In 1984, the author of this book brought his wife and one-month-old infant daughter to the NBA meetings in Salt Lake City. Meeting the young mother for the first time, Auerbach looked at the tiny baby girl and said, "Lady, you got a lot of balls bringing that baby all the way out here. Yes, sir, a lot of balls."

Compliment? Probably.

In 1984, an angry Auerbach blocked *Boston Globe* (and now CBS) reporter Lesley Visser from entering the Celtic locker room after a Madison Square Garden playoff loss to the Knicks. This was just two years after Auerbach, Celtic head coach Bill Fitch and Bill Russell had attended Visser's wedding reception at the Ritz-Carlton in Boston.

Jackie MacMullan, who played women's basketball at the University of New Hampshire and today covers the NBA for the *Boston Globe,* remembers her introduction to Auerbach:

"I was covering a college game and he was sitting right next to me at the press table. I was pretty nervous, and I tried to appear as professional as possible. Finally, during a time-out, when the cheerleaders were on the court, Red turns to me and says, 'What do you think?' I started going into great detail about the specifics of the game and he said, 'No, what do you think of the cheerleaders? Aren't you the cheerleading coach?' "

He kept great distance from his players' wives and families. Wives never made road trips, not even in the early days when Auerbach would take All-Stars on State Department junkets. It was a team rule; it remains a team rule. Wives were a distraction. They could be like agents, telling players that they were underpaid, underplayed or underappreciated. Wives wanted the ballplayers to buy homes in greater Boston. Auerbach wanted his players to rent.

Ballplayers' girlfriends could also be trouble. Red-the-liberal didn't like girlfriends hanging around, and black players who had white girlfriends sometimes felt especially uncomfortable. Robert Parish remembers bringing a white, female companion to a Celtic function and being greeted by Auerbach with, "What did you bring her for?" Parish told a friend that he believed Auerbach disapproved of mixed-race couples. He said that Auerbach only mentioned it once, but that he always received annoyed looks from Red when he showed up with a white woman on his arm.

"I don't think that was ever a problem," says Cousy. "I think Bill Russell broke Arnold down early with that one. Russ would have chimpanzees up there; Russ didn't miss anybody. I think Arnold realized early on he wasn't going to control the Russells of the world."

Auerbach says his politics are democratic. He's met every president since Harry Truman, and he's lived in Washington for almost sixty years. Yet, he has never voted. "I never got around to it," he says.

He's terrible with names. He always referred to Dallas player personnel director Rick Sund as "Mike." Dallas GM Norm Sonju says, "To Red, Rick will always be Mike. If Rick doesn't want to change his name, that's too bad." Folks around the Celtic offices understand Sund's dilemma. With few exceptions, everybody is "What's his name?" Auerbach knows longtime secretary Mary Faherty, Volk, Rosensweig and a few others, but many of the Celtic employees are nameless minions. In the old days, there had been only three people in the office, only three names to remember.

Still vain, he removes his glasses when someone asks him to pose for a picture. His favorite song is "Night and Day." He likes Rockport Shoes and Hershey's Kisses. He is incapable of taping a program on his VCR. He sometimes cries at the movies. His all-time favorite television shows are "Hawaii Five-O," "Magnum, P.I.," "The People's Court" and "Jeopardy!" He likes Jimmy Durante, Bill Cosby and George Jefferson. He loves martial arts movies and anything starring Chuck Norris. He collects engraved cigar boxes, letter openers, silver, ivory, and cloisonné—and he remembers where he bought each item and how much it cost. He doesn't eat much before games, not even now, not even as a seventy-seven-year-old president emeritus. He believes your mind is sharper when you're a little bit hungry.

Auerbach's offices and his homes (his home is in Washington; he keeps an apartment in Boston) could serve as wings of the Basketball Hall of Fame. Celtic CEO Dave Gavitt says this about Auerbach's main office at Celtic headquarters in Boston: "We use it as a museum. If somebody comes in from out of town, we take them in and show them around."

On the shelves of Auerbach's office are books—books by Red, books about Red and books about the Celtics and the NBA. On the walls there are photos—Red with presidents from Truman to Reagan, Red with his ballplayers, Red with the gang from Miller Lite, Red on the sidelines, Red in the boardroom, Red on draft day, a still shot from "Red on Roundball," Red in a cap and gown getting

an honorary doctorate, Red with people in tuxedos. He looks at a
life-size cardboard cutout of himself. He has his videos, his carica-
tures, his endorsements. He has his Washington Capitols jacket and
a miniature statuette of his Faneuil Hall statue—the official trophy
handed out to those who are named NBA Coach of the Year.

Dick Johnson, curator for the New England Sports Museum, in
all seriousness says, "I'd like to take his entire office and move it
over here as a permanent exhibit."

Randy Auerbach on her parents' love of bric-a-brac: "He loves
stuff. Collecting. My mother, too. And there's no consistency to the
stuff. She likes her stuff and he likes his stuff and there's no cross-
over stuff. She's like, "Why did he buy that and what are we going
to do with that?' And she goes to the flea market and he's like, 'Why
did you buy that? You'd throw that out.' When he traveled, he really
enjoyed picking up things. And a bargain. He remembers what he
paid. And then I'll take him shopping and it's like, 'How much?' "

With the memorabilia, there is pedestrian clutter.

"Every time we move his office, there's been more stuff," says
Celtic marketing director Rosensweig. "We recently moved again
and there was a box that just said, 'Red.' We opened it and it was a
boxful of hundreds of key chains from our thirteenth world championship. That was 1976. These things were almost twenty years old.
He's always loved stuff. We'll have a clinic that has nothing to do
with Red and he'll call me the next day and say, 'Get me some of
those T-shirts.' "

"He's a sucker for these things," adds Celtic GM Volk. "If the
right salesman gets him, he's a sucker for almost anything you can
put the logo on. He used to buy office pens. They were terrible.
He'd give you a whole box and he'd think he was giving you gold,
and they're awful. And it goes the other way. Anytime we have a
promotion of any sort, he needs to get fifty of whatever the item is.
Ten years later, he'll still have forty-eight of them and he'll call and
say, 'Where is that stuff? I got to send it out to Randy.' "

Draft picks often leave Auerbach's office with a couple of bags
of Celtic trinkets and giveaways from past promotions. Ex-Celtic star
John Havlicek once said a Celtic rookie leaving Auerbach's office
resembled a young man who'd just had a big day at the boardwalk.

Auerbach's Washington telephone numbers always have been in the phone book. His office number on New Mexico Avenue is under "Arnold Auerbach" and the home phone number on Massachusetts Avenue is under "Arnold Red Auerbach." He answers all of his mail personally, because he believes it's the only way to do business. When he has a problem with any service or industry, he directs his complaint to the president of the company. He knows that if you write to a junior executive, your letter gets tossed. Red will tell you: *That's why the man will never be more than a junior executive.* His fifth and latest book, *Management by Auerbach,* is stored in the business section of bookstores and libraries. Lee Iacocca wrote the foreword. It's difficult to imagine Iacocca writing the foreword for a book written by Billy Martin or Al Davis.

Auerbach is frugal, but he's an easy touch for friends in need. "He'll never loan you ten dollars," says Volk. "He'll only loan you a hundred. He knows that you might forget about ten. He might forget about ten. But he knows you'll both remember a hundred dollars.

"He doesn't lavish money on himself. When people in the office get married, he buys nice, personal gifts, and he pays for them himself. He's thoughtful. He actually is a thoughtful guy. He doesn't want people to know that. Put him in a basketball environment and he's a killer."

Auerbach likes to help young people get into college. He has connections at universities across America and it gives him great joy to make phone calls on behalf of the sons and daughters (or grandsons and granddaughters) of his cronies. Perhaps it is kindness. Perhaps it is a chance to show off and flex his muscles. "I think of him as the ultimate godfather," says Celtic coach Chris Ford. "He loves doing little favors for people."

Early in the 1990s, a young woman who knew only a professional, working relationship with the gruff Auerbach was surprised to get a phone call from him. She had recently suffered a miscarriage and was unaware that Auerbach knew her sorrow. "He just called one night, out of the blue," she recalls. "He just made small talk and said, 'You okay?' I knew what he meant. It was really sweet. We never talked about it then, or any other time, but it was really a sweet thing to do."

In 1982, he selected Indiana's Landon Turner in the tenth round of the NBA draft. Turner would have been an NBA player, but a car accident had made him a paraplegic, and Auerbach wanted to do something to lift his spirits. Landon Turner can forever say he was drafted by the Boston Celtics.

For more than a half century, Auerbach's primary food groups have been doughnuts, cookies, Cokes, southern fried chicken, brisket of beef, pastrami sandwiches, chocolate milk shakes, shrimp with lobster sauce, wonton soup, roast pork, beef with snow peas, and cigars. Hang around with Auerbach for any length of time, and you inhale secondhand smoke and eat chow mein.

In 1977, former Celtic center Dave Cowens, something of a health nut, stood outside a team bus, inhaled a healthy heap of Seattle atmosphere and proclaimed, "Ahh, fresh air."

"Awww, that clean living. It'll kill you every time." Auerbach snorted.

He smokes Hoyo de Monterrey cigars. He also smokes cigars that he gets in the mail, by the box, for free. He often takes the free ones and turns them around as gifts. If your wife has a baby, Red might go to his office closet and pull out a box of Dutch Masters Corona de luxe.

"You learn not to get downwind," says Gavitt. "I just look to see which way the smoke is going. We were at a wedding together with David Stern and his wife. We were all at the same table and Red was needling David. He says, 'You know, I used to like you when you smoked cigars,' and David says, 'Well, you know, Red, the reason I gave them up is because I had two secretaries who were pregnant at the same time,' and Red says, without batting an eyelash, 'So you get new secretaries.'"

Greg Kite, who broke in with the Celtics in 1983, says, "One of the things I'll always remember about practicing at Hellenic College with the Celtics is the cigar smoke. Of course, nobody was going to say anything about it, but by the end of practice, it would get kind of thick."

Volk adds, "If I've driven with Red for any appreciable period of time, I'll come home and my wife, Lisa, knows immediately that I've been with Red. My suits have to be cleaned."

Auerbach loves gadgets, but is mechanically inept.

"It's always been a problem," Volk says with a sigh. "He's intimidated by mechanical things. He absolutely won't allow himself to read and understand it. It just overwhelms him. He cannot play a tape. If the TV isn't on and set to the right channel, he's got problems."

Rosensweig says, "He wanted a portable phone. He saw somebody with one and said, 'I've got to have one of those.' We got him one. It's not very complicated. The instructions are, 'Charge the battery, use the phone.' Well, he doesn't charge the battery and he calls practically every day saying that the damn phone doesn't work."

"He's got a phone number which he can use to plug directly into our radio broadcast," adds Volk. "But he rarely uses it. He'd rather talk to someone. He usually calls Dave Zuccaro [director of publications] at courtside and has him do a play-by-play. That way he can say, 'How's so-and-so playing?' or 'Why isn't so-and-so in the game?' "

Auerbach's never been a snappy dresser. He wears plaid sport coats and camel sport coats. He wears brown on brown, plaid on stripes. Listen to Rosensweig, hired by Auerbach in 1974: "My father went to college with Red. I knew Red when I was a little kid. His daughter, Randy, is a year younger than me. My father and Red share an office in Washington. You can safety say they are best friends. They've always invested together. My father is a very handsome, distinguished-looking man. He dressed beautifully and always did. You know how Red dresses; it doesn't matter to him. Well, my father bought a chain of clothing stores in Washington—Brooks Brothers types. At one point, Red asked my father if he should invest. My father said, 'I don't know about that, but the one thing I don't want is you wearing our clothes.' "

Cousy says, "It was always a deal. Typical jocks. We went to the plain pipe racks. He would search out people for these wholesale deals. You'd go in through the back and they'd be thirty-five dollars a jacket. He wasn't style-conscious at all; none of us were. It was just because it was a good deal."

Daughter Randy says, "It's a big issue with us. I'll go in and say, 'You can't wear this.' Last summer, I visited and I went to his closet and I said, 'I'm going to throw some things out.' His reaction to everything was, 'No, no, that's my favorite.' I kept saying, 'Dad, these are bell-bottoms, you can't wear these things.' And he'd say, 'I know, but they're my favorites.' So I'd say, 'Okay, I'll save them.' Then we'd get to the T-shirts and there's stains and cigar holes and he's saying, 'No, no, Bobby Knight gave me that from the NIT,' or 'This is going to be worth something someday.' Most of it is still there. But I think now that he's gotten older he realizes the plaid sport jackets are out. Now he's more into gray slacks and blue blazer."

His former players remember him as one of the world's worst drivers. They talk of the foggy night he whizzed off a Maine highway and ripped through a Howard Johnson parking lot going eighty miles an hour. According to former Celtic Gene Conley, who was riding shotgun, Auerbach never even knew he'd left the highway. He once borrowed a car for a drive to Maine, then left this note on the car owner's window: "You'd better have this checked. The front end shimmies when it goes over a hundred."

Ex-Celtic Ed Macauley says, "That was Red. He wanted to dominate the car, dominate the road, dominate the whole damned state of Maine."

Volk says, "I think he's just fast and aggressive. He does have one unsettling habit: Red is not the paragon of manners, but for some reason while he's driving he insists on having eye contact with you when you're sitting in the backseat."

Auerbach can be a road menace even when he isn't driving. One day during the Larry Bird Era, Auerbach was running late for a Celtic game in Hartford, Connecticut. Celtic employee Mike Cole was doing the driving and Auerbach told him to step on the gas. Connecticut state troopers are famous for ticketing Massachusetts vehicles, and Cole expressed some concerns. Auerbach told Cole, "Don't worry, you're with me." Predictably, the car was pulled over by a radar-wielding state cop, and Cole swallowed a speeding ticket while Auerbach sat silently. After the episode, pulling back onto Route 84, Cole said, "Hey, Red, I though you said everything would be all right." Auerbach shrugged and said, "I guess he didn't recognize me."

In Boston, without his family, on the road with his ballplayers,

Auerbach dodged the traps that catch so many of the rich and famous people in professional sports. He was too committed. He has
too much discipline.

"I have never seen Red take a drink," says Jeff Cohen, who has
known Auerbach for more than forty years and worked side by side
with him for fifteen seasons. Cohen's dad, the late *Boston Herald*
sports editor Sammy Cohen, was one of Auerbach's best friends.
"Maybe once in a blue moon Red would have a cocktail, but that
would be it. I also never saw him with another woman. Never."

"That was not a priority in his life at all," says Cousy.

Everybody knew who the other woman was. The other woman
was basketball.

Auerbach believes in loyalty, change and teamwork. He loves it
when his guys come back to visit or call. The Celtics are a family.
They are a family business. Auerbach is the grandfather.

Chuck Daly, coach of the Detroit Pistons when they won back-
to-back NBA titles between 1988 and 1990, before coaching the
New Jersey Nets, says, "I've only gotten to know Red in later years,
because we were so competitive and there was an obvious dislike.
But down deep we all knew he was the original patriarch. And he
had really the right idea about what an organization was about: Loyalty. There are few people around still doing that. Some teams are
trying to emulate it. It just doesn't work. I think Dean Smith is able
to do it at North Carolina. They have that in Boston, and Red understood how important that was to create an atmosphere for winning. He was very unique in terms of the game and his relationship
with people. In the communicative aspect of it, he was very far ahead
of everyone else. He really was an unusual communicator."

World-famous as a shrewd general manager and a successful, ref-
heckling coach, Auerbach, before he was anything else, was a
teacher. He earned a master's degree in education at George Washington University and started his career as a high school teacher and
coach. He never lost this love of teaching. He still lives to give instruction to those who want to learn. He's proud of his instruction
book, the oft-copied obstacle course he developed, his basketball
videos, and the seven honorary degrees he has received since leaving
the bench. Attorney Alan Dershowitz recruited Auerbach to help

teach a course in sports law at Harvard, where Bill Russell's daughter and former NBA center Len Elmore were two of Red's students. Today, Auerbach earns up to $15,000 delivering his management theories to captains of industry.

His detractors claim that he was lucky, simply an okay coach who rode the coattails of the indomitable Bill Russell. But Auerbach did his homework when nobody else was doing homework. Before the 1956 NBA draft, Auerbach gave up two terrific players, got his owner to pledge the Ice Capades to Rochester and landed the greatest center in history. No one knew what Russell was going to be. Only Auerbach was willing to stake his reputation and his future on a nonshooting center who played his college ball three thousand miles from Boston. The acquisition of Russell took smarts, guts and foresight. Even Auerbach critics admit that Red has plenty of all three. The ones who say he was lucky are also the ones who could never beat him.

Hollywood director Bill Friedkin in 1993 directed *Blue Chips,* a movie that starred Nicke Nolte as a basketball coach. Auerbach was brought on board as a highly paid consultant. Friedkin told Volk that he had thought about doing a movie on Auerbach, but there wasn't enough failure to make the project work. A good film needs the main character to fall and rise again. Auerbach hardly ever fell. Too much success. Too boring.

He's always loved movies, and going to the show with him is a noisy and stomach-filling experience. Randy Auerbach, who works in Hollywood, enjoys artsy films that one might find at the Cannes Film Festival. Her dad likes Chuck Norris movies and popcorn.

"I took him to see my friend's movie, *Total Recall,* she remembers. "We bought popcorn, hot dogs, Chunkies, ice cream. We bought about twelve dollars' worth of food. Watching the movie, every five minutes he'd say, 'I don't get it. It's pretty good, but I don't get it.' And I'd say, 'Dad, just watch.' Finally, at the end he says, 'It was okay, but I still don't get it.' And I said, 'That's the point.' "

He can be very petty. Halberstam remembers the painful process of interviewing Auerbach for *The Breaks of the Game:* "I called him because I wanted to talk about his view of [former coach Jack] Ramsey and he just was extraordinarily unpleasant. I had credentials. His daughter works for a friend of mine. I had been with him before. I had gone out to dinner with him twenty years earlier with George Plimpton. We knew each other. You could make the connection and he just tried to bully me over the phone and I just said, 'What is this? I'm asking a simple thing. There's nothing at stake between coaches.' And he just came at me and bullied me and it was about power and about territory. And it was dumb in a way because it would have been so easy for him to be graceful, tell stories, to reminisce. And instead he took something that should have been pleasant and made it very unpleasant. You saw that part of him which is fighting for every piece of turf. But there's a part of Red that's very primitive and very crude."

Auerbach wouldn't let any Celtic wear No. 13 because he didn't like Wilt Chamberlain, who wore that number. He went two years without speaking to NBA publicity man Haskell Cohen. He detested the late Bill Mokray, Boston Garden owner Walter Brown's basketball director. In the 1980s, Auerbach stalked out of a charity testimonial for Curt Gowdy when he discovered he hadn't been seated at the head table. He long has lived with a persecution complex. He thinks the league is out to get him. Who other than Red Auerbach would scream at retired officials while serving as a coach in an NBA All-Star legends game?

In cities throughout the NBA, he was considered a bully, a sore loser, and an ungracious winner. This is a badge of honor for a man who believes that any good loser is merely a loser. One competes only if one is interested in winning. Otherwise, what's the point?

He particularly hates to lose in New York. It puts him in a nasty mood. Writer Irv Goodman, researching a 1965 *Sport* magazine profile on Auerbach, sat next to the Celtic coach on a shuttle flight to Boston after a loss in Madison Square Garden. Goodman described this exchange between Auerbach and a flight attendant who attempted to have him extinguish his cigar.

Flight attendant: "You'll have to put out that cigar."

Auerbach: "Honey, that sign doesn't say no smoking cigars."

Flight attendant: "Sorry, but for the comfort of all passengers, we don't permit cigar smoking."

Auerbach: "So, why don't you ask the passengers if my cigar smoking bothers them?"

Flight attendant: "I'm sorry, sir, but I'm afraid I'll have to insist."

Auerbach: "Don't be afraid, honey, and don't insist."

He smoked his cigar. All the way to Boston. Years later—ten thousand cigars later—an annoyed diner at Boston's renowned Legal Seafoods waved smoke from her face and demanded that the man at the next table, Red Auerbach, extinguish his cigar.

"Read the menu!" she scolded.

"No, lady," he snapped. "*You* read the menu!"

He had her. The menu at Legal Seafoods specified that cigar smoking is not permitted—except for Red Auerbach.

# 1

# THE EARLY YEARS

*In 1986, the day before they won their last championship, I went to lunch with Red, K. C. Jones and Jimmy Rodgers. After lunch, we came out and I looked in Red's car and the backseat was loaded with all kinds of clothes. Suits, jackets, pants. They were all piled up, all wrinkled. I said, 'What are you going to do with that?' He said, 'I'm going to go up and clean and press the suits. I used to do this when I was a kid. It was one of my jobs. I know a guy in Brookline, he's got a place up on Beacon Street and he lets me do it. I go over and do it for fun maybe once or twice a year.' I said, 'Why don't you just let him do it?' Dead serious, he said to me— 'I do this because it makes me think of where I came from.'*

WILL MCDONOUGH, Boston Globe *Columnist*

THE TWENTIETH CENTURY HAD JUST BEGUN WHEN HYMAN Auerbach, still a teenager, left his parents in Minsk and made the long, hopeful journey to the land of opportunity. Eastern Europe was becoming increasingly unfriendly to Jews. Thousands fled. Hymie and his older brothers, Sam and redheaded Louis, settled in the Williamsburg section of Brooklyn, New York's largest borough. Descendants of Hymie and his brothers say that the boys never thought of their journey as daring or remarkable. It was a chance to get out. It was a chance to make a new life.

Many Russian immigrants settled on New York's lower East Side of Manhattan, but there also was a Russian subculture in Brooklyn.

They assimilated quite well. Like all others who came over on the boat, Hymie was in America to make money. He took a job working the counter at Rosoff's Restaurant in Manhattan. He'd been educated in Russia and spoke a little Polish and English when he came to the States. An insatiable reader of New York newspapers, he quickly mastered the English language. He was outgoing, friendly and always willing to work.

He courted a pretty American Jewish girl named Marie Thompson (yes, a Jewish Thompson) who worked as a cashier at Rosoff's. They married, worked hard and saved their nickels. They bought a home on Lynch Street and settled into a third-floor apartment. The Auerbachs had four children in eleven years. Victor was born in 1914, Arnold on September 20 in 1917, Zangwell in 1921 and Florence in 1925. Victor was the top student in the family. Zang was artistic. Arnold, the middle boy, was athletic.

In 1920s Brooklyn, everybody had a nickname. Pickles, Boomie, Peaches, Dasmo, Ions, Bondo, Stinky, Shorty, Giggles, Buzzy, Lefty. Arnold was easy. Arnold Jacob Auerbach had his uncle Louis's hair. Arnold was Red.

Two forty-six Lynch Street was a short walk from the elevated trains that rumbled over Broadway toward New York City. Elementary school PS 33 was across the street from the Auerbach's home. Their piece of Brooklyn was in a mixed neighborhood of blacks, Russian Jews, Germans, Poles, Italians and Irish. There were the usual territorial scraps in the street. Red remembers hearing an occasional, "Hey, you lousy Jew!" but on the whole, everybody learned to get along. They had to.

When Red was about nine, he got into an argument with an Italian kid. The other boy swung first and Arnold went down. Lesson learned. Never again. Auerbach is seventy-seven years old, and it's been sixty-eight years since he waited for the other guy to hit first. Ask Ben Kerner, former owner of the St. Louis Hawks.

When the Auerbach children were young, Hymie owned his own delicatessen in Brooklyn. The old man was good with his hands, and one of Red's earliest memories is watching his dad surgically dissect breads and meats. Hymie got out of the deli business in 1931 and bought into a cleaning and drying plant. The company failed. He had a chance to buy an apartment building, but backed away because the cost seemed prohibitive (the daring move would have made him wealthy, but Hymie wasn't about to take chances with four children at home). Undaunted, Hymie bought a truck and entered into a dry-cleaning commission deal. His Manhattan pickup route stretched from the 50s down to the lower East Side, and sometimes young Red would make the rounds with his old man. All the clothing had to be numbered, and mistakes could not be made. Arnold learned to pay attention to detail. After a few years of this, Hymie went back into business for himself and opened his own dry-cleaning shop. "It's not how much money you make," he told his sons. "It's how much you've got left."

Red Auerbach spent a good part of his teen years pressing pants for Sunset Cleaners. The hotshot athlete wasn't too big to help out at home—there were nights when he'd come home from (Seth Low) college and press pants from ten at night until eight in the morning. Sunset charged 15 cents for pressing a suit. Red knew the math: One hundred suits meant $15 for Sunset Cleaners. Fifteen bucks for dad.

Red was a hustler, even as a child. The Auerbachs lived in a neighborhood where taxicabs lined up to get gas, and young Red would clean cab windows in hopes of getting a nickel tip. Today, stopping at city traffic lights, we recoil in fear when young men assault our cars with Windex. It's an unwelcome, bullying scam for tips. It was different in Brooklyn in the twenties. There was nothing intimidating about young Arnold. The drivers were happy to toss him a coin for his trouble.

Zang Auerbach remembers that his older brother always seemed to have four jobs. And Arnold always had a penny or a nickel for his younger brother—he kept spare change in hiding spots throughout the house. Red took care of his younger brother and sister. Even as a child, he was the godfather.

There were lessons learned. One day while riding the subway, young Red encountered a man selling socks for 5 cents per pair. Knowing a good deal, Auerbach paid 60 cents for a dozen pairs of socks. When he got home, he discovered that none of the socks matched. He had been taken. Research indicates that the long-gone, anonymous sock-peddler in the New York subway might have been the last guy to put one over on Red Auerbach. Today there are NBA front-office executives who no doubt would like to buy dinner for the sock-swindler who duped Red, if only to find out his secret.

"When I was in high school, my mother used to give me the money to pay the electric bill," Red says. "It was in the Bedford-Stuyvesant area. I used to roller-skate from my house to Myrtle Avenue and pay the bill. Our high school was quite a ways from Williamsburg. So I used to go on roller skates. I'd go up to get the trolley car and I'd hitch on the back with the roller skates. Other times, we'd hitch on the fender. When we played ball on the lower East Side in New York, we'd take the streetcar, which cost two cents to go over the Williamsburg Bridge. Once, I didn't have the money, but you could climb over the top of this tall fence. I did it twice, but then I thought about it and decided it was too goddamned dangerous—if I fall, I'm dead—so I stopped that. But we used to sneak into Ebbets Field and the movies. One day I was at the Loews Broadway and I had to go to the bathroom. When I came out, I got lost. I went down some steps and all of a sudden, I'm outside in the back of the theater. I went back in to see the show and then I said to myself, 'Why can't I sneak into this place?' Which I did, from then on."

The Auerbachs lived only a block off the East River. Auerbach remembers his father pointing out gangsters down by the docks on Forty-sixth Street between Eleventh and Twelfth avenues. There was a guy everybody called Swanee who made sure no harm came to the Auerbachs. According to Red's recollection, Swanee was put to death by electrocution.

Young Red steered clear of the neighborhood gangs, rackets and cellar clubs. He didn't play hooky. He didn't even smoke. It was out of respect for his parents. There were no policemen knocking on the Auerbachs' apartment door.

Auerbach's was a Neil Simon, Depression Brooklyn. Always, there were kids playing games in the streets and on vacant lots. It was never baseball, football or soccer, because there was not a blade of grass in the neighborhood. They couldn't even play stickball. For stickball, you needed tall buildings to keep the ball in play, and

Williamsburg didn't have high rises. Stickball was the province of those lucky kids near the tenements on Manhattan's lower East Side. Kids in Auerbach's neighborhood had to be creative. They played punchball, boxball, and handball; in high school, Red would captain the handball team. But most of the time, they played basketball. They played it on a rooftop, enclosed by wire.

Victor and Zang Auerbach were not into sports. Victor played a little high school basketball. Zang boxed a few times. Arnold was naturally competitive, and athletic competition provided him with a chance to excel. He would work at the games the way his dad worked at making money. In elementary school, Auerbach won a medal for compiling the most athletic points. It was an afternoon program that called for shooting baskets, doing broad and high jumps, performing chinups and competing in any other activity the gym teacher could invent. Points were compiled over the course of the entire school year, and Red set his sights on the No. 1 spot. He got it.

He played his first organized basketball on the roof of Public School 122. (Games were called off on days when it snowed or rained.) He went on to Eastern District High School, where he played varsity handball and basketball. He was only 5-9 and not especially fast, but he was smart enough to know his shortcomings. He suffered from asthma, but never to a point where it stopped him from playing ball. He made himself faster by running sprints long after the other kids went home.

The work paid off. One of Auerbach's greatest thrills was getting his picture in the *New York World-Telegram*'s Schoolboy Hall of Fame, becoming the first boy from Eastern District so honored. As a senior, he was named to the All-Brooklyn second team. Much later in life, Red Auerbach's place on the All-Brooklyn second team became a source of some ridicule from some of his Celtic ballplayers. Bill Russell would say, "All-Brooklyn? That's not even a whole city?" Red still likes to point out that Brooklyn, then and now, has more people than many states in our union.

Hymie thought all of this basketball activity was a waste of time. He indulged his boy, because the kid put in hours of work, but clearly there wasn't any future in basketball. In the Depression 1930s, a career in basketball seemed no more likely than a career in handball, boxball or punchball. Hymie wanted Red to take over the cleaning business. Red couldn't see himself standing behind a counter being nice to customers all day, every day, for the rest of his life. Red wanted college, and he was able to show his dad that basketball could help get him there.

Early in his high school career, a physical education teacher named Alvin Bolton reminded young Red that basketball wasn't the only ticket he'd need to get to college. Studying didn't come easily for Arnold, as it did for brother Victor, but Red cracked the books and got his average up to 88. The B-plus average enabled him to run for school president. Eastern District in the 1930s was a school of approximately twenty-five hundred students, most of them girls. Prior to the school election, candidate Red had to give a campaign speech. His knees buckled and his voice cracked, but he got through it. Backed by a $5 campaign war chest, he led the ticket of Auerbach, Rizzo and Rabinowitz and won the election, defeating Saul Ritter. His first duty was to read the Bible at school assembly. Again, he quaked. Ever bent on self-improvement, Red pledged to take a public speaking class when he got to college.

Auerbach always was resourceful, and he had a terrific head for numbers. In 1934, when he was seventeen, he needed uniforms for his neighborhood club team, the Pelicans. The uniforms cost $75, and money was tight in post-Depression Brooklyn. Young Red organized a ball game and dance day at the local YMHA. He rented the building for six hours on a Sunday afternoon, promoting three ball games capped by a dance. He hired a seven-piece band. He charged 25 cents a head and got five hundred kids to come. Five hundred patrons gave him gross receipts of $125. The rent was $25, shrinking his wad to $100. The band charged $14, a couple of dollars per man.

Paying the band would have left Auerbach with $86 dollars, $11 more than he needed for the uniforms, but one of the committee members lobbied to stiff the band and keep the extra cash. Red called for a vote and was beaten by a vote of five to three. The band didn't collect. The manager of the YMHA stepped in and told the committee that the building was off-limits if the band wasn't paid. Finally, the band was paid. There were hard feelings and Auerbach was embarrassed about the matter. The band's leader went on to become a famous comedian, Alan King. Auerbach and King still joke about this teenage joust from sixty years ago. King got his $2. Auerbach got his uniforms for the Pelicans.

Auerbach *loves* to tell this story about himself. Spend time in his company and you will hear the Alan King, stiff-the-band story. Maybe twice.

Auerbach graduated from high school in 1935 and enrolled at Seth Low Junior College, a Brooklyn branch of Columbia University. Seth Low was tucked into a couple of floors of the Brooklyn Law School. Red felt he was kept out of Columbia because he was Jewish. He didn't apply to New York University because the school required that all scholarship athletes had to go to the School of Business. Auerbach wanted physical education. He wanted to teach and coach. Nat Holman, the big-name coach at CCNY, called Auerbach about a scholarship, but Red was disappointed to learn that CCNY scholarship candidates needed an average of 92. (One wonders what type of program any school would have today if it implemented old-time requirements. Do the players at UNLV average 92 in the classroom? How good is MIT's basketball team?) Auerbach figured he didn't have any shot at Long Island University, so he enrolled at Seth Low, where tuition was $250 and they were offering a $100 scholarship. To earn the rest of his tuition, Red took a job with President Roosevelt's National Youth Administration. It paid $19.08 a month. His dad sent him $15 a month.

There were only 175 students at Seth Low. One of Auerbach's classmates was future science fiction writer Isaac Asimov. Everybody had to participate in athletics, even Isaac. "Asimov wasn't much of an athlete, but he tried hard," says Auerbach.

It was at Seth Low that Hymie finally got to see his son play basketball. After watching his first game, the father told his son, "You're in the living room and all the action is in the kitchen. You're too far away from where the action is." Red liked that. The old man didn't know basketball, but he knew where the action was.

"My father was a hard worker," says Red. "He paid a price. He was a thinker. The difference between me and my father is that he loved people. He'd make friends wherever he'd go, very quickly. I wasn't an introvert, but I wasn't a hail-fellow-well-met who went out and was buddies with everybody. My father was a very friendly man. He liked people and people liked him, and I'm just the opposite. I've got a lot of real good friends, but basically, I'm an introvert. I couldn't go to a bar and sit around and talk to people. I couldn't go on an airplane and by the time I leave the airplane, the people next to me are my buddies. My father could do that. I can't do that. I know this: I didn't do anything to disappoint my dad."

Brother Zang (a Washington artist who designed the official Celtic logo in the mid-1960s) says, "My father was like a lot of immigrants of that period. They were all gonna solve world problems. They knew everything. And remember, this was the Depression. My father worked seven days a week, twenty hours a day just to survive. Around our house, it was pretty much, 'Who's the stranger?' And the stranger was my father. Mom was pretty much everything. She was the disciplinarian, the comforter. You couldn't possibly do something that was against the law. There was always that feeling—'What would my mother say?' We had great fear and respect of the law, and the respect was my mother."

Fate played a hand in the career of Red Auerbach, in the person of Bill Reinhart.

William J. Reinhart was born on August 2, 1896, and grew up in Salem, Oregon. He played on Salem high school teams that won state championships in baseball, basketball and football. His high school nickname was "Dollar Bill." In 1915 he enrolled at Missouri Wesleyan College in Cameron, where he matriculated for one year. In the fall of 1916 he transferred to the University of Oregon, but he left in 1917 to join the army. He served in France during World War I, then returned to Oregon, where he quarterbacked and captained the mighty Ducks. He led Oregon to the 1919 Rose Bowl (a 7–6 loss to Harvard, of all teams) and served as captain of the baseball and basketball teams in his senior year. After graduating from Oregon, he went to work for Standard Oil as head of the statistical division. He wanted to be chairman of the board of Standard Oil. Two years later, he went back to Oregon for graduate work and was offered head coaching jobs in baseball and basketball.

Reinhart later said, "I took the jobs because they involved working with kids and there were a lot less competent men than I who were successful as coaches. Sports are simple and logical. Coaches are the only teachers who are *given* tests."

Reinhart was successful at Oregon, and in 1935 he was lured to D.C. by George Washington University football coach and athletic director Jim Pixlee. One of Reinhart's former Oregon players, Gordon Ridings, was head coach of basketball at Seth Low. When George Washington came to New York to play LIU, a scrimmage was arranged at Seth Low's humble home court, the Plymouth Church.

Reinhart was impressed by Seth Low's fiery guard, the kid with the red hair and the hollow eye sockets. He took young Auerbach aside and asked if he'd be interested in playing college basketball at George Washington, in the nation's capital. Red had only one consideration. He wanted to know if he'd keep his scholarship if he failed to make the GW team. Reinhart told him that if he kept his marks up—regardless of his basketball fortunes—he would leave GM with a diploma. It was the kind of deal Red later struck with many of his own players. It was a promise, a handshake agreement between men of goodwill. It was enough. Auerbach went to Washington . . . and never left. Almost sixty years later, home in D.C., Auerbach still goes to George Washington University almost every day. He sometimes plays racquetball, sometimes works out and sometimes just schmoozes.

In the fall of 1936, Auerbach walked onto the GW court and saw a lot of competition. A 5-9 Jew from Brooklyn, he was a target. He was a street kid, a city player who knew his way around any court. The other candidates for the team thought he was a dirty ballplayer. Some of the well-mannered kids from the farms didn't know how to set picks or shoot off a screen. Brooklyn Red got into four fights in his first two weeks of practice. He made the team.

What he'd learned at home from watching his father, he learned at the gym watching Reinhart. Auerbach believes his college coach invented the modern fast break: *Snatch the rebound, fire the pitchout to the guards, then fill the lanes down the floor while passing the ball back and forth. Go for the three-on-two advantage. No dribbling—it takes too much time.* Auerbach credits Reinhart with the invention of the long-pass drill. Larry Bird in the 1980s was one of the best practitioners of the Sammy Baugh, court-length, TD bomb. Reinhart-to-Auerbach-to-Bird. Praise the rebound and pass the ball the length of the floor.

GW's practices were tough. All of Reinhart's strategies required that his ballplayers be in the same condition as long-distance runners. You had to be in shape; it gave you an edge over your opponent. Watch the other guy get winded before you did. Don't sit down during time-outs. Show the other guy that you're never going to get tired. It was a nonskill; it simply was a product of dedication and commitment.

Reinhart was a teacher, and he had a special way of communicating his message. He once benched Auerbach for several games without any explanation. Red kept his mouth shut and came back with a vengeance.

The GW coach didn't smoke or drink. He was tough on his players, but treated them with respect. He wasn't too proud to admit a mistake. During Auerbach's early days at George Washington, Reinhart had the players running the streets of Washington as a conditioning exercise (he made them wear school colors, and Red suspected this might have been a promotional tool as well). When a couple of players went on the shelf with shinsplints, Reinhart discontinued the practice. Thereafter, all of GW's conditioning work was done in the 90-by-50-foot space of the basketball floor. Auerbach later applied the same technique with the Celtics. Red's team ran, but only on the hardwood.

In thirty-one years at George Washington, Reinhart won 525 varsity games as a head coach of baseball, football and basketball. His baseball teams went 193–133. In football, he was 16–17–1. Basketball was Reinhart's game, and in twenty-four seasons his teams went 315–239, earning two trips to the NCAA tournament. His GW days were interrupted by a stint in the navy, commencing in 1942. While in the navy, Reinhart established new training programs for naval personnel. Boxer Gene Tunney trained under Reinhart. Commander Reinhart left the navy in 1946 and took over as football coach and athletic director of the U.S. Merchant Marine Academy in Kings

Point, New York. He coached at Kings Point for three years before returning to GW in August 1949.

Reinhart didn't go back to football when he returned to GW, but he coached baseball and basketball for almost two more decades. His 1953–1954 Colonial hoopsters went 23–3. Even in years when they were down, Reinhart's GW teams got tough when it came time for the Southern Conference tournament.

He and his wife, Roslyn, loved duckpin bowling. His son, William Jr., became an army helicopter pilot and served as President Eisenhower's personal pilot in the 1950s. It was not unusual for one of Bill Reinhart's baseball games to be interrupted when Bill Jr. flew overhead, carrying the most powerful man in the world.

Reinhart retired as GW basketball mentor in 1966, the fourth-winningest active coach in NCAA history (at least 475 victories, although Oregon's records are incomplete). At the time of his retirement, he trailed only Kentucky's Adolph Rupp, Oklahoma State's Hank Iba and Butler's Paul Hinkle. After leaving the bench, he went to work as a substitute teacher in chemistry, math and shop. At seventy years old, he said, "Sports have been a way of life for me since I made the decision to forgo a business career and started coaching at Oregon in 1924."

He told the *Washington Post,* "The only way to make sense to a kid is to be a kid yourself. One thing, you won't find me sitting on my fanny."

In 1966, by which time Auerbach had become the most successful coach in the history of professional sports, he said, "A lot of Reinhart rubbed off on me. Not the tantrums I throw, of course— Bill seldom lost his poise. But I've got red hair. Still, even when I threw my fits on the Celtics' bench, I never lost control of the game. He was a wonderful proselytizer. He could adapt himself. If he visited a family of a coal miner's son in Pennsylvania, he could sit and drink beer in the kitchen with the best of 'em. If it was some rich kid's house, Bill could handle a little itty-bitty teacup, too."

By all accounts, Reinhart was a man without prejudice. A German-American raised in Oregon, he finished his career coaching at a Catholic elementary school. Reinhart died on Valentine's Day,

1971. He was buried as a Catholic. Twenty-two years later, he was inducted into the George Washington Sports Hall of Fame. His nephew, Robert F. Reinhart, is at work on a biography of Bill Reinhart's life. Robert says, "The fast break and the outlet pass originated on the kitchen table at One Sixty-eight South Twenty-fourth Street in Salem, Oregon, on a piece of paper and pencil in the hands of my uncle, Bill Reinhart. He drew up the fast break and the transition defense right there."

Strategy was one thing, but Auerbach was most impressed with Reinhart's discipline and his loyalty. The coach made sure his players got degrees, and he kept tabs on most of his former athletes. Many became coaches. If you were one of his guys, you were one of his guys for life. A lot of the alums came back to watch GW play. At the tiny college in our nation's capital, Reinhart built the same kind of basketball family that Auerbach later brought to Boston. The things that Auerbach became famous for—winning, teaching, loyalty and a prestigious private club of former players who became lifelong friends—were all characteristics of Reinhart. When Reinhart was inducted into the George Washington University Sports Hall of Fame in the spring of 1993, Auerbach was one of those who put him up for consideration. Arnold Auerbach is Bill Reinhart's legacy.

"Reinhart was Red's first real hero," says brother Zang. "He was like his priest, his rabbi, and he unquestionably made a great impression on him. I don't think I've ever heard him speak without giving Reinhart some credit. This was his mentor. Red's not a follower, he's a leader. But he always was quoting Coach Reinhart. He genuinely loved this guy. He became the same guy."

"I wouldn't say I modeled my personality after him," says Auerbach. "I liked his coaching philosophies. I liked the way he ran the break, conducted the practices and had control. There were a lot of things I liked about him. He was a great coach, way ahead of his time. But he was a little more reserved. He was a quiet, bright guy. He coached football and baseball, too. I looked up to him, the way he conducted himself and his knowledge of the game. He knew the game, and after I left we were in touch all the time. I used to give him credit."

Seventy-six-year-old Mo Siegel, who in 1946 covered Red Auerbach's first pro team, the Washington Caps, says, "I'll say one thing about Red: He lavishes every bit of credit on Reinhart. He'd have the Caps practice one hour. At the most. He said, 'If you get sixty minutes out of an hour, it's as good as practicing five hours and farting around.' That was from Reinhart."

"There are coaches in the [pro basketball] Hall of Fame who couldn't carry his jock," says Auerbach.

Auerbach played three seasons at GW, serving as captain in his senior year. He was a heady guard who ran the offense and averaged 10 points per game. George Washington went 38–19 in his three years and in 1937–1938 beat Minnesota, Ohio State and St. John's. According to Auerbach, in his sophomore season the Colonials were aced out of an NIT bid because the tourney committee didn't want the little Washington school upsetting a big-draw team from New York. Auerbach has never forgotten this slight. A Brooklyn kid who worked hard to become a major-college basketball player, he never got to play in Madison Square Garden. For more than forty years, Auerbach's always made his teams play a little harder in New York. Only Red could watch a 1990s Celtic victory in Madison Square Garden and think of it as payback for an NIT slight from almost a half century earlier. But it's true. All of Auerbach's Madison Square Garden wins are a little payback for Reinhart. Losses to New York, and particularly losses *in* New York, remain the toughest to take.

Auerbach has never abandoned his George Washington Colonials, even when they went 1–27 in 1989–1990. In the spring of 1993, GW advanced to the NCAA Sweet 16, beating Coastal Carolina and UCLA before losing to Michigan in the West Regional. The NCAA games were televised into the student center at GW. When George Washington beat UCLA in Tucson at the west subregional, students at the GW campus center in Washington pulled out cigars and lit up.

It was at GW that Arnold Auerbach met his lifelong companion, Dorothy Lewis. When Red was a junior, Dot was a sixteen-year-old freshman, an education major who wanted to be a newspaperwoman. In the summer before her freshman year, she worked at the *Washington Times Herald*, writing an advice column for the lovelorn. ("I loved it," she says. "I learned to set the type, write the answers and sometimes make up the questions.") She was a strikingly beautiful brunette, the daughter of Washington pediatrician Dr. Edward Lewis.

Auerbach first spotted her in the Student Club at GW. "She was sittin' there with a bunch of kids and I said, 'Man, that's a good-looking chick,'" remembers Auerbach. Quite taken by her long legs and fiery black eyes, he bought her a cola and took her for a walk on the small patch of grass outside the Student Club. She knew he was a basketball player, and a member of the TEP fraternity. He seemed to know what he wanted in life. He wanted to teach and coach. He had plans and was going to see them through. A young woman from a good family was impressed by these traits of dependability.

"I don't remember what he said that first day," says Dorothy. "We just started to talk in the Student Club and then go out on dates; in those days it was either games or movies. We'd get something to eat after the movies. He was a big man on campus, but nice, sort of quiet and reserved. He was not a blowhard."

In those first years away from Brooklyn, Auerbach was very much into self-improvement. He wanted to be a teacher, and worked to eliminate his Brooklyn accent. In his new world, nobody said "foist" for first, or "thoid" for third. Meanwhile, as always, he worked, supplementing his scholarship with a variety of part-time jobs. He swept buildings and washed windows for 40 cents an hour. He was a camp counselor and athletic director on D.C. playgrounds. He answered the switchboard at the *Baltimore Sun*'s Washington bureau (sportswriters who've wrestled with Auerbach through the years no doubt chuckle at the thought of Red at a newspaper switchboard). For $25 a month, he worked in the National Training School for Boys, where young car thieves and other delinquents were rehabilitated. At the school, Auerbach learned lessons of discipline, authority and the human condition. Kids took advantage. Kids stole. But sometimes, *when kids got respect, they gave respect.*

"That was one of the greatest experiences of my life for learning about people," he says.

He needed a car for his job at the School for Boys, and he went to his dad to ask for $125—an advance on his monthly $15 stipend from home. He bought an eight-year-old Ford convertible with the $125.

In the spring of 1940, Auerbach was awarded a bachelor of science degree in physical education. He made a deal with GW to direct intramurals in exchange for tuition for his master's degree. Red and Dot wanted to get married, but that wouldn't happen until he got a job. While in the master's program, he landed a position as basketball coach at the prestigious St. Alban's Prep School. His first days of coaching were disastrous. His preppy players were woefully green and he overestimated their abilities. He was barking orders that they could not understand. It was a rookie mistake. After watching them flounder for four days, he told his players to forget everything he had told them. His next words were: "This is a basketball . . . " They proceeded from square one and staggered through a losing season.

Red still winces at the recollection of the final game of his first season on the bench. St. Alban's led, 17–16, and had the ball with five seconds to play. Incredibly, the kid who threw the ball inbounds decided to try a behind-the-back pass. The fancy maneuver was intercepted and St. Alban's lost by one point. Auerbach never has been a fan of razzle-dazzle basketball. Years later, he would balk when he had to coach a fancy-pants hotshot from Holy Cross College—Bob Cousy. Some players would rather look good and lose. Auerbach didn't care if he looked bad, as long as he won.

The St. Alban's experience was the beginning of Auerbach's long career on the bench. More important, it was a job. It was income and respectability. It made young Arnold Auerbach a legitimate provider. He and Dorothy got engaged in October 1940—Dorothy's grandparents' fiftieth anniversary. Arnold and Dorothy were married in a rabbi's home on June 5, 1941, a rainy Thursday in Washington, D.C. The reception luncheon was held at the Old Wardman Park Hotel on Connecticut Avenue (now the Sheraton Park). It was somewhat of a mixed marriage: Dorothy Lewis was the daughter of a prominent Washington pediatrician; Arnold Auerbach was the son of a Russian immigrant who owned a cleaning store in Brooklyn. All four parents attended the wedding, along with Auerbach's brother, Zang, and Dorothy's brother, and one of Auerbach's GW teammates. No one remembers why the wedding was on a Thursday.

"In retrospect, it was probably because everybody else got married on Saturday," says Dorothy. "We're really not conventional people. And we're definitely not chic. I'm not a great one for big displays. I hate 'em."

The newlyweds moved in with Dorothy's parents for nine months while she completed her studies toward an education degree at George Washington. When Dorothy graduated, they took an apartment at Cathedral Mansions, a block and a half from Dorothy's parents' home. She worked for the government, briefly, then took a position at a junior high school library. After a short spell, she walked off the job and went to the Pentagon, where she was a clerk in the motion picture division of the Air Corps. She turned down William Wyler's offer of a Hollywood screen test for $75 per week for six weeks. Legendary movie star photographer George Hurrell walked into the Pentagon office one day, saw the fiery brunette sitting at her typewriter and said, "Come on, Dorothy, I'll take your picture." The picture, a young Dorothy in all of her starlet beauty, today sits on Red Auerbach's office desk. He points to it and says, "People would give their right nut for a picture like that."

Randy Auerbach describes her diverse sets of grandparents: "It's so funny, because there was such a gap. My mother's parents were southern, refined, gentle. And my father's parents were New York Jews. And it was a real contrast for me in that sense. But my father was very wonderful to my mother's parents. He really liked them.

"My father's parents were from Brooklyn. Growing up, I remember they would come visit, and it was like they just got off the boat with bagels and all sorts of nuts and candies from the lower East Side. Lox and all that. My grandfather was tremendously energetic. He would get up very early and have something ready and take a walk and buy a paper. If we went to New York to spend the weekend with him, we'd see the Staten Island Ferry and the Statue of Liberty. I was exhausted. He just wore me out. He was a guy in the true sense of that New York period. He'd be up and having coffee at six

A.M. and reading the paper and arguing and talking. My grandmother was very devoted, but I don't remember that much about her. He was more overpowering. She was very proud."

A married man with new responsibilities, young Arnold got his master's degree and was named to the faculty of Roosevelt High School in Washington. He would teach history and hygiene, while coaching basketball and baseball—all for $1,800 a year. When he started the new job, he had to get one thing straight: Some of the students who knew him from his summer playground job started calling him "Red." Other teachers with similar conflicts permitted informal salutations, but Auerbach would have no part of it. He told his students that the position of teacher warranted the title of "Mr." He expected to be called "Mr. Auerbach."

Patrolling the corridors of Roosevelt, Auerbach encountered a student who later would have a tremendous impact on professional sports. Always looking for talent, the young coach in 1941 corralled a sturdy, 6-5 kid named Bowie Kuhn. Auerbach invited the tall youngster to come to basketball tryouts. Kuhn said he was quite clumsy and would not be of any use to the coach. The coach insisted, and so the kid came out for the team. It didn't last. Auerbach cut him after one day. Kuhn went on to become commissioner of major league baseball; Auerbach went on to find other tall ballplayers.

The new coach stressed rebounding and running. In two seasons at Roosevelt, his teams went 13–1 in conference play, but each time were eliminated in the first round of the local tournament. The playoff losses were by one and two points, respectively. This meant that in three seasons of high school coaching, Auerbach's teams had lost their last game each year, by an aggregate total of four points. Close. No cigars. In light of what happened later on, when he made sports history, it's easy to forget that unsatisfactory finishes dogged Auerbach for the first fifteen years of his coaching life. Red never forgot.

He doesn't remember much about his brief tenure as a baseball coach. "I was the worst," says Auerbach. "I coached it one year. I'd never played baseball as a kid. I would tell the kids, 'Look, there's nobody to do this here except me. I'll do the best I can and that's it.' I'd played a little in junior college, a little first base and second base. I think my batting average was .142."

He didn't rest in the summers during his high school coaching years. Three months gave him time to make extra money, so he took to the playgrounds and began a career as a basketball official. There are a lot of NBA referees and administrators who no doubt would pay big money for a photograph of Arnold Auerbach wearing the zebra stripes. For seven bucks a game, the most celebrated referee nemesis of all time worked the whistle himself. This is a little like Ralph Nader doing commercials for General Motors.

Auerbach on his career as an official: "When you get out of school, you've got to do a lot to supplement your income. I had a lot of jobs. I was intramural director at the school and I worked the playground and the Boys Club and I was a cashier. Some of those jobs dissipated after I went for my master's, so I started refereeing. I took the test for the association and failed, because it was a clique and they didn't want to let me in. I got forty-seven out of fifty true-false questions right and they said I needed forty-eight. It was one of those bullshit things.

"So I said, 'I'll fix these guys.' I talked to friends of mine and they gave me their whole schedule to work. Girls' and boys' games. So it turned out I was making as much, if not more, than these other guys. I had the industrial league at night. So finally, they saw what was happening and said they'd take me in the organization. Within a year, I was doing college games—Georgetown, the Naval Academy, Catholic University, American University. I was a pretty good official. I always felt that when the coach sees you're in control, you don't have any problems."

While he was at Roosevelt, Auerbach published his plan for an obstacle course. In the March 1943 issue of the *Journal of Health and Physical Education*, there is an article written by "A. J. Auerbach." Auerbach's model later was used to design obstacle courses for the U.S. Navy. Red still keeps a copy of the publication, and is fiercely proud of his plan.

Like most young men of his generation, Auerbach heard the call after Pearl Harbor. He was a citizen, a patriot and a man. This meant he had to sign on. After he finished his second year at Roosevelt, he joined the navy in May 1943.

Red's Washington connections have always served him well, and when he joined the navy, George Washington's athletic director, Max Farrington, had him placed in the Physical Fitness Program under former heavyweight boxer Gene Tunney. Auerbach took his boot training at the Great Lakes Naval Training Station outside Chicago. He made third-class petty officer, then was transferred to the Physical Instructors School at Bainbridge, Maryland. At Bainbridge, he was in the same unit with future college basketball guru Pete Newell, big league slugger Johnny Mize and Red Sox infielder Johnny Pesky.

"I was being processed," remembers Pesky. "I was just going through Bainbridge to go to Atlanta to get my commission. It was in the wintertime, during the basketball season, and I got to know Red. I think he was a chief petty officer, but he put this team together with a bunch of college guys. You could tell he knew what he was talking about. He must have had good schooling. He used to talk about Billy Reinhart a lot."

After Bainbridge, most of Auerbach's pals got cozy assignments conditioning navy fliers at universities. Those officers were allowed to bring their wives with them and live on campus. Auerbach was shipped to the Norfolk Naval Base, which he considered the worst stateside post. There had been some negative press about too many famous athletes at Norfolk, so the navy sent some of the big names out and sent Auerbach in to set up an intramural program for sailors. Auerbach had written his fellowship thesis on intramural sports. He had run camps and clinics. He'd been a coach, a teacher and an official. He was perfect for the position. Norfolk in the early 1940s was not particularly sailor-friendly, but there was one great benefit for Arnold J. Auerbach: Reinhart was a full commander there.

Bob Feller and Phil Rizzuto were among the baseball stars at Norfolk. Basketball players included Bob Feerick (Santa Clara), Red Holzman (CCNY), Matt Zunic (George Washington), Jim Floyd (Oklahoma A & M), Ralph Bishop (Washington), Johnny Norlander (Hamline), Belus Smawley (Appalachian State) and Bob Carpenter

(East Texas). Auerbach had a pretty good team. He took his guys "off campus" a few times and they won some impressive exhibitions in arenas in Washington. He got forty bucks a game to coach against the all-black Washington Bears at Turner's Arena. The Bears had just won a national tournament in Chicago, but Auerbach's sailors won two of three. Washington arena owner Mike Uline noticed.

Meanwhile, Auerbach's mental file cabinet was growing. He remembered the names and the abilities of all the players he saw. This was going to come in handy very soon; professional basketball was only three years away.

In the winter of 1944 Auerbach earned his ensign stripes and was sent to the Sampson Naval Base in upstate New York, then to Bethesda Hospital in Washington for rehabilitation work with the wounded. Back in D.C., he formed a basketball team of Washington Redskin football players. He took them to Uline Arena in Washington and they played a couple of exhibitions against the Philadelphia Eagle football/basketball team. Mike Uline again was impressed by the brash young coach.

In 1946, Arnold and Dorothy gave birth to their first child. Daughter Nancy was born in February, just a few months before her dad was scheduled to be discharged from the navy. The folks at Roosevelt were waiting for him to return to his old job, where he would be paid $2,900. The Auerbachs were living in a $65-a-month garden apartment in Buckingham Village in Arlington, Virginia.

A young couple could hardly have been more settled. The breadwinner was an honorably discharged veteran, a husband, a father, a teacher and a coach of young people. His father-in-law was a local pediatrician. It looked like Arnold was set for life in a profession he loved.

It was all there, waiting for him . . . when he heard about the formation of a new professional basketball league—a league that was going to have a franchise in Washington. Auerbach wanted to make a bid. He wanted to coach the Washington franchise.

Everything about the embryonic Basketball Association of America was risky. Pro basketball hadn't made it in the past. Another pro league, the National Basketball League, was decidedly small-time.

In the NBL there were franchises in Fort Wayne, Rochester, Anderson, Oshkosh and Sheboygan. Players made between ten and forty bucks a game and most of them had real jobs outside of basketball. Games were played in dance halls and crummy old arenas. Americans had been slow to embrace the pro game.

"I always felt during that time, why couldn't the great stars of basketball be put on an equal level with those in baseball and football?" Auerbach said forty years later. "I wondered: Whatever happened to the heroes of college basketball? They were still young people when they stopped playing. I felt that if somebody had the idea of getting a league together that featured these great stars in continual performance, it would have public appeal. I believed in the concept of professional basketball."

On a personal level, he saw the formation of the new league as a one-time opportunity. He figured if it flopped he could go back to teaching or refereeing; he'd seen his father fail and start over. He talked it over with Dot. She encouraged him to take the chance. She was the one who would sacrifice the most, since the basketball life meant nonstop travel, but she knew it was what he wanted. Red, Dot, Dot's parents and her aunt and uncle held a family conference. Dot's uncle, Selig Brez, a Washington lawyer, told Red, "If you're ever going to take a chance, do it now, while you're young. If you don't you're going to be a teacher for the rest of your life without ever knowing what you might have done in a highly competitive field. The worst thing you can do is go into civil service and then let things like pensions and retirement benefits take precedence over your ambition. It just doesn't suit your kind of personality, Red."

"I think it was his vision of a way out," says Zang Auerbach. "Everyone thought basketball was a waste of time. Red was one of the biggest crapshooters in the world, but how could you have the stupidity to leave a high school teaching job to go into pro basketball?"

Red posed one more question to his ever-understanding wife. He knew that if he became a pro basketball coach, he might someday have to relocate in order to stay in the profession. He did not want to start this new career, then abandon it because his wife wouldn't move. She heard this warning and still told her husband to go ahead. If he eventually got a job in another town, they would find a way to work things out.

Mike Uline owned the franchise rights to Washington's professional basketball team. He had made his fortune on patents for ice-making machines. He didn't know a thing about basketball, but he knew he didn't want to go to New York's Ned Irish or Philadelphia's Eddie Gottlieb for advice. He didn't want to have to ask them whom he should hire to take charge of his basketball operation, since these were the people he'd soon be trying to beat.

In May 1946, Uline looked across his desk at a twenty-eight-year-old, redheaded navy officer who was selling himself as the man to coach a team that still had no players.

"Mr. Uline, I think I can do the job for you," said Auerbach. He then explained how he could get top players without spending buckets of money. He knew where the players were, and in the navy he'd shown what he could do with top talent. Uline had seen the talented and well-coached service teams that Auerbach had brought into his arena.

On paper, it was a little silly. Auerbach was very young and hadn't even coached college ball. St. Alban's to Roosevelt High to professional basketball? How could professional basketball have any credibility if owners were handing teams over to high school coaches?

A cautious man, Uline could see the practical benefit of hiring Auerbach: The kid would come cheap. It was done. Uline gave Auerbach a one-year contract worth $5,000.

"I was always a bit brash," Auerbach said years later. "I don't know why, but Mike bought my brag."

"Who knew what it was going to become?" says Dorothy Auerbach almost fifty years later. "He was here; it was a Washington team. Other than road trips, it was a home base. I didn't want him to be in sales—real estate, insurance—where you make a killing and then you sit for six months. That's not my style. I'd rather have less and know I'm having it."

In the fall of 1946, Red Sox shortstop Pesky was busy hitting .335

for the first-place Boston team. The Sox were on their way to their first World Series appearance since 1918. In Washington to play the Senators, Pesky picked up a newspaper and read about his service pal from Bainbridge. Twenty-eight-year-old Arnold J. "Red" Auerbach was the coach of a new professional basketball team, the Washington Capitols.

# 2

# PROFESSIONAL BASKETBALL

---

*Red was an original. He came in one night and held up
the game because he had to measure the goddamned baskets.
He had somehow brought in this big tape measure and
claimed we had a shorter basket.*

SID HARTMAN, *representing the Minneapolis Lakers, 1948*

Washington Capitols. Boston Celtics. Cleveland Rebels. New York Knickerbockers. Philadelphia Warriors. Providence
Steamrollers. Toronto Huskies. Chicago Stags. Detroit Falcons.
Pittsburgh Ironmen. St. Louis Bombers.

These were the original eleven franchises in the Basketball Association of America. Three of the original eleven are alive today
(Washington, Cleveland, Chicago and Detroit's 1994 franchises are
unrelated to the original eleven). The Philadelphia Warriors moved
to San Francisco and today play as the Golden Gate Warriors. The
New York Knicks and the Boston Celtics are continuous. The Celtics
are the only NBA team still playing in the same gym they used in
1946.

The league was officially born on June 6, 1946 (the second anniversary of D day), when representatives of the eleven sites convened in New York City at the Commodore Hotel on East
Forty-second Street next to Grand Central Station. Ten of the eleven
original league members had ties to professional hockey clubs in
their respective cities. Arena owners were looking for alternative
forms of entertainment to fill their big barns on the cold winter

nights when there were no hockey games. There were only so many ice shows, boxing matches, circuses, rodeos and track meets. Postwar Americans had new leisure hours and a little bit of pocket change, and they wanted to go out and be entertained. The arena owners and hockey honchos decided to give professional basketball a major push.

There had been pro baseball before the BAA. The game was invented in Springfield, Massachusetts, in 1891, and by 1898 there was a National Basketball League with teams in New York, New Jersey and Pennsylvania. The disorganized league dissolved after little more than a decade. George Preston Marshall, George Halas and Max Rosenblum in 1925 organized the American Basketball League, which featured nine teams between Brooklyn and Chicago. This league of the roaring twenties was shut down for several years during the Great Depression, and never fully recovered. The strongest and most famous franchise in the old league was the New York Original Celtics. Teams routinely went on barnstorming tours, and legend has it that in 1922 the New York Celts went 193–11. There was an all-black team known as the New York Rens (named after the Renaissance Ballroom), and the Harlem Globetrotters were formed in 1927.

Pro basketball effectively vanished during the Depression; games were played in dance halls, and there usually was a dance before and after the contest. Home teams almost always won. In 1937, the National Basketball League followed the American Basketball League. The next year, the NBL eliminated the center jump after each basket—a decision for which the world is forever grateful. The league shrunk to three teams during World War II, but it was back up to a dozen franchises in the fall of 1945. America was feeling good about itself. A crowd of 23,912 came out in Chicago to watch the two-time NBL champion Fort Wayne Pistons play a team of college all-stars. This kind of action, and the regular sellouts of college doubleheaders in Madison Square Garden and Boston Garden, buoyed the hopes of the men who ran professional hockey—the men who were starting up the new professional basketball league.

The Washington Capitols were the only BAA franchise with no links to hockey. Five BAA teams were associated with the National

Hockey League, five with the American Hockey League. Maurice Podoloff, a New Haven lawyer who served as president of the AHL, was the first commissioner of the BAA. Podoloff's promotion came at the insistence of Chicago owner Arthur Wirtz. Wirtz owned the NHL Black Hawks and said he wouldn't join the new basketball league unless Podoloff was in charge.

In innocent, ignorant fashion, this new pro basketball league borrowed from the National Hockey League. Owners wanted games that would last around two hours (similar to hockey in the 1940s), so they extended the forty-minute college game and settled on forty-eight minutes. (We can be thankful the BAA didn't push for pro basketball games to be played in three periods. Basketball didn't require twenty-minute breaks for the Zamboni to clean the ice.) It's ironic that pro basketball in its early days chose to borrow from the NHL, because in the 1990s the National Hockey League consistently copied the progressive, marketing-friendly NBA. In an effort to borrow some of the NBA magic of the nineties, the NHL in 1992–1993 anointed Gary Bettman as commissioner. Bettman had been one of the best and brightest NBA minds working under Commissioner David Stern.

The BAA of 1946–1947 played four quarters of twelve minutes each. It was established that the ballplayers would be signed to exclusive contracts—just like in major baseball. Each year, teams would draft from the pool of college talent, and the draft order would be the reverse of the final standings from the year before. To build up local interest, teams could exercise territorial draft picks.

Washington's Uline knew nothing about hockey or basketball. This would work in Auerbach's favor. An owner who didn't interfere was preferable to an owner with a little bit of knowledge—an owner who could stick his nose in just enough to screw things up.

Uline gave young Auerbach two orders: Find enough players to field a team, and don't spend too much money.

Auerbach knew exactly how he wanted to go about assembling his team, and again, Reinhart was his model. Basketball in the 1940s was still a regional game. It was played differently in different parts of the country. New York and Jersey had the smart guards, the Midwest had runners and power players, while the big tough rebounders were coming from the West. Most of the BAA franchises in 1946 carved teams from local colleges. New York loaded up on kids from New York area schools, Boston went for players from the New England colleges, and so on. Coaches felt comfortable recruiting players they had seen, and local players were liable to draw more fans. As a result of this provincial approach, teams of similarly skilled players were built. New York had the ballhandlers. St. Louis had the one-handed jump shooters, Detroit and Cleveland had the runners. Auerbach had a different idea. Because of his navy background, he knew players from all over the country. Red wanted a mix of talents, the kind of team Reinhart had built at George Washington. Auerbach figured his fans wanted winners more than local attractions.

The assumption that certain parts of the country breed certain types of players was, at best, a gross generalization. There might have been something to it in 1946 (we still hear of typical "Philly guards" and "Big Ten Rebounders"), but it's much like saying all Swedes have blond hair or all Kenyans are good distance runners.

Though the generalizations are less true now than they were in the 1940s, some believe Auerbach still sees geography as a facet of a ballplayer's game. This is not only politically incorrect, but it can lead to a disastrous draft pick. In 1989, the Boston Celtics drafted a 6-10 forward named Michael Smith. Smith was from Brigham Young, and Auerbach pegged him as a guy who might someday play a little like Larry Bird. He was supposed to be sound on fundamentals, team-oriented, and a good weapon in a running, passing offense. But Smith was a fraud. He was a slow, fundamental-bound NBA player of the fifties, not one suited for the run-and-jump nineties. In picking Smith, the Celtics passed on future All-Star guard Tim Hardaway. No one has ever taken full blame for the Smith pick, but there's a real possibility that Auerbach was simply employing the same type of thinking that worked so well for him when he carved out his first team in 1946.

Auerbach says he no longer believes in regional typecasting: "It all was neutralized about thirty-five to forty years ago. At one time, you didn't have any tennis or golf. Nobody played hockey in the cities. In New York, very few of 'em had high school baseball. So everything was basketball. So your best players were from your urban areas."

In Washington in 1946, Auerbach's first starting lineup was Bob Feerick, John Norlander, John Mahnken, Bones McKinney and Freddie Scolari. Feerick was a navy buddy, one of Red's studs from the base at Norfolk. Norlander was from Minnesota. Auerbach remembered Mahnken as a 6-8 center who had played for Elmer Ripley's pre-war Georgetown teams. McKinney was a 6-6 All-American from North Carolina. When Auerbach called him, the star had already agreed to sign with Chicago. Auerbach talked McKinney into stopping in Washington on his way to Chicago. He took him to dinner at the Blackstone Hotel and stuffed ice cream into him until he agreed to sign with Washington. In the men's room of the Blackstone restaurant, McKinney signed with Washington for $6,500.

Scolari had played one year at the University of San Francisco, and arrived on the recommendation of Feerick. Auerbach didn't know anything about the little guard, but he believed in recommendations and he believed in Feerick. The first sight of Scolari made Auerbach stare in disbelief. Scolari was a 5-10 butterball with skinny arms and legs. Auerbach pulled Feerick aside and said he didn't think this was very funny. Feerick said it was no joke. Feerick told Red to watch Scolari play. Auerbach watched, and became a believer. Scolari had great hands, played tough defense and could bury one-handers from every spot on the floor.

Feerick made the top salary: $8,500. The bottom salary was $4,000. Auerbach's recruiting costs, including phone calls and ice cream for McKinney, came to $500. Uline had his team. On the cheap.

"In the first years, many of the stars were known only in the area where they played their college ball," says Auerbach. "So we had to go into a selling-type thing. A lot of big-name college coaches were involved. We did clinics all over. We did them in supermarket parking lots. I'd get the team in uniform and demonstrate certain things."

He was a twenty-nine-year-old high school coach going up against the big boys of basketball. Philadelphia had Eddie Gottlieb. Chicago had Harold Olsen (Ohio State). Boston had Honey Russell. Auerbach was nobody.

"I was a punk kid competing against proven coaches," he said.

He knew how to prepare a team. These were professional athletes. They had to do what he asked. He pledged to get them in shape, in better condition than any other team. He ran them up and down the court, forward and backward, sometimes sideways (Auerbach always had an aversion to players whose complexion turned beet red when they exerted themselves. He thought they must not be in good shape, and usually they were cut early). He didn't care who vomited. That was your fault. He wanted his team to run the fast break, spread the scoring around and play good defense. One of his practice drills was a four-on-four full-court scrimmage. The losers had to play two-on-two—full court. The losers of that match had to play one-on-one—full court. It was torture. You did not want to lose, not even in practice.

He stressed conditioning, discipline, teamwork and loyalty. He did not have a complex system. He kept it simple and encouraged input from his players. He did not treat all of his players the same. This flies in the face of everything most coaches preach, but it's what worked for Auerbach. Some guys need to be whipped, some need to be babied.

During games, Auerbach grasped a rolled-up program in his left hand—it kept him from pounding his right fist into his left palm and blistering his knuckles on his wedding ring. The program became a permanent prop.

He could motivate officials as well as ballplayers. Always looking for an edge, Auerbach found loopholes wherever he could, and the NBA rules committee constantly had to make modifications to stay one step ahead of him.

Jack Ramsey grew up watching Auerbach coach. Ramsey was a child of the Great Depression. He went to St. Joseph's in Philadelphia and started coaching high school ball in Pennsylvania in 1949. He became a college coach, then moved up to the pros and coached against the Celtics for seventeen seasons, winning 864 games. He ranks third on the all-time NBA victory list, trailing only Auerbach and Lenny Wilkens.

"I think Red did anything that was legal that would help his team win," says Ramsey. "If you were inconvenienced in your dressing room, too bad for you. I probably would not have liked to have coached against Red. I think he would have irritated me as a coach. In those years, I think he got an advantage by the way he badgered the officials. He got away with it because he was Red. He had a certain way about him that was accepted because of who he was. But I've watched Red Auerbach since I was a high school coach. Later, when I got into a position in my basketball life where I could talk to his former players, they all talked about Red. That was very impressive to me. A lot of times players don't want to accept the role or the impact of a coach, but to a man, all these guys talked about Red. So I know the profound influence that he had on those teams, and at the professional level, that's not an easily accomplished task. I was intrigued about what made his teams great teams. The frequency of the mentions of Red Auerbach made me believe that he was the key guy."

Auerbach's 1946 team had some features that have become a permanent part of the NBA today. There was, for instance, a little-remembered player named Irv Torgoff. Torgoff was one of Auerbach's best players, but he did not start. He came off the bench to average 8 points per game. He usually was able to take advantage of a more tired player. Auerbach's strategy was fairly simple: Keep one of your best players on the bench at the start of the game. Said player comes off the pine when everybody else is tired and torches the other team for a few easy baskets. All you need is a guy with big talent and small ego. Irv Torgoff was a smart player who did not have a huge ego. He was the forefather of Frank Ramsey, John Havlicek, Kevin McHale and Bill Walton—great Auerbach ballplayers who stayed on the bench at the start of the game. Auerbach made his sixth men feel tall. He'd say, "It isn't important who's in the game when it starts, what's important is who's in there when it ends." The NBA today annually hands out a Sixth Man Award. The award should be a bust of Red Auerbach, or maybe Irv Torgoff.

Washington's young mentor was the first pro coach to take his center out of the middle and allow a smaller player to score inside. He brought the high-post passing game to the NBA. Auerbach loved the full-court press, and was the first to use strategic fouling in the second half when he had a lead. He designed a series of out-of-bounds plays, something no other coach had done. He also invented the "lonesome forward" play—sending one of his frontcourt players to the other end of the court when the opponent was shooting free throws. Watch any game today, at any level: Auerbach's lonesome forward is still standing. He encouraged low-cut shoes and discouraged knee pads, elbow pads or anything that might increase weight and decrease speed.

The 1946–1947 Capitols blasted out of the gate, winning seventeen straight early in the season, and finished 49–11, a percentage of .817. They went 29–1 at home. Feerick averaged 16.8 points per game, second only to Philadelphia's Joe Fulks, the pioneer of today's jump shot. The Caps played switching, helping, team defense. Their average margin of victory was 9.9 points, and they surrendered the fewest points in the league.

Mo Siegel was one year younger than Auerbach when he was assigned to cover the Washington Capitols for the *Washington Post*. He remembers, "Red introduced something to the NBA, which was New York-style basketball. I never knew that Red knew that much about basketball, but apparently he did. He had one guy he didn't like—John Mahnken from Georgetown. One night we were in a hotel in Philadelphia, drinking until three in the morning. Not Red. Mahnken. And Mahnken was telling me how much he hated Auerbach. He said, 'Auerbach makes me want to jump out of a hotel window.' And I said, 'Go ahead.'"

In these days, there was a lot of beer drinking by players. In St. Louis and Detroit, management supplied free beer in the locker room after games. After some New York doubleheaders, it was not uncommon to find up to twenty ballplayers drinking together at a bar near Madison Square Garden.

Auerbach discouraged the drinking and fraternization. He didn't want his players making friends with players on other teams. He encouraged teammates to eat together, go to movies together and take cabs together. There were no team buses in the 1940s (many NBA teams today have their own airplanes). Auerbach claimed he knew the exact cab fare from every NBA hotel to every arena. Play-

ers had to come to him for reimbursement, and he guarded the
purse carefully. If you were a big tipper, that was *your* problem. To
get from city to city, players sometimes traveled by car. De Soto
Suburbans were the unofficial cars of pro basketball teams. They
were long cars, and the back was open for luggage space. Hotels
were hardly plush; Bob Brannum, who started with Sheboygan and
finished with Boston, remembers a team hotel which used ropes in
place of fire escapes. In 1992, NBA Dream Team All-Stars stayed
in $900-per-night suites in downtown Barcelona.

Auerbach's first team finished twenty-seven games ahead of the
pitiful Boston Celtics. The last-place Celtics went 22–38 in 1946–
1947 and drew only 3,608 fans per game. Boston's top crowd was
6,327—less than half of the number of fans who regularly watched
Holy Cross in a full (13,909) Boston Garden. The Celtics were the
worst. Who would want to coach them?

"The public reaction to our league was cool at first," says Auerbach. "In a lot of towns, the top writers knew very little about basketball. They were concerned with football, baseball and the fights,
and all of their columns were geared that way. We had a difficult
time getting acceptance as a big league sport. But I think one of the
reasons basketball became successful is because, while you couldn't
get the respect of the media, you nevertheless had the respect of
the athletes from other sports. You'd hear people saying that basketball was all freaks—big skinny kids but nothing more. But a lot
of baseball and football players dispelled that theory. They'd say,
'Hey, these guys are not big goons. These guys are well-conditioned,
well-coordinated athletes.' This feeling from other athletes gradually
started to turn the media around. They began to believe that these
guys were great athletes and were deserving of big-league status."

The pro game offered some advantages over the college game.
The BAA was much more physical and deliberate. A player had to
be tough (a 1949 playoff game between New York and Baltimore
featured a hundred personal fouls and three fistfights). Pro teams
spread out the offense, put everybody in motion and set bone-
rattling picks. Some players thrived, other college stars disappeared.
For the truly talented, the pro game offered more opportunities to

showcase one's skills. This is still true. Michael Jordan's talents were smothered in the Dean Smith system at the University of North Carolina; it wasn't until Jordan got to the pros that he was able to unleash his entire arsenal. It took fans a while to see this in the early days. Joe Fulks, Max Zaslofsky and Auerbach's Feerick and McKinney were the first stars of the new league. None of these players had a multimillion-dollar sneaker deal.

The Capitols, who had lost only one game at Uline Arena in their first season, dropped two straight home games in their first playoff series, against Chicago. They never recovered. Chicago took a 3–0 series lead and eliminated Auerbach's team in six games. The Philadelphia Warriors beat Chicago in five to win the first BAA championship. Cleveland, Detroit, Pittsburgh and Toronto folded after that first season. The Baltimore Bullets were added to the seven surviving teams, and Washington was moved from the east to the west division for the second BAA season. The sixty-game schedule was reduced to forty-eight games. Auerbach's team went 28–20 in its second season, and again was eliminated in the first round of the playoffs.

The two-year-old Basketball Association of America got a break after that second season when several flagship NBL teams defected. The NBL champions, the Minneapolis Lakers, brought star center George Mikan to the BAA. Fort Wayne and Rochester also switched leagues. Washington moved back into the eastern division and finished first, even though the Caps did not have any scorer in the league's top ten. This would be an Auerbach trademark. His ball clubs stressed team play, not individual accomplishment. He never coached a scoring champ—only team champs.

While coaching the Caps, Auerbach had an audience with President Harry Truman. "That was one of the greatest thrills of my life," Auerbach says. "He was my favorite. We're standing there and he says, 'Come on, Coach, get in here closer or they'll cut you out of the picture.' Then he says to me, 'Look at these glasses. They're like Coca-Cola bottles. That's why I was never an athlete. I couldn't see.'"

The parents of Dorothy Lewis had to be a little impressed with this young Brooklyn man who had married their daughter. The kid wasn't particularly refined, but he was succeeding in this new field, and he had his picture taken with the president of the United States.

Despite Auerbach's success, he was a little restless and had se-. rious doubts about the future of the new league. In January 1949, he told the *Boston Globe*'s Harold Kaese, "Pro basketball is a cut-throat business. I'd coach college basketball for less money—if I could get an assistant professorship for security."

Dorothy made a decision early on: There would be no road trips for the coach's wife. "I made a couple of trips," she remembers. "I was excess luggage. It was, 'Here's your ticket, you'll eat with so-and-so and I'll see you after the game.' Un-uh. I'd say. 'Maybe I don't want to eat with so-and-so. Maybe I want to eat back in the room.' Un-uh. So that was the end of that."

In his third season as a professional coach, Auerbach's team went 15–0 at the start of the season, still an NBA record (the Houston Rockets tied the mark in 1993). For the first time in his coaching career, his team advanced in the playoffs. The Caps beat Philadel-phia, then New York, before facing mighty Minneapolis in the cham-pionship finals. The Lakers won it in six. It was the second of five championships the Lakers would win in six seasons. In the early years of the BAA and NBA, the Lakers were pro basketball's mar-quee team, and it's possible that without the notoriety of the Lakers, the fledgling league might not have survived long enough for the Boston Celtics to take over.

The 1949 finals represented the only playoff series Coach Auer-bach would lose to a Laker team. Red's Revenge would prove to be hell on the Lakers after they relocated to the West Coast.

In three seasons with the Washington Capitols, Auerbach's rec-ord was 115–53 (.685). He established himself as smart, shrewd and in control. He didn't care if his players liked him; he commanded respect. He didn't care if fans in other arenas liked him. He was brash and cocky on the bench. He had the suspicion of a native New Yorker (what you do want from me?). He assumed the other guy was out to screw him.

The estimable Irv Goodman, in a lengthy *Sport* magazine profile, described Auerbach's bench demeanor this way: "He lunges upward and outward from the bench on most of the calls against his team. His face, hardly a smiling countenance in the best of situations, contorts into a snarl as he rasps his pet phrases at the referees. Familiar, too, is his habit of storming over to the scorer's table for a suspicious look at the records, or flicking cigar ashes at the feet of the officials. It requires little more than a palming call against Cousy for the balding, Brooklyn-born ex-redhead to go into his act, which, in milder moments, consists of hands raised to the rafters, a loud foot stomp, a furtive turn to the stands for sympathy, a deliberate stride toward the referee, a martyred return to the sidelines at the urging of the official, a determined jam of his cigar into his mouth and, with hands on hips, a heavy sigh of utter disbelief that such injustice could be taking place here and now—and to him."

Auerbach was tough with his players, but asked only that they stay in shape and try to remember the plays. He would not let any player ask him "Why?"

In 1948 Matt Zunic made the mistake of asking for an explanation. "Why'd you sit me down?" Zunic shouted as he came to the bench. Auerbach waited a few seconds, called the player over and said, "I'm going to tell you this just once: Don't ever do that to me again. Don't ever ask me why I took you out of a game. Don't ever talk to me like that after I take you out. I hired you and I'll fire you. I don't have to explain what I'm doing to you or any other ballplayer. If I'm wrong, I'll get fired. Till then, I run this club."

This was the manner in which a coach earned respect in 1948. Auerbach says it still works today. Good luck. Can the coach du jour of the Charlotte Hornets fire star forward Larry Johnson, who in 1993 signed a twelve-year, $84 million contract?

Officials couldn't stand Washington's coach. Auerbach was convinced that Lapchick, Gottlieb and the other marquee coaches were getting breaks from the refs. Early in games, he would pick up strategic technical fouls, trying to get inside the ref's head. He was going for the next call—the one he would need late in the game. Before Lombardi said it, Auerbach lived it: Winning wasn't just the most important thing—it was the only thing.

In his second autobiography (1977), Auerbach addressed Grant-
land Rice's famous line—"It matters not that you won or lost—but
how you played the game."

Red wrote, "It's a good poem, but the philosophy is a lot of crap.
So is that baloney about losing coaches building character! As far as
I'm concerned, it is important whether you win or lose. And who
says you can't build character when you win? As long as you're going
to keep score, you've got to go out there with the idea of winning.
I've always believed that . . . I'd break or bend every damned rule in
the book if I thought it would help me win a ball game!"

He did win, but he didn't win a championship. It was starting to
get to him. What had happened in high school was happening in the
pros: Auerbach's teams were the best over the long haul, but folded
in the pressure of tournaments. After the championship loss to Minneapolis, he had to deal with dissension in the newspapers. Ev Gardner wrote a story in the *Washington Daily News* that was headlined:
"Player Revolt? Auerbach on Hot Seat." According to Gardner, five
players wanted out and had gone to Uline to complain about Auerbach. They didn't like his substitution patterns. They felt the team
had lost close games because there were too many reserves on the
floor at the end of games. Feerick, Auerbach's old navy buddy, was
believed to be at the core of the dissent. He was thirty-two years
old, hindered by a leg injury and had his eye on the coach's job. He
already had gone to Uline.

Complaints from ballplayers about their coaches are as old as
sports, but that didn't change the fact that young Auerbach had to
address the situation immediately. He went to Uline to see where
he stood.

In the owner's office, Auerbach asked,"Have I done a good job?"
Uline paused, then said, "You've done all right."

Auerbach could see what was happening. A coach always knows.
It was time to go for a vote of confidence. It was time to find out
where he stood with his owner.

"Okay, Mr.Uline," said Auerbach. "I want a three-year contract.
I intend to buy a house and I'd like to have some assurances that
I'll be here long enough to live in it. We'll need to do some rebuild-
ing, and one year is not enough."

Uline wouldn't go for it. He said one year was his policy.

It was an offer Red could only refuse. Uline wanted to fire him, but was too much of a gentleman, so he was making an insulting offer. Behind the scenes, Feerick was being groomed as a player-coach. It would save Uline's paying a coach's salary. Feerick was in. Red was out.

"I wish you and Feerick luck," said Auerbach. "I'll see you sometime."

He walked out. When he got home, he was greeted by Dot and their baby daughter, Nancy. At thirty-two years old, he was starting over. He made calls. He phoned George Preston Marshall, owner of the Redskins, to see if Marshall knew of any available college jobs. Marshall said to check out Dartmouth. Arrogant Red said, "Too cold." Ditto for Michigan State.

Auerbach's phone kept ringing. According to Red, Lou Pieri, owner of the Providence Steamrollers, called. Providence (12–48 in 1948–1949) was the joke team of the league, and Auerbach was blunt with the wealthy owner. He needed the job, but he couldn't go to Providence unless the owner was prepared to do what it would take to win. Auerbach told Pieri that Providence had the worst collection of ballplayers he had ever seen in the pros. He said Pieri should be prepared to lose $400,000 to keep his franchise afloat while building a team from scratch. It would take two or three years. The options were fold or lose a fortune. So much for Red's job offer. Pieri thanked him for his honesty and wound up folding the franchise. But the candid conversation stayed with Pieri, and soon he'd have a hand in hiring young Mr. Auerbach for a lifetime job.

There was another call. Former Red Sox third baseman Billy Werber was a member of the Duke alumni association, and Duke was looking for somebody to assist head coach Gerry Gerard. It wasn't a very attractive assignment. Gerard was dying of cancer and wasn't expected to last the season. The salary was $7,500 and Auerbach could move his wife and baby to Durham, North Carolina, at no expense. His daughter Nancy was asthmatic (a condition she'd inherited from her dad) and the family hoped she'd have an easier time breathing in a warm climate. Auerbach took the job.

He was not comfortable at Duke. He felt like he was waiting for a nice man to die. It didn't seem right. Mrs. Auerbach was even less happy. Her short time at Duke represents the only time of her life in which she lived outside of Washington, D.C.

"I hated it," she says. "I was not there long. I'm a homebody, and back in Washington I had everybody around me."

They had decided to return to Washington when he got a call from Ben Kerner. After the 1948–1949 season, the Basketball Association of America had officially changed its name to the National Basketball Association, and Kerner was owner of the new franchise in Tri-Cities (Moline, Illinois, Rock Island, Illinois, and Davenport, Iowa). Kerner was a hustling advertising executive from Buffalo who'd run the Buffalo Bisons before moving his team to Tri-Cities, where it played in the NBL. Tri-Cities was one of five survivors of the old NBL (Anderson, Sheboygan, Waterloo and Denver were the others) to join the NBA in 1949–1950. Auerbach was excited when Kerner called. He wanted to get away from Duke and he wanted to get back into pro basketball. He checked with Duke athletic director Eddie Cameron, and Cameron gave him his blessing. Auerbach called Kerner back and accepted a two-year, $17,000 contract. Dot and Nancy packed for Washington, and Red was on his way to Moline.

In a 1968 letter to the Basketball Hall of Fame, Cameron wrote, "I wish to advise that Red Auerbach did serve as a coach here for about two months when Gerry Gerard was sick. He really would have become head coach, but accepted a position with the pros in anticipation of Gerry's recovery. He had a fine influence on the basketball team at Duke and was particularly effective in training Dick Groat as a sophomore. Groat later became All-American."

At Tri-Cities, Kerner was the George Steinbrenner of his time. He fired three head coaches in his first three years. The Blackhawks were 1–6 at the start of the 1949–1950 season when Auerbach was summoned. Introducing Auerbach to the Tri-Cities media, Kerner said, "Auerbach is the answer to our problems. He's going to look over this club, decide who to keep and who to let go. Because of his reputation in pro ball, he will be given full authority to trade and build as he sees fit. This is the man to tell us what we need here."

In the *Davenport Democrat*, Auerbach was described as "the Easterner."

The Easterner went to work. The Blackhawks were not a good team. In six weeks he made deals involving twenty-eight players. Of the players on his original Tri-Cities roster, only three survived the season. Tri-Cities was involved in more player transactions than all the other sixteen NBA teams combined.

"I'll give these customers a real show if you'll pay the fines," Red told Kerner.

Red game 'em a show in Sheboygan one night. Bob Brannum, then with the mighty Sheboygan Redskins and later with Boston, remembers it well:

"We had an auditorium that seated about thirty-five hundred people and the teams had to sit on a stage at one end of the court. Both teams and the scoring table were up on that stage and the crowd sat down beneath. When Red wanted to say something to the officials, he had to jump down to get on the floor. At the opposite end of the court they had swinging doors. One of his players got knocked through the swinging doors while going down on the fast break and the ushers sort of stood in front of the doors and the guy couldn't get back in. Red came off the bench like a rocket. He went screaming down the side of the court at the officials and the ushers. One of our fans, I think he was the mayor of the town, he jumped up and hit Red with a program as Red went running by. Red turns around and starts to belt him. Then there were two or three cops in on it and they were going to drag Red away. I got in between them and told them to let him go. He didn't do anything. I liked Red, even then, because he was a competitor."

The feeling was mutual. Two years later, Auerbach paid $10,000 to bring Brannum to the Boston Celtics.

Red's Blackhawks won their first game under their new coach, defeating Waterloo, 99–89, and setting a franchise record for points in a single game. Two weeks later, the Hawks drew a record crowd for a 104–88 victory over the first-place Indianapolis Olympians. In late January, the Blackhawks went to Uline Arena and beat Bob Feerick's Capitols, 85–81. The Caps were near the end. They went

32–36 in one season under Feerick, then disbanded the following year.

Auerbach and Kerner had their own Waterloo on the horizon. The owner liked Boston forward Gene Englund, a former Wisconsin star. Boston wanted John Mahnken in exchange, and Red didn't want to make the deal. While the Blackhawks were on the road, Auerbach got a telegram that read, "HAVE TRADED MAHNKEN FOR ENGLUND—WILL ASSUME RESPONSIBILITY."

That would be it for Red in Tri-Cities. Kerner had done the one thing that Auerbach could not tolerate from ownership: He had made a deal without his consent. Red wasn't going to be anybody's dummy coach. Auerbach finished the season. The Blackhawks went 29–35, but Auerbach's record with them was 28–29—the only losing season of his professional coaching career. After the Hawks got bounced in the playoffs by the Anderson Packers, Auerbach quit.

"I had two degrees," remembered Red. "I felt I could get a job teaching or I could get a job somewhere. I didn't want to be a stooge coach. Once you're a coach and you're afraid of your job, you'll never make it. You got to lay it all out up front. What do you want me to do? Do you want me to win or do you want me to kiss ass and please the personalities of everybody around? You can't be worried about getting fired and who to please. You do the best you can. The worst thing a coach can do is start to kiss fannies because he's afraid of losing his job. I was never afraid of my job."

And so he walked.

He'd coached four years of pro basketball. He'd been squeezed out of one job and quit another. He had a reputation as a fiery coach who could get his team ready, bait the refs and win a lot of games. But when he walked out the door in Moline, Illinois, it looked a little like the end of coaching a professional team for Red Auerbach. He was thinking about retreating to the college ranks.

There is no reason he would have paid any attention to what was happening with the team up in Boston. In four seasons of BAA and NBA play, the Boston Celtics had posted a win-loss record of 89–147. John Davis "Honey" Russell had coached the first two seasons, followed by Holy Cross legend Alvin "Doggie" Julian.

The Celtics were owned by gentleman Walter Brown, son of

George V. Brown, the man who brought the marathon to Boston. George Brown was at the first modern Olympics in Athens in 1896 and was fascinated by the twenty-six-mile race. The first Boston Marathon was run a year later, and from 1906 to 1937 George Brown fired the gun to start the race. Born in 1905, Walter was one of George V. Brown's three sons. When Walter was fifteen years old, his dad was general manager of the Boston Arena. The Boston Garden was built in 1928, and when the Great Depression smothered America, the Arena Corporation bought the Garden and George Brown took over as general manager.

George Brown passed away in 1939, and thirty-three-year-old Walter became general manager of the Garden-Arena Corporation. In 1941, Walter Brown became president of the Garden, hockey's Boston Bruins, the Boston Athletic Association (which ran the marathon) and vice president of the Ice Capades. In 1945, it was Brown who pushed some of the reluctant hockey owners to give pro basketball another chance. In the early years, Brown struggled with the rest of them, but he never abandoned the NBA. When Julian resigned at the end of the Celtics' fourth season, Brown already had lost more than $450,000 on the Boston basketball team. Brown had to sell his home and other private investments to keep the team afloat, and he was seriously considering doing what Mike Uline had done in Washington: cutting his losses and folding the franchise.

While Auerbach was winning in Washington, the Celtics had been scuffling to win games and build a fan base. New England sports fans followed the Red Sox, the Bruins, boxing and Holy Cross basketball. Holy Cross is a small (2,400 students) Jesuit college in Worcester, forty miles west of Boston. The Crusaders won an NCAA championship in 1947 and annually represented the region in the NIT at Madison Square Garden. Basketball was not played by Boston high schools in the 1940s, and Brown had been unable to sell his product without offering sideshows, doubleheaders and special discounts.

Brown was president of the Bruins and founded a popular amateur hockey team called the Boston Olympics. But the Celtics were his pet invention. He'd even named them. When the BAA was formed in 1946, Brown sat in an office with his PR man Howie

McHugh and they kicked around possible names for the new basketball team. They considered clunkers like "Unicorns," "Whirlwinds" and "Olympics" before Brown sat up and said, "I've got it. The Celtics. We'll call them the Boston Celtics! The name's got a great tradition, and besides, Boston's full of Irishmen. We'll put them in green uniforms and call them the Celtics."

In 1977, Marjorie Brown, Walter's widow, told Auerbach cobiographer Joe Fitzgerald, "Friends were begging Walter to give it up. And truthfully, I was, too. We had just finished paying off our house mortgage when the Celtics came along. Walter owned stock in the Ice Capades, and we used those dividends to buy the home. By 1950 he had sold most of the stock in the Ice Capades and remortgaged the home. Almost everything we owned was locked up in the Celtics. One day I said to him, 'Walter, what's going to happen to us if it's all lost?' I was worried. All of our friends were worried, too. But Walter loved that team. I've heard people say he hung on because he was stubborn, or because he was too proud to admit failure. That wasn't it at all. The Celtics were his idea from the beginning, and he just never stopped believing in them."

Brown decided to give the Celtics one more try, but on Wednesday, March 22, 1950, after another nonplayoff Celtic season, Boston coach Doggie Julian announced that he was leaving the team to take over as head coach at Dartmouth. "I don't think I am tough enough for professional basketball," said Julian. "Another reason for my change was the fact that with the pros you travel too much. I was away from home most of the past winter. I don't care for this."

A proven college coach with an NCAA championship on his resume, Julian had been devoured by the pro game. The NBA wasn't looking for teachers or molders of young men. The pro game called for a savvy bench coach; one who could think quickly while under siege. One had to be suspicious and aggressive. Julian was neither. Making matters worse, Julian's health was failing.

John Bach, former assistant coach with the Chicago Bulls, played for Julian's Celtics (Bach wore No. 17, later worn and retired by John Havlicek). Even as a young player, Bach could see that Julian was not long for the pro game.

"He came in with a college system and college mentality," says

Bach. "He really was disappointed by the professional game, and maybe by the respect that they rendered to him. He had some real old pros. This was a guy who would get all fired up, almost every day. We'd lose three in a row and he'd say, 'We're going to be looking for a job.' He was a very likable man if you were a young player. I think the veteran players felt he was too emotional. And he had a great deal of dogmatic thinking about the game. He used an open middle, and this was a time when the pro game was a hard-assed, pivot game—the game the best team in basketball, the Minneapolis Lakers, were playing. So he wanted his college philosophy to work against the professional champions. It didn't work, and I thought he was pretty disappointed."

On the threshold of bankruptcy, out of the playoffs for two straight years, Brown was saddled with the additional headache of hiring a new coach. This time, he needed to find somebody "tough enough" for pro basketball.

Brown was asked if he had any interest in hiring Nat Holman, coach of CCNY's basketball team. Holman had rejected the Celtics when the league was first formed in 1946. In 1950, Holman was a hot item, but Brown said, "I wouldn't have the crust to ask him. As bad shape as we're in, it wouldn't be cricket to go after Holman."

More than that, Brown knew he didn't want another college coach. He needed a man who knew professional basketball. He needed a guy like Red Auerbach.

# 3

# COMING TO BOSTON

*I don't give a damn for sentiment or names. That goes for Cousy and everybody else. The only thing that counts with me is ability, and Cousy still hasn't proven to me that he's got that ability. I'm not interested in drafting someone just because he happens to be a local yokel.*

RED AUERBACH, 1950

WALTER BROWN ROUNDED UP HIS FRIENDS. ON MARCH 23, 1950, he summoned trustworthy reporters from local radio stations and newspaper sports departments and asked them to meet with him at his Boston Garden office. He had one question for each of them—whom should he hire to coach his Celtics?

It's an unthinkable scenario today. Imagine any self-respecting club owner lowering himself to rely on the opinion of lowly newspaper and radio reporters. In the nineties, the owner-media relationship is often adversarial. At best, both sides keep their distance to avoid conflicts of interest. But these were the early days of professional basketball and Walter Brown was an old-fashioned owner who took care of those who took care of him. These were the days when teams often paid reporters' travel and hotel expenses. There were a lot of perks for the sportswriters, and most had no trouble accepting gifts and favors from the teams. In exchange, the team got the coverage and publicity it desperately needed. In more than one instance, moonlighting reporters worked for ball clubs in their spare time.

Brown's ten-man search committee was made up of Jack Conway Jr. (*Boston American*), Les Smith (radio station WNAC), Jack Malloy (WEEI), Roger Barry (*Quincy Patriot-Ledger*), Leo Egan (WDDH), Red Marston (WHDH), Sam Brogna (*Boston Record*), Joe Kelley (Associated Press), Dinny Whitmarsh (WBZ) and Joe Looney (*Boston Herald-Traveler*).

The event was hardly secret. A picture of Brown and his ten "advisors" appeared in the *Boston Herald-Traveler* the next day and the caption read, "Walter Brown and his ten-man advisory committee . . . " Looney, who'd been at the meeting, wrote this story in his paper:

"Walter Brown and his newly formed brain trust (sportswriters and radio men) discussed the problems of the Celtics for about two hours yesterday afternoon and eventually agreed that the new coach should be a man of experience from within the ranks of the National Basketball Association.

"In an almost unprecedented gesture, Brown called in Boston sportswriters and radio men to hear their version on what should be done to aid the Celts in the 1950–1951 campaign. It was an off-the-record session, because the men suggested for the coaching position, vacated Wednesday by Doggie Julian, are still under contract elsewhere.

"The writers made numerous suggestions on players who should be drafted from the college ranks, but Brown asked that the names be withheld perchance some other teams might become suddenly interested in those players.

"Brown admitted he received 'two applications' for the coaching position yesterday. He also explained he could not take a chance with 'an untested coach.' That statement would seem to eliminate Art Spector, who has been with the Celts for four years, but lacks coaching experience."

Roger Barry in 1950 was a a thirty-year-old Red Sox beat reporter for the *Patriot-Ledger*. During the winters he had covered Celtic home games, and unlike most writers of his era, he'd actually played high school basketball. When he was in his mid thirties, Barry went to work part-time for Walter Brown in the public relations department of the Bruins' front office. This is his recollection of the meeting that brought Red Auerbach to Boston:

"Walter was one of these guys who thought basketball writers knew something about it. Reading the morning *Globe*, he'd found out that Doggie Julian had taken the Dartmouth job. The season was over, he hadn't made the playoffs and now he didn't have a coach. The Celtics were in a disruptive state. They didn't have much of a future. [Celtic PR man] Howie McHugh called us all and asked us to come into the Garden Club and have a meeting. So we all showed up. What did we know? What the hell, I felt like I knew it all, like everybody else. I felt like I knew everything about the sport. Only two or three of us in that room had played, but everybody was very much interested in the Celtics. Walter was the great white father of New England sports.

"Our group quickly divided into three camps. One camp was guys who favored Art Spector. He was the last suviving member of the first Celtic team. A couple guys favored Buddy Jeannette. He had coached the Baltimore Bullets and he was a real personality.

"I brought up Auerbach. A couple of us liked Auerbach. I had become a big Auerbach fan when he coached the Washington Caps, because he won. I also remember one summer when I was traveling with the Red Sox in Washington. Red came over to the Wardman Park hotel to say hello. He'd had a falling-out with Uline and had quit. I think he was going to coach at Duke. The Celts had drafted Tony Lavelli from Yale, and Walter wanted to get him. Tony was a fine musician, and at this time he was playing the accordion at the Paramount in Washington. Jack and Red and I wound up going to this theater where Tony was playing. And I stood there listening to Red giving Tony a helluva sales talk for the Celtics, with whom he had no connection. He talked to him for twenty minutes, and it was a real sales pitch. That impressed me. It made me aware of Red's sincere interest in the game and the league in general. I became a big Auerbach fan.

"So I was the first one to bring up his name, because I was prejudiced. I thought he was the best guy. I really did. I used to sit next to the visitors bench and I thought he was a helluva coach. So after Walter got everybody's opinion, I went up to him and said,

'You know Auerbach's situation. Why don't you call Red and see if
he's interested in the job.' He said, 'Goddammit, Roger, you know
I can't do that. He's still under contract to Ben Kerner in Tri-Cities.
Why don't you get hold of him?' I think maybe Walter'd had a
couple of scotch and waters by this time.

"So I went home and I wrote Auerbach a letter telling him that
the job was open here. I let him know that the job was available
and I wanted him to tell me if he was interested in it. I didn't know
what his plans were. I wrote one to Jeannette, too. I sent them off
airmail.

"Three days later, I've got a golf date at Scituate. Someone came
in and said, 'I just saw an old friend of yours at the Garden. Red
Auerbach.' I was steamed. Later Walter told me that Red got the
letter and got on a plane and came to Boston. You didn't have to
have an appointment with Walter. Anyway, Walter told him there
was nothing he could do until he talked to Kerner. So he did. He
talked to Kerner and he made Ben happy and Red came to the
Celtics. He had a big press luncheon to greet him, and he started
off by thanking me publicly for bringing Red here.

"For some reason, over the years, Red has denied the sequence.
He has never mentioned that letter to me."

"I don't remember the letter," Auerbach says. "I might have gotten one. If he says I did, I did. But what the hell, that's forty years
ago."

Brown's summit meeting with the Boston media was held on a
Thursday. The night after that meeting, Auerbach's Tri-Cities Blackhawks were eliminated from the NBA playoffs, dropping a 94–71
decision to Anderson. This put the sequence in good order. Auerbach was still involved in a playoff series when his name was first
mentioned. By the time he would have received Barry's letter, his
season was over, and he was committed to leaving because he was
mad about Kerner's going over his head to make the Mahnken-
Englund trade. Brown called NBA Commissioner Maurice Podoloff
to get permission to talk to Auerbach. Unaware that Kerner and
Auerbach were feuding, Podoloff called Kerner to see if he'd release
Auerbach. Kerner happily flashed the green light, and Brown was
free to negotiate. It was win-win for everybody.

"Walter called Ben and Ben released me," says Auerbach. "Ben loved me and we got along very well, but he didn't feel that the coach was that essential."

There's one other theory, advanced in Auerbach's autobiographies, which may explain Brown's interest in Auerbach. While Brown was looking for a coach, he also needed a partner. Directors of the Boston Garden had withdrawn all support of the team and Brown was forced to buy the fledgling franchise. He went to see Lou Pieri, owner of the Rhode Island Auditorium and the AHL Rhode Island Reds, a hockey team. This was the same Lou Pieri who Auerbach claimed tried to hire him to coach the Providence Steamrollers. Auerbach's version is that he talked himself out of the position by telling Pieri that it was going to cost too much money to keep the franchise. The theory holds that Pieri never forgot the good advice he'd gotten from young Auerbach, and that when Walter Brown came to Pieri, the Rhode Island businessman agreed to invest $50,000 in the Celtics on one condition: Brown must hire Red Auerbach as head coach.

"I've read where Lou Pieri supposedly wanted Auerbach to coach the Celtics," says Roger Barry. "That's crazy. Pieri hated Auerbach. He called him 'the wiseguy from Brooklyn.' Later, they became friends, but at that time, Pieri didn't like him at all."

"I always got along with Pieri," says Auerbach. "I got along with Lou because Lou was a very bright guy. Everybody looked at him, because he was short and fat. But Lou was a professor and a teacher. I got along with him. I liked him."

Auerbach went to Boston and tried the same Bogart demand that had failed with Mike Uline. Auerbach told Brown he would require a three-year contract to make the move.

Then he listened. He listened while Brown explained the fiscal facts of the Boston Celtics. He heard how Brown and Pieri had put their necks on the line, borrowing $250,000 to take the Celtics out of the hands of the Garden. There could be no three-year contract for any employee, because there might not be a team next year. All Brown could offer was one year at $10,000, plus a piece of the profits, if there were any. The Celts had lost $460,000 in four years, so there didn't seem to be much prospect for profit-sharing. Auerbach had nothing in writing, only the good word of Walter Brown.

In sixteen years under Brown, Auerbach never had a contract. Sixteen handshakes. All of them good as gold.

Red got one more guarantee: total authority. Brown knew nothing about basketball and promised not to interfere with personnel or game-related situations. It would be like working for Uline instead of Kerner.

"I thought it was a great opportunity," remembers Auerbach. "It's a step up. Would you rather coach in Tri-Cities or Boston?"

In Boston, Auerbach was not thought of as an "Easterner," as he was to those nice folks at Tri-Cities. In the Hub of the Universe, Red Auerbach was a brash, Jewish New Yorker. Too brash for some.

"We thought he was a no-good, arrogant Jew," recalls the *Boston Record*'s Sam Brogna. "He still is. I don't know how well you know him, but I knew him from the old days. He didn't have a friend in the world. He didn't care. I remember his first year with us, he lived in the Hotel Lenox. That's where we used to have our weekly basketball meetings. I made a trip with him to Providence. I rode down with him. He was a maniac behind the wheel. We got back to the hotel and while I was waiting for my wife, he said, 'Let's go and have a drink. This is on Walter Brown.' Everything was on Walter Brown. He wouldn't spend his own money. He tried to hold Water Brown up a few times. Red never had the friends. Just the Chinese food."

Clif Keane is an eighty-two-year-old former sportswriter for the *Boston Globe* and has been an Auerbach basher for forty-five years. This is his recollection: "Auerbach. Bad story. Bad guy. He lived in the Lenox and he had no friends. He was stuck in a corner room and nobody in town liked him. I'm telling ya. Believe me. You may think I'm juicy, but I'm not. I saw that thing grow, and he's full of shit. He was a faking son of a bitch, really a bad guy. His wife was a lovely girl and I don't know how she put up with him. When he'd eat, he was like a pig. I had to sit with him a couple of times at breakfast. Christ, he was belching and burping. He really was. He was unbelievable. You wouldn't believe it, but I saw it. It was true.

This is exactly what happened with this guy. Walter Brown used to talk to me about him, Walter wanted to get rid of him a couple of times. I never liked him, and I don't to this day. He's no god of mine. Ninety-nine thousand guys will tell you he's some genius. I thought the guy was a fraud."

Auerbach says this about Keane: "What his problem was, was that he was Catholic and he was so pro-Cousy. I honestly believe that he didn't like anybody unless they were Catholic and Holy Cross. The extent of what he disliked, I can't talk about, but nobody liked the guy."

Auerbach doesn't use anti-Semitism to dismiss his enemies; he knows it's too easy. He's felt the arrows of those who think every white man is antiblack. Around greater Boston, the Celtics always have drawn heavily from the local Jewish community. A dinner sponsored by the B'nai B'rith Sports Lodge has been the team's traditional kickoff bash, and the franchise has a long-standing relationship with Brandeis University (located in Waltham, Massachusetts), a nonsectarian college funded by the Jewish community. The new gym at Brandeis's Gosman Sports and Convocation Center is named after Auerbach, and serves as the team's regular practice site. At any given time, there are usually a handful of Brandeis grads and undergrads working in the Celtic offense. Auerbach has been the overseer of this affiliation.

GM Volk says, "Red's not observant, but I think he feels religious. I think he might be more religious than he wants you to think he is. While he doesn't observe kosher laws, he's very respectful of people who do. He doesn't ridicule. He's convinced that he didn't get into Columbia because of a quota system. When he was put up for the Madison Square Garden Club at the Boston Garden, he was blackballed because he was Jewish. I believe he has a strong religious identification."

Mo Siegel, a Washington sports columnist for almost fifty years and a former roommate of Auerbach's brother Zang, says, "Red lives half a block from the biggest and most affluent temple synagogue in Washington, and I've never seen him at services. It's not any part at all of his life."

There may have been some anti-Semitic feelings about Auerbach in his early days in Boston, but he's never complained about the dominance of Irish-Catholic names in the Boston press corps.

His first two friends in the Boston media were *Herald-Traveler* sports editor Sam Cohen and columnist Dave Egan.

"The guy who had the most influence on me in Boston at that time—and on the success of the team, I thought—was Sam Cohen," says Auerbach. "He was just a basketball guy that really loved the game, and he wanted to see the sport succeed. Egan? Sure, he was tough on Ted Williams. He was tough on Harvard. He was tough on a lot of people. But he liked basketball, and he liked the way I operated, I guess. He'd come to games, very quietly. He didn't go to baseball games or football games. The only thing he used to go to was fights, and basketball."

Jeff Cohen was eight years old when his father first brought Red Auerbach to the family home in Newton. Jeff remembers playing pickup basketball in the driveway with the feisty New Yorker. "He'd push me all over the place to make sure he beat me," says Cohen, who later became assistant GM of the Celtics. "My father used to call him a 'fresh bum.' My father and Walter Brown were very close, and I think Walter asked my father to make this guy comfortable. They were kindred spirits right from the start. I saw how my father used to handle him. He'd threaten to kick him down the stairs."

In 1980 Sam Cohen told the *Herald's* Joe Fitzgerald, "He reminded me of a sailor who had been out to sea for three years and had just gotten back onto land. Fresh? You wouldn't believe it. But the funny thing was, he had his wife with him [on a visit], and she was the complete opposite. I remember thinking the guy couldn't be all bad if he was married to a girl like that. If his wife wasn't with him, I think I'd have punched him in the nose. That's how fresh he was. Red's idea, and he told us this right away, was that if your heart and soul weren't into basketball, you were no damned good."

Sam Cohen's interest in basketball had little to do with his love of the game. Editor of the Hearst papers in Boston, he saw a chance to sell more copies of the 7 P.M. Payoff Edition of the *Boston Record*. Anytime there was a Garden event, the Payoff Edition paid off. Accordingly, Cohen was a Celtic booster.

The Lenox Hotel, located on Boylston Street, just a block from the Boston Public Library, was Auerbach's home for the entire sixteen seasons he coached in Boston. He had a two-room suite on the ninth floor, room 900, which today is a nonsmoking room. He kept the place stocked with bottles of Chinese noodles and jars of nuts and candies. He kept potatoes in a refrigerator. He had a hot plate and he liked to make french fries or heat up leftover Chinese food. His bathroom had a pull-chain toilet and a marble sink. The chambermaid kept tabs on his laundry, which included dozens of pairs of argyle socks.

Backup center Gene Conley first came to the Celtics in 1952, lived at the Lenox for a year and never saw the inside of the coach's hotel room. "We'd practice at the Cambridge Y and he'd give me rides," said Conley. "He'd say, 'Meet you in the lobby, and you better be there or you catch a cab.' He'd come out of the elevator and look over, and if you weren't there, he'd be gone."

Dot and Nancy stayed behind when Auerbach moved to Boston, just as they stayed behind when he lived in Moline, Illinois. In 1951, with the help of a $3,000 loan from his father, Auerbach purchased a row house on Nebraska Avenue in Washington, D.C.

"I knew I could pay it back," says the coach. "It didn't really bother me that much. I just said, 'If you got it, it would get me off the hook,' so I borrowed it."

Daughter Randy was born in April 1952. Arnold Auerbach was a homeowner, a husband and a father, but he never really would live in his house with his family. It was the ultimate sacrifice in the name of career.

"You got to face reality," Auerbach says. "My kids couldn't move up there. Nancy has asthma, and she was in the hospital most of the time she was in Boston. Plus, my father-in-law was a pediatrician for more than thirty years. It made sense for them to stay in Washington. I stayed at the Lenox. I was like a horse. There wasn't a day that wasn't planned. I was either going out scouting, or I was home. Today, coaches are different. They try to lead a normal life. They play golf. To me, it wasn't like that at all. Christ, I had to go overseas to unwind. I'd go away with my family. But then I'd go back to work."

In his 1966 autobiography, Auerbach wrote, "The simple fact is that Dot, a third-generation Washingtonian, never wanted to live anywhere else, and once I hit the professional trail for good, I didn't argue it because I didn't want her with me. I don't mean to put it that way, of course. I mean I knew it would be too rough on her. Suppose she had come to Boston with me when I was set there. How much would she have seen me?"

Randy says, "It made me very independent at a very early age, because he wasn't around so we didn't have that authoritarian figure. My mother was more of a friend. So I never heard that 'Uh-oh, wait until your father comes home.'"

Nancy's asthma has always been her father's first explanation for the family's reluctance to leave Washington. Auerbach has always maintained that it was difficult for his daughter to breathe in the Boston climate. Today, Nancy says, "I think that's a myth, but I've always lived here in Washington."

Dorothy says, "I'm a great family person, a great roots person. And fortunately, he went along with me and it worked out. I had no desire to tackle a new environment. And furthermore, coaching is like vaudeville. At least here, I had support. There, I may have had support, but I wouldn't have felt the same."

When Dot was asked if the lengthy separation helped the marriage, she replied, "It doesn't hurt."

People have forever wondered about this marriage. Dorothy says, "First it bothered me, then it didn't. I don't care what they think. I never had any bitter feelings. I never said, 'Why do I have such an odd setup?' No. I loved my kids and being with them. They had a good childhood, I think. My dad was a doctor and my brother's a doctor. That makes you feel pretty secure."

Ten years after Auerbach arrived in Boston, he bought a center-entrance colonial at 1301 Legation Street in the Northwest section of Washington. This would be the only single-family, unattached house that the Auerbachs would own. It had a basketball hoop over the garage (Nancy was the better shooter of the two Auerbach girls. Once, when she played at Wilton High School and the Celtics were in Baltimore, she got her dad to bring some of his players to watch a game. She remembers that Frank Ramsey brought a book. They left early. Her dad's observation: "Those kids are terrible.") and a lawn to cut. Auerbach hated house maintenance. When the neighbor across the street would cut his grass, Auerbach would sit up in his chaise lounge and snort. "What's he trying to do, anyway, make me look bad?"

"He's certainly no Harry the Homeowner," says Dorothy. "The man is not handy. I am the maintenance worker around this house, not Red."

Auerbach assumed control of the Celtics in April, a few days before the 1950 college draft. Every basketball fan in New England wanted the Celtics to draft Holy Cross guard Bob Cousy. Holy Cross had just completed a 27–4 season and made it to the NCAA tourney for the third time in four years. Cousy was a 6-1 guard with long arms and the kind of fancy-pants style that infuriated Auerbach. The Cooz had revolutionized college basketball, and his HC teams regularly sold out the Boston Garden while the lowly Celtics struggled to draw six thousand fans in the same building, playing the same sport. New England fans truly believed that Holy Cross's team played superior basketball to that played by the NBA Celtics. This infuriated Auerbach. These people didn't know anything about pro basketball. And they certainly didn't know who the best college players were.

Sizing up the needs of the 1950 Celtics, Auerbach decided that Bowling Green's 6-11 center Charlie Share would be the No. 1 selection. Like a lot of basketball old-timers, Auerbach has always been in love with height. The cliché is "You can't teach height," and Red is a believer.

In 1984, he made this comment about tall people: "Our attitudes about height have changed. Years ago, most guys 6-8 or 6-9 were considered a little bit eccentric, because there was no one around who was their size. There was nothing geared for bodies that size, as there is today. They felt self-conscious and walked about real stooped. Most of them were uncoordinated. But when tall men began to play basketball, they realized more and more that height is an asset, something to be proud of. They started not only to play tall, but to talk tall. They had pride."

Share had height. Share no doubt had pride. But Cousy had style and he was local and that's what the Boston sports fans wanted. The prospect of Share over Cousy was outrageous. Brown was ridiculed. Auerbach was mocked. The down-and-out Celtics had a chance to snatch local legend Cousy, and were going for a string bean from Bowling Green. Who'd ever heard of Charlie Share?

On Thursday, April 27, 1950, a little more than a month after the Walter Brown advisory committee meeting, and a few days after the sacrilegious draft, wiseguy Auerbach was officially named the third coach of the Boston Celtics. The press conference was held at a noontime luncheon at the Lenox Hotel. The afternoon edition of the *Boston Globe* ran the story in small type, under a pair of stories about high school sports and next to the racing results from Suffolk Downs.

Despite the scant coverage, the unveiling of Auerbach brought out the largest media assemblage in the brief history of the Celtics. All the writers wanted to hear an answer to the Cousy question.

"How come you didn't want Cousy?" asked one.

Auerbach was ready, uttering his famous "local yokel" quote. He made it clear that he was not into sentimentality or provincialism. He insulted the local college hoop god.

"[Cousy] won't bring more than a dozen extra fans into the building," Auerbach said. "What will bring fans into the building is a winning team, and that's what I aim to have . . . Proof is that eleven, at least, of the dozen teams would have selected Share as their first draft choice. I'm sure he will make the grade. Right now, I don't regard Cousy as good as Ed Leede. Remember, Leede has already made the grade and Cousy has to prove he can. He still has to learn what to do when he doesn't have the ball. Maybe he will, but I think it was more important for us to get a big man like Share."

"I don't remember having any specific reaction to it," Cousy says, forty-four years later. "I've tried like hell to take Arnold off the hook on that over the years. The difficulty arose because I had been a so-called media darling all those years. And Walter Brown, God bless him, used to stand up at those luncheons and say, 'I'll tell you how smart we were'—'we' being himself and Arnold, he'd point to me and say—'we never picked that guy.' And I used to sit there with

my head down, thinking, 'Please don't do this.' But I don't remember that Arnold and I ever had a discussion about it. It was just his
choice of words."

After the introductory "local yokel" remark, Auerbach went on
to say, "I always had a hankering to come here, and I was on your
Boston payroll as a scout while coaching at Duke last year before
moving to Tri-Cities. I think we've got some real ballplayers now."

In 1993, Auerbach explained the "scout" remark: "That's sort of
correct. You're not allowed to do that, I found out later. I didn't
know. Doggie had asked me to help him because Doggie was a
notoriously poor drafter. He drafted [George] Hauptfuehrer from
Harvard. He picked him as the Number One pick in the whole NBA
draft in the whole country. The guy would have been taken in the
fifth round. Imagine blowing not just the first round, but the first
pick. That was before I got here."

Tossing bombs from the podium was an Auerbach trademark in
that first season. Embarrassing local college coaches was an Auerbach specialty. At a basketball luncheon, when Boston College coach
Al McClellan talked about a new NCAA rule that allowed substitu-
tions only during time-outs, Auerbach suggested having players fake
injuries in order to get time-outs. When McClellan protested that
such a tactic would not be ethical, Auerbach bellowed, "Don't give
me any of that crap about college ethics. I know plenty of college
coaches who'll bend the rules just as far as they will go." Later in
the year, at another public function, Colby College's Lee Williams
said the officials in his league were so good that he hadn't found
reason to complain about any calls all season. Auerbach snapped,
"Any coach who doesn't complain to the referees once all season
just isn't doing his job."

"Local yokel" is the phrase that stuck. Auerbach, the smart-ass
New Yorker, was a pro basketball know-it-all, and he didn't care
whom he offended. He had the credentials.

His rejection of Cousy was backed by the rest of the league.
Seven NBA teams passed on the Holy Cross flash after Boston used
its top pick to select Share. Auerbach could have soothed the masses
by pointing out that seven other teams didn't want Cousy, either,
but that's not his style. He did what he felt was right and that was

that. Those who didn't agree with him simply knew nothing about basketball. Meanwhile, he didn't hesitate to point out that Holy Cross stars George Kaftan, Dermie O'Connell and Joe Mullaney—all teammates of Cousy's—had failed to make it in the NBA.

It was old friend Ben Kerner who drafted Cousy, with the ninth pick of 1950. Kerner offered Cousy $7,500, and the Cooz figured he could do better than that without playing pro basketball. A bright young man with a Holy Cross degree, Cousy was prepared to open a driving school in Worcester. Unable to sign the star guard, Kerner traded Cousy's rights to Chicago. When the Chicago Stags folded, the NBA called a meeting in New York to divvy up Chicago's roster. The final three Chicago players to be placed were Andy Phillip, Max Zaslofsky and Cousy. The Knicks, Warriors and Celtics were the final three teams in the bidding. Auerbach wanted Zaslofsky. His second choice was Phillip. Stubborn to the finish, he simply did not want Cousy. When the teams were unable to agree on who'd get whom, Commissioner Podoloff put three names in the hat of Syracuse owner Danny Biasone. The Celts were in line to pick first, but Walter Brown deferred. New York's Ned Irish drew Zaslofsky. Philadelphia's Gottlieb went next and drew Phillip. Brown took Cousy's name out of the hat and dropped it on the floor. The local yokel belonged to Boston. Red Auerbach was going to be Bob Cousy's coach—the only one he'd ever have in the pros.

"I think I held out for about eighty-five hundred dollars," Cousy jokes today. "Arnold was making all the money in those days."

Nemesis Keane says, "He didn't want Cousy. I was part of the thing. Cousy was in college, getting out of Holy Cross. And Brown said to me, 'I want to get Cousy. Do me a favor. Call him up and tell him that I want him and I'll get him. I don't want him to sign with Tri Cities.' So I called Cooz and said, 'Don't sign. Walter Brown wants you and he's going to get you, despite Auerbach.' He said, 'All right, I'll hold out.' A couple of days later I saw Brown and he asked if I'd reached him and I said I had. I said I told him to hold off, and Brown said he was still working on it. Then Cousy went to Chicago somehow and they folded. Then, when the Celtics finally got him, Auerbach still didn't want him, and he talked about trading him for Freddie Scolari a couple of times."

The folding of the Chicago Stags was no small story in the NBA. It delivered Cousy to the reluctant Auerbach, but it also left the league without a team in one of the country's biggest cities. In four seasons, the Stags had gone 145–92 (.619) and had made the playoffs every year. Chicago was the sixth team to fold in 1950, joining Sheboygan, Waterloo, Anderson, Denver and St. Louis.

In Boston, the Celtics were hanging on only because they were Walter Brown's dream. And now this brash young coach was going to show everybody how he'd handle the hotshot from Holy Cross.

Bob Cousy had to audition for Red Auerbach. Before the first practice, Auerbach again goaded the local media by announcing that the young guard would have to "make the team." The greeting for Cousy at the first practice was typically Auerbachesque. At Holy Cross, players wore T-shirts under their uniform shirts, and when Cooz walked onto the court for his first Celtic practice, Auerbach hollered from the other end of the gym, "What the hell is that T-shirt? Get your ass downstairs and get that thing off."

Auerbach was determined to establish that he was the boss. It was important that he show the know-nothing writers that he wasn't going to cower to a rookie All-America. He'd had one bad experience when he was undermined by Feerick; this time, he had to make it clear that he alone was running the show. He had no way of knowing that Cousy actually was a very bright young man, eager to take instruction. Cousy's receptive, unassuming attitude turned out to be a nice surprise for the young coach intent on proving himself in a new town. When Cousy's dazzling passes started clanging off the heads and hands of intended receivers, Auerbach took the guard aside and explained that the best passes in the world were no good if they weren't caught. He asked Cousy to tone it down a little until his new teammates got used to him. Cousy followed orders.

Cousy turned out to be a far better player than Auerbach had projected. In his first season, Cousy was NBA Rookie of the Year and finished ninth in the scoring race with a 15.6-point-per-game average and 341 assists, second in the league to Andy Phillip (414). In his 1966 autobiography, Auerbach wrote, "There was no question, even then, that Cousy was going to be the greatest passer that ever lived, even better than Dick McGuire. This kid was learning all the time. He might get sore when I threatened to bench him if he lost the ball, but he kept digging. He never sulked, and we never got into the kind of situation he had with Doggie Julian in college, where they wouldn't even talk to each other for weeks at a time. He knew if he listened and he worked at it, he could play any type of game with the best of them—and nothing was going to stop him, not even my own special brand of needling."

The needling was obvious to everyone, especially Cousy. In his interaction with the young guard, Auerbach adopted the philosophy that more is expected of those to whom more is given. The thoughtful parent is hardest on his most gifted child. Cousy had uncommon, God-given skills, but when talking about his starry guard in public, Auerbach never failed to accentuate the kid's flaws. Cousy later admitted that his fueled him. He'd mutter, "I'll show this guy," then work even harder.

"I used to carry Cousy's bag out of the arena," says Keane. "He'd be crying. With two minutes to go, he'd be in the game and Auerbach would take him out and put Sonny Hertzberg in to freeze the ball. They'd kill two minutes. Nothing would happen. Fans would be screaming for Cousy because Cousy'd put on a show. Instead, Auerbach wanted them to play this possession ball. It was driving people out of the building. Hertzberg was one of his sweethearts. Cousy'd be crying. I don't know how many times I carried his bag out of the arena. I'd say, 'You'll be all right, Cooz. Forget about it.' They later became pals. He joined Cousy in a couple of business operations."

Auerbach says, "I don't ever recall bawling Cousy out, because whether I'm an amateur psychologist or I deal in common sense, who knows, but I felt he was an emotional guy. He was sensitive and introverted. I felt I could accomplish more by talking to him. There were other guys that you had to get on, like [Tommy] Heinsohn, [Jim] Loscutoff, Ramsey. I don't ever remember getting on Cousy."

Cousy agrees. "All that about Arnold riding me was overdone. I was and still am sensitive about what I perceive to be unfair criticism. I don't remember that he was on me. Arnold didn't have that kind of relationship that he would tell me what to do or what not to do. He didn't have one-on-one relationships with players. And certainly he was not the traditional coach. He wasn't a guy you'd go to with your problems. It was business. And he dealt with us as a group. He wasn't telling you to 'do this, do that.' There was no individual repartee at all, from the beginning. We never discussed it. It was just 'come play.' Run us through the drills, get us in shape. Play the game. Take you out. Put you in. It was minimal.

"Arnold was the most successful coach in the NBA and he deserves what he got, but I think he did it with the least amount of wasted motion. The X-and-O guys all put him down. He wasn't an X-and-O guy. He didn't have sophisticated defenses. He didn't have varied offenses and all that shit. He knew how to win. He did know how to motivate. It wasn't like a system he designed. He was a ghetto rat like a lot of us and he'd scream and holler and we'd be afraid of that and that's how he'd motivate. He used fear, that's all."

Pesky, Auerbach's navy pal, who was still with the Red Sox in 1950, says, "The thing that I liked about Auerbach was that he knew his business. He was a good coach and players liked him. They say he was rude and crude, but to me he was a fine man. We got along good. He was sharp. He was a lot like our Dick O'Connell [then Red Sox GM]. I always thought O'Connell was one of the brightest guys I ever met, and Red and Dick got along extremely well. Auerbach had a sixth sense about a player. I went to a dinner with him one time. It was a B'nai B'rith dinner. Red got up and told a story about this Jewish kid that was trying out for the Celtics. The kid went up to Red and said, 'You and I are the same kind.' And Red said, 'Well, if you can play basketball, we'll be all right.' But the kid insisted, 'You and I are the same kind,' and Red supposedly said, 'Go fuck yourself.' And I can see Red saying that. He was one of those guys that could say things and get away with it. I enjoyed being around him a lot."

There was another rookie of significance on Auerbach's first Celtic team. In April 1950, on the same day that Auerbach passed on Cousy and took treetop Charlie Share, the Celtics used a second-round draft pick on Duquesne forward Chuck Cooper. Cooper was the first black drafted by an NBA team.

Where do we place this on the list of historical firsts? It is laughable to think of the NBA today without black players, but for four full seasons the league was a whiter shade of pale. Auerbach doesn't dwell on this particular first, but in the wake of charges that he faced in later years—charges that the Celtics preferred white players—it's handy that he can always claim he drafted a black player when nobody else would do so.

The selection of Cooper was hardly on a par with Branch Rickey's introduction of Jackie Robinson to baseball in 1946. The Washington Capitols selected Earl Lloyd of West Virginia State in the ninth round of the 1950 draft and the New York Knicks quickly signed Nat "Sweetwater" Clifton from the Harlem Globetrotters. Lloyd beat both Cooper and Clifton onto the floor. Lloyd played his first game for the Caps on Halloween 1950, a few days before Cooper played for Boston.

Auerbach had not yet been announced as Celtic coach when he huddled with Brown to go over plans for the 1950 draft. After talking the owner into the controversial Share-over-Cousy selection, Auerbach said, "There's a kid coming out of Duquesne who can help us. Chuck Cooper. I've mentioned him to you before. He's 6-6 and real good, but you know he's a Negro."

NBA owners worried about the gate impact of integration. They also feared retaliation by Abe Saperstein, the man who ran the Harlem Globetrotters. Still, Brown felt it was time. Cooper had led Duquesne into the semifinals of the NIT and everybody in New York knew about him. He was a shooter. The day after the draft, Cooper sent Walter Brown a telegram that read: "THANK YOU FOR HAVING THE COURAGE TO OFFER ME A CHANCE IN PRO BASKETBALL. I HOPE I'LL NEVER GIVE YOU CAUSE TO REGRET IT."

In present-day context, it's fascinating to look back at some of the reaction to the drafting of Cooper. One of the persons most outraged was Saperstein. He never before had been forced to compete to sign a black player. After the draft, the Trotter owner informed the NBA that he would not be taking his show into Boston. When Brown was told of the threat, he said, "He is out of the Boston Garden now, as far as I'm concerned! It would be different if we were signing an established Globetrotter."

Sid Hartman, who served as personnel director of the Lakers in the 1950s, says, "I was in the meeting when Walter Brown drafted Cooper, and they immediately called a recess. Eddie Gottlieb was sitting next to me and he said, 'Oh-oh. Abe's gonna go crazy.' Everybody knew that Abe Saperstein would cut out all the doubleheaders, and in those days they couldn't get along without the doubleheaders. Abe Saperstein would come to Boston and play three doubleheaders and that was their biggest gate of the year. Sure enough, Abe pulled out, and Walter Brown stood up to him."

Auerbach certainly had no problem coaching a black player. Players were players. He'd grown up in the melting pot of Brooklyn. Auerbach knew about discrimination. Chuck Cooper wasn't going to get any special treatment from his pro coach. In an era when integration was still a dirty word in much of America, Auerbach had no trouble assimilating a black ballplayer into the closed society of the Boston Celtics. Cooper roomed with Bones McKinney, the only southerner on the Celtic team.

Cooper (who died in 1984) played four seasons for the Celtics. He did not develop into the consistent rebounding forward that Auerbach wanted. Privately, Auerbach questioned the kid's hustle. Cooper knew. In a 1978 interview with the *Amsterdam News,* he charged Auerbach with contributing to the perception that black players had a low threshold of pain. Cooper said, "If I was hurt, they got suspicious. Auerbach, in fact, had labeled me a hypochondriac. In my four years in Boston, I never had an X-ray—lots of stitches, but never an X-ray. There were one or two white players on the Celtics that if they jammed a finger it was a cause of great concern. But then, you know how strong black skin is. We don't hurt. Ha!"

Auerbach says, "What happened with him is this: He was one of these guys who'd give me a great game. But you know he's got the potential. He lacked consistency, but all in all, he was a damn good player."

Mo Siegel says, "Red should be remembered for more than winning a lot of championships. Red did as much for the integration of basketball as Branch Rickey did for baseball. Red doesn't know the difference between black and white. Never did."

Cousy, Cooper and Auerbach were not the only new Celtic faces of 1950. Auerbach kept the bodies flying. He was like a fresh college graduate with a degree in physical education, taking his first job as a high school gym teacher-basketball coach. The new coach inherits a team of lazy, hotshot seniors—kids who lose most of their games and don't particularly care. These players are ready to come back for another mediocre season when the bold new coach cuts them from the team and elects to go with hungry underclassmen who've not yet been infected with the losing ways of the old program. Parents and administrators are furious with the young coach, but he wants to win and he needs to do it his way. This was Red Auerbach when he came to Boston in the fall of 1950.

Tony Lavelli, a 6-3 Celtic who sometimes played the accordion at halftime (his favorite number was "Lady of Spain"), was immediately dumped. A popular local product of Somerville and Yale, Lavelli wasn't tough enough for Red. "He's gone," said Auerbach. "He's not tough enough to play pro ball, and I've got no time for sentiment."

Lavelli had company. Ushered out the door along with him were Holy Cross alums George Kaftan and Joe Mullaney (Auerbach was "stuck" with Cousy, but he didn't want too many ghosts of Holy Cross haunting the premises). Howie Shannon, Jim Seminoff, Johnny Ezersky, Bob Doll and Art Spector were also sent packing. Only two players—Sonny Hertzberg and Ed Leede—survived the purge.

The best new player to join the team was Ed Macauley, a big forward who came from the folded franchise in St. Louis. Macauley was a 6-8 center who could score. He was awarded to Boston on the basis of the Celts' desperate need for talent. Macauley was a gift, one of the last gifts the NBA would bestow after Auerbach came to Boston. Macauley's presence enabled the Celtics to sell the immortal Chuck Share to Fort Wayne for $10,000-plus (which was used to purchase Sheboygan's Bob Brannum), Bob Harris and the rights to a University of Southern California guard named Bill Sharman. Share never played a minute for the Celtics, but he certainly made a contribution to future titles.

The new coach took his new Celtics to Fort Wayne for their first game and they were beaten by the Pistons, 107–84. Auerbach's Celtics lost their next two games. Same old Celtics. Brown had to be thinking about folding the team.

Suddenly, the Celtics turned it around. They started playing like Auerbach's old Washington teams. They ripped off seven in a row, ten of twelve. Over the course of the season, they challenged Philadelphia for first place, "Easy" Ed Macauley averaged 20.2 points per game, the C's went 39–30 and attendance improved by two thousand fans per game. The first NBA All-Star Game was played at the Boston Garden. By every measure, it was a successful season, even if the Celts were bounced by the Knicks in the first round of the playoffs.

Egan, the tough *Boston Record* columnist, wrote this after watching Auerbach's first Celtic team: "We know that a winner has been forced upon us in the person of Red Auerbach of the Celtics, and that he will do for professional basketball in this town of ours what Frank Leahy did for intercollegiate football . . . We know this not by anything he ever has said, but by the performance of his team . . . This is not a team of ballerinas and prima donnas and temperamental, selfish stars. They are young and hungry and full of heart, and they play the rambunctious, enthusiastic, blood-and-thunder basketball which only the young and the hungry and only the hearty can play."

Egan was a minority. Most Boston sportswriters continued to concentrate on baseball, boxing, hockey and college sports.

Broadcaster Curt Gowdy recalls, "I first got to know Red when I came up here to work as a Red Sox broadcaster in '51. Red looked at me and said, 'Look, nobody cares about basketball in this town. I want you to work our games if you can. We've got to educate the people in Boston about basketball and make them fans.' The Red Sox let me do it that first year, and there was never a dull moment with the Redhead. I've known him a long time, and he's one of the greats of sports."

Sharman was not part of Auerbach's first season in Boston. One of many two-sport stars who've played for the Celtics (Chuck Connors, Gene Conley, K. C. Jones, John Havlicek and Danny Ainge come to mind), the West Coast marksman was an outfielder in the

Brooklyn Dodger system when Auerbach guided the Celts to their first winning season. Sharman played thirty-one games with the Washington Caps in 1950–1951, and his rights were awarded to Fort Wayne after the Caps folded. He became Celtic property when Auerbach dealt Share to Fort Wayne.

Sharman was part of Boston's backcourt when the Celtics went 39–27 for a second-place finish in Auerbach's second season. This was the year that the lane was widened from six to twelve feet, resulting in less clogging underneath the basket. The Celtics again were eliminated by the Knicks in the first round of the playoffs. The deciding game was a one-point, double-overtime defeat. Auerbach's playoff record in the pros dropped to a dismal 10–16: He'd won two of eight playoff series. The Celtics averaged only 5,523 fans per home game, down about 600 per game from Auerbach's first season.

Leaguewide, there was good news. The 1951–1952 season was the first in which the NBA fielded the same ten franchises for two consecutive seasons. Brown invented the annual East-West All-Star Game and Celtic Ed Macauley was MVP of the first midwinter classic, a 111–94 win for the East in front of 10,094 fans at the Boston Garden.

In 1952 Auerbach published his first version of *Basketball for the Player, the Fan and the Coach.*

"I got a big royalty on that book," Auerbach says. "I wrote it in longhand. Each subject was like a term paper. It first sold for twenty-five cents and I got a penny a copy for the first hundred fifty thousand. Then I got a penny and a half, and then I revised it and they sold it for thirty-five cents and I got two and a half cents. They they sold it for ninety-five cents. Then it was a dollar ninety-five. Then it went into hardcover, then softcover again for three ninety-five. It sold way over a million copies. I got copies of it. It's in Polish, Russian, Italian, Japanese and Burmese. It was a good book, it really was. I worked on it myself; nobody helped me."

Common sense prevailed in the book. You don't bounce the ball without a purpose; a pass is the fastest way to advance the ball; if a pass is not caught, it's usually the fault of the man who threw it; when your man has the ball, watch his hips.

Other suggestions told coaches and players how to use gamesmanship and even to bend the rules in order to gain the edge. Here are some coaching tips from Red's international bestseller:

- When a player notices an official's indecision as to an out-of-bounds ball, he should run over and pick it up with the full confidence that it is his.
- Us[e] the hands to hold and block cutters under the basket.
- Faking injuries is used for many reasons such as stalling for time and giving the impression that a player will not be at his best.
- Some players may agitate their opponents by incessant chatter, refusing to talk to them at all, or even ridicule.
- If the opposing team has a high scorer, keep reminding the other players of their uselessness because the scorer takes all the shots.
- Grabbing or pulling the pants or shirt of the opponent can be very aggravating.
- During the held or jump ball a player can go in and out of the circle with the purpose of getting the opposing jumper's timing off.
- When an opponent needs one more foul to be disqualified or has a light injury, keep reminding him about it.
- Very often slight movement of the body is used to distract the opposing foul shooter.
- Jockeying from the bench can be very annoying.
- When a player has only one foul left before being disqualified, some member of his team should mention it loud enough for the officials to hear. This may result in an official hesitating to call a slight infraction.
- When your opponent makes a good play, don't congratulate him, merely mention that he was lucky.
- Place the scorer and timer's table near your bench.
- It is not advisable to announce your starting lineup until just before the game. If you are away from home, it might be wise to see your opponent's lineup before you give your own.
- Help organize the cheerleaders if necessary. It will help, especially at home.
- Wait until the other team has started warming up and then re-

quest their basket. This request must be honored away from home.

Pure Auerbach. Is it any wonder he was hated by many rival coaches and copied by all the rest? He is not suggesting cheating, but he wants his players and coaches to stretch the rules to the limit. It is unsportsmanlike, yet effective, and most of it has become gospel in every dimly lit gym in America. Auerbach trained America's high school coaches to make the home team relocate during warm-ups. It's a small thing and fairly rude, but Auerbach knew that the rules specified that the visiting team could choose which basket it wanted for the first half. You still see this today. The Westford Gray Ghosts will be warming up at the south end of their home gym while cheerleaders do cartwheels and the pep band plays. Suddenly, the visiting Groton Crusaders spill onto the floor and run right over to the end of the floor where the Gray Ghosts are doing lay-up drills. Westford yields. Grudgingly. It's the rule. It sets the tone. It agitates the home team and it keeps Westford away from its own bench in the second half. It's one of Red's lasting gifts to high school, college and pro basketball.

"What's dirty?" Auerbach asks. "What's tricky? Hell, what's winning basketball? If it's legal and it helps you win, you do it."

In Orrville, Ohio, 1952, Auerbach's instructional book caught the eye of a twelve-year-old basketball enthusiast. Young Bobby Knight bought the book off the newsstand rack at the Homestead restaurant.

"If you played basketball," legendary Indiana University coach Knight says today, "how could you not know Red Auerbach? He's really smart. You've got to start with that. He's a helluva lot smarter than most guys coaching are, and I think he really understood the mental side of competition, the psychological part of competition. That's a whole new area now. I think Red may have been the absolute forerunner in sports psychology. Red and Vince Lombardi. Red just had a great determination for his team to win, and I think that carried over to the players he had. It all goes back to his intelligence. You're dealing with a really smart guy. He spent time think-

ing about how to get people to play. He realized with talented
players, you could utilize the break and score off the break. Get the
ball down the floor. Talent is gonna score."

Auerbach was selling books and theories, but he wasn't winning
championships. Walter Brown started getting a little impatient during the 1952–1953 season, during which the Celts improved to 42–
25 and battled the Knicks and Syracuse Nats for first place. Boston
finished third, then dumped Syracuse in the playoffs, but lost to the
Knicks in the second round. After the playoff loss, Brown told the
press, "Some of our players are going to be playing for a lot less
money unless we get up where we belong."

Cousy was making a team-high $15,000. Speaking at a weekly
press luncheon, Auerbach directed some criticism at the All-Star
guard.

"Cousy is back where he was three years ago," said the crusty
coach. "He makes a spectacular play, but we lose the ball. Cooz can
make the club go, or he can kill it. He has been trying too much of
that behind-the-back razzle-dazzle. The other clubs are wise to us,
and they're jamming the middle and making us eat the ball. I've got
to go to work on Cousy's game."

Needless to say, this did little for the player-coach relationship.
Yet Cousy and Auerbach have worked together, on and off, for more
than forty years. Other than Mrs. Auerbach, Cousy remains the only
person on earth who refers to Red Auerbach as "Arnold." He's
learned to understand and tolerate Auerbach's mind games.

"Arnold runs away from confrontation. When he screams out his
edicts, that's fine. But as tough as he is, there's insecurity. The first
couple of years, he used to scream out when we'd come into a hotel
lobby. He'd yell, 'Hey, you guys, where've you been?' Like he was
the boss and everybody's supposed to shake. I don't know what trig-
gered it—I think I must have been with friends—but it embarrassed
me and I screamed back at him in the lobby in front of people. That
was the last time he ever did it."

Still struggling to take the Celtics to a higher level and establish
himself in Boston, Auerbach continued to be sensitive about local
players and local college basketball. In the winter of 1951–1952,
Auerbach arranged a scrimmage with the Holy Cross Crusaders. He

made sure all the writers were there to see it, and he made sure his
team won big.

Ron Perry Sr. grew up in Somerville and played high school tournament games in the Boston Garden when the Celtics were struggling through their early years. In 1954 he was co-captain of Holy
Cross's NIT champs. He was later drafted by the Celtics, but military
service and injuries ended his pro career. Today he is Holy Cross
athletic director. In 1951–1952, he was a college sophomore guard
who found himself playing in a scrimmage against a very motivated
Boston Celtic team.

Perry: "It was a good battle. In those days, we'd play anywhere
from six to eight games in the Boston Garden against intersectional
teams. We'd always draw well, and I think that was a carryover from
the Cousy years. There was a lot of interest. The Celtics weren't
taking hold at that particular time. So when we came down to scrimmage, I can recall some real shoving and pushing going on. It was
not discouraged. Bill Sharman was involved and three or four others.
I was kind of going at it myself. We were all playing aggressively
and I think the practice didn't end up to be what [Holy Cross coach]
Buster Sheary would have hoped. You could see there was that feeling that the Celtics were going to show us. I understand now why
Red felt that way. He felt that he had the best players in the world
and yet fans still wanted to see Holy Cross."

In the next three seasons, the Celtics won forty-two, thirty-six
and forty-four games—finishing second, third and second—while
Brown struggled to keep the franchise afloat. They annually scored
more points than any other team, but each spring, they were beaten
by Syracuse in the playoffs. A pattern had developed. Auerbach's
well-conditioned teams would fly out of the gate, but lose steam
around mid-February.

Syracuse's Dolph Schayes remembers, "The Celtics were a blood
rival, and in almost every game there was a fight. I think Red was
the instigator. He'd tell them, 'Go knock him on his keister' and
'Don't let them lay it up' and that kind of stuff. There was bad blood,
but it was good, tough, hard-nosed basketball. They were definitely
our big rival. The Celtics were more like the tough guys, and our
fans definitely wanted to beat them the most."

Auerbach hated Syracuse. He wanted to win every game at the War Memorial. He'd threaten his players: Win the game or we'll spend New Year's Eve in Syracuse.

From 1949 to 1958, Syracuse beat the Celtics 52 times in 102 meetings, including playoffs. There was a nationally televised ten-minute riot during an Eastern Conference Finals Celtic-Nat game in 1961. Auerbach taunted the crowd throughout the fracus. Referee Sid Borgia said the officials should have received combat pay for working Boston-Syracuse games.

The 1954–1955 NBA season marked the introduction of a momentous rule change: the 24-second shot clock. In the days before the shot clock, there was a lot of "stall-ball," and too much fouling, since you had to send the other team to the foul line in order to get the ball back. This made it difficult to come from behind. The shot clock solved these problems and made the game much more exciting for fans. Stall-ball was eliminated. Fouling was reduced. And there were plenty of thrilling comebacks, because the team with the lead was forced to keep playing. The shot clock was the brainchild of Syracuse owner Danny Biasone, the same man who offered his hat when Cousy's name was mixed with those of Andy Phillip and Max Zaslofsky. Auerbach initially resisted the idea, because he had the ultimate run-out-the-clock weapon in Cousy, but it was clear from the outset that Biasone's invention made the NBA much more attractive to fans. In the 1954 playoffs, one year before the shot clock was instituted, in only three of twenty-three NBA playoff games did a team crack the 100-point barrier. One year later, with the clock ticking away, eighteen teams broke the 100-point mark in playoff competition.

There was another reason for the rising popularity of NBA basketball. A 1951 investigation revealed that ninety college games had been fixed between 1947 and 1951. Thirty-three players from six different colleges were implicated. American sports fans lost some of their trust in the college game, and there was a shift toward the NBA.

The *Globe*'s Will McDonough says, "Red told me the thing that irritated him most in life was when he was coaching and some guy would come up and say, 'Well, you gonna win tonight?' That used to drive him nuts. He always suspected the guy was a bookie. He never wanted anybody to ask him that."

"When I'm in Boston I have to be careful who I associate with," Auerbach told *Sport* magazine in 1956. "I'm always making sure to avoid gamblers or flashy characters. I don't go into restaurants that have a reputation for serving the gambling crowd. And a coach can't have many friends."

One would have to be naive to believe Auerbach when he says he's never known any gamblers. He's been in basketball at the college and professional level for almost sixty years. He knew the coaches who were foiled by scandal. One of his best players, Cousy, in a 1967 *Life* magazine article, was fingered for friendships with a pair of known gamblers. Auerbach says he proposed a regulation that prohibited NBA officials from going to Las Vegas.

"My dressing room was clean as a pin," Auerbach says. "There was none of this 'friends' stuff. The hangers-on bothered me because it related to the college-game manipulations and drugs. I swear to you that I couldn't place a two-dollar bet with a bookie. Ever. I was never approached. They know. Gamblers obviously are not stupid. They know who to approach. I remember one incident at the Touchdown Club, way back in about 1948. We're at the bar having a beer and a guy says, 'Hey, Red, we could do some business together. You're the coach. We could bet on some games.' I turned around toward him and said, 'Look, if you ever talk to me again about betting or anything else, I'm gonna deck you. And furthermore, one more word out of you and I'm going to turn you in to the FBI.' Boy, everybody in the joint was shocked. There's no such thing as kidding when it comes to that."

The Celtics in the spring of 1955 were drawing almost seventy-five hundred fans per game. It was an improvement, but Brown still had trouble meeting the payroll. The Celtics had barnstormed, it seemed, through every small town in New England. In an effort to get his hockey fans to watch pro basketball, Brown tried dozens of promotions. There was a midnight game against the Detroit Pistons after an ice show. Brown called it the "Milkman's Matinee." The Celts played doubleheaders, sometimes sharing the bill with the Harlem Globetrotters. For a game at the Boston Arena, Brown

charged $1, first come, first served. He sold six thousand $1 seats.
It was never enough. After one of the playoff losses to Syracuse, he
asked his players for some extra time to get them their money. Celtic
players settled for IOU notes instead of playoff shares.

Cousy remembers, "We went to the other players and said, 'The
guy's in trouble. Let's give him a break.'"

In 1963, when Cousy was honored during his final season, Walter
Brown told the Garden crowd, "Things weren't always so good with
the Celtics, and one year they were so bad I couldn't pay 'em their
playoff money. And I didn't pay it to 'em for nearly a year. Bob
never said a word, and neither did Ed Macauley, Bob Brannum, Bill
Sharman or Chuck Cooper, all those great guys we've had. And they
permitted the club, by this action, to exist. It was the greatest tribute
I ever had paid to me."

During this period of fan lethargy, financial instability and post-
season mediocrity, Auerbach continued assembling the nucleus of
what would become the most dominant team in the history of professional sports. In 1953, he used a first-round pick on junior Frank
Ramsey, a Kentucky forward. Ramsey had been redshirted—forced
to sit out for a year—which made him eligible for the draft even
though he had one more season of college ball. Auerbach knew
Ramsey from the summer camps; Auerbach was a summer coach in
the Catskills and Ramsey was a ballplayer-busboy. Ramsey liked the
demanding Celtic coach, and Auerbach reminded Ramsey of Kentucky's legendary Adolph Rupp.

Versions differ, but moments before the 1953 draft, either Auerbach or Philadelphia's Eddie Gottlieb proposed a rule change that
would make players eligible for the draft before they were ready to
graduate. This allowed teams to take a college junior who had been
redshirted. The change was adopted, and Boston immediately selected Kentucky players Frank Ramsey (first round), Cliff Hagan
(third round) and Lou Tsioropoulos (eighth round). Seeing what
Auerbach was doing, New York Knick boss Ned Irish protested, and
after the 1953 draft, the rule went back to the way it was—you could
only take players who had used up all their college eligibility. (This
changed again when the NCAA returned to freshman eligibility, and

Auerbach employed the tactic a second time to land a player named Larry Bird.)

*Minneapolis Tribune* reporter Sid Hartman, who doubled as a personnel director for the Minneapolis Lakers in the early 1950s, remembers it quite differently.

"I was there, and we fought like gangbusters," says Hartman. "Red pulled that fast one for Hagan, Ramsey and Tsioropoulos. I was at every meeting. I tangled with Red at those meetings all the time. Red was a smart son of a gun. The rule was never changed; he just did it. I was there. He picked those players and Ned Irish was screaming about it. But Podoloff let it go because he liked Walter Brown and Brown was going bankrupt."

In the summer of 1954, Ramsey was in Boston with a group of college all-stars who were playing the Harlem Globetrotters at Fenway Park. It was in the Red Sox dugout that Ramsey negotiated his first contract with Auerbach and the Celtics.

"Red and Rupp were almost alike," says Ramsey. "They both demanded discipline. You had to dress appropriately. They were both dictators. I thought Red's strength as a coach was the way he drafted personnel. He got the talent and meshed the personalities into a winning team."

"Red really liked Ramsey," says Conley. "Ramsey was like a general manager. He's very dependable. He looked after everybody. If you went to Syracuse and it was snowing he'd made sure everybody had a driver for their car and make sure we stayed in line. He was like an old mother hen, and Red liked that.

"As much as Red liked him, he got on him one time, and it really shocked me. We were in New York. Red was a commission salesman for a company [Cellu-Craft, a cellophane-plastics outfit]. He didn't like people coming in the locker room before a game too much. But this particular night, these guys he was in business with were in there with him, talking business and meeting all the players. It was almost time for the game and Ramsey made a comment. He said, 'I don't understand—we get up for a ball game and we have to put up with all these guys in here. How can a guy concentrate?' And Red lit into him, saying, 'I'm the coach of this ball club, Ramsey. It's my business what I do, and if these are my friends, you have nothing to do with it,' and he really let him have it.

"Frank really felt bad, because he thought he was the favorite. Everybody thought they were the favorite of Red. He made everybody think they were the favorite. And to this day I'm still trying to figure out if Red used that, 'cuz he used to use different things to motivate us before a ball game."

The sales position was Auerbach's hedge against dismissal. Because of his lack of playoff success, and the ever-fragile nature of the NBA and the Celtics in particular, he needed a parachute. Through broadcaster Marty Glickman, Auerbach had hooked on with a major cellophane-packaging company owned by Sam Levy. Chicago Bear quarterback Sid Luckman and New York Giant football coach Allie Sherman also worked for Levy. Auerbach sold in his spare time, and he was pretty good at it. His accounts included Lever Brothers and General Mills. This gave him the security he needed to run the Celtics the way he felt they had to be run. He would not be a stooge coach. He would not worry about getting fired.

"I was on straight commission, and I was good," he recalls. "I opened up a lot of big accounts. I learned a little of that from Rupp. When I was in Kentucky, he explained to me how he had a tobacco farm, and he had some cattle, and he had an insurance business. You're at the mercy of the owner. I loved Walter Brown, but he was a guy that would get excited once in a while, and I wasn't the kind of guy to take it. So I figured we could eventually get into some disagreement. I didn't want to be out on the street. I wanted something that you could fall back on."

Cousy says, "On one hand he'd tell us not to get involved with a lot of things, then he'd be selling that goddamned cellophane. Almost everything after a while took second place, including the game. Nobody was allowed to have anybody in the locker room, but he'd have the buyer from General Mills in with his little kids and we'd have to shake hands. There was that kind of hypocrisy."

There would be many other ventures. Auerbach later bought part of a Chinese restaurant, Anita Chus, on 1366 Beacon Street in Brookline. At the urging of the Lenox Hotel manager, he invested in a Cape Cod hotel, the Seacrest in Falmouth. He endorsed a line

of athletic shoes. He opened a basketball camp in Marshfield. With
baseball pal Dick O'Connell, he bought into a franchise in the national Professional Soccer Football League. And of course, there was
his instruction book—at every newsstand in every airport on the East
Coast.

"I remember when he had the shoes," says Conley. "After I left
the Celtics, when I was playing for the Knicks, Red asked me to
wear these shoes he had. I put the shoes on and had a couple of
good games. One game I was really hot and scored about twenty
points and we beat the Celtics in New York. I saw Red and said, 'I
like the shoes,' and he said, 'Kiss my ass.'"

Sales, shoes, restaurants, hotels. In the end, Auerbach wouldn't
need any of his backup jobs. He had Cousy, Sharman and Ramsey.
The pieces were falling into place. The Celtics had a pair of Hall of
Fame guards. They had the shooters and the running forwards. But
they couldn't move ahead in the playoffs. Red Auerbach had been
coaching ten seasons in the pros and he'd made it to the finals only
once, where he'd lost in six games. In Boston, he had won only three
of nine playoff series and had never made it to the finals. After a
full ten seasons as a head coach, no small tryout, the book on Red
Auerbach was that he couldn't win the big one.

Woe to the hoop historian who ever put that thought to paper.

Auerbach says he was never in danger of being fired. Brown is
dead and can't comment. The two men were not very much alike.
Brown was generous, a tad naive and very outgoing. Auerbach was
petty, street-smart and almost always kept to himself.

"He always had hangers-on," says Auerbach. "That's the only
thing that used to bother me. You'd go into his office and there's
always some schmoe sitting there. I'd come in and say I wanted to
talk about my next contract and he'd say, 'All right, let's talk.' And
I'd say, 'Can't we have any privacy?' So he'd say, 'All right, let's go
into the bathroom.' He wouldn't kick the guy out. I'd say I wanted
a five-thousand-dollar raise and he'd say, 'Okay.' I never had a written contract. Year by year, it used to be in the toilet every time. I
couldn't believe it."

The coach and the owner got along well, but would often argue
about league matters. Brown frequently made sacrifices for the good

of the NBA; whereas Auerbach worried only about what was good for the Celtics. Auerbach hadn't wanted the shot clock because he had Cousy to dribble out the clock; Brown favored it. In the 1960s, Auerbach and Brown clashed over the propriety of the NBA's territorial draft—the rule which allowed teams to deal with one local college player apart from the draft. Auerbach never wanted to lose an edge, but Brown could see that the territorial draft was unfair to teams that played in remote regions. Auerbach's response was, 'Tough. That's their problem."

Keane, who gave Auerbach an especially tough time in the early years, holds that Auerbach was close to being fired twice. Auerbach believes Keane holds a grudge because he tossed him out of his dressing room after a playoff loss to Syracuse.

Keane: "Brown was losing all his money. Howie McHugh called me one day and said, 'Clif, come on down. I want you to be here, because Auerbach's going to be fired.' I came down to the office. I'm standing outside the door. Red went in. Dave Egan went in. Sammy Cohen. They came out in about an hour. Red was going to be fired, but Egan talked Brown out of it. About a year later, Syracuse killed 'em again in the playoffs and Walter Brown came up to me and said, 'Clif, who can I get to coach this team?' I said, 'He's your guy. Keep him.' "

After the 1954 playoff loss to Syracuse, Brown ordered a pay cut for Auerbach, saying, "I hold him partially responsible for the poor showing of our team this year." He also said, "He's not rising or falling on the outcome of the playoffs." (Auerbach's Celtic playoff record at this hour was 6–11.)

*Boston Globe* columnist Bud Collins remembers, "Walter would host those luncheons at the Lenox and he'd have two or three drinks before the thing got started and then he'd be up there telling us that everybody was gone. I was young, and I was off to write about it one time when Howie McHugh pulled me aside and said, 'Walter doesn't mean any of that.' "

Cousy agrees. "By that time, even though we hadn't won anything, Arnold had cemented his relationship. Arnold is a survivor. It's possible but I would have been very surprised if Walter had ever gone that far. Walter would say things, then regret them in the morning."

Keane says, "Al Cervi would outcoach him. Cervi would come in here with the worst load of garbage you ever saw and he'd beat Red. Auerbach was afraid of him. He was afraid Cervi was going to come over and punch him in the mouth. He'd look down the floor at him . . . My thought is that if Russell had ever failed, the franchise would have been out of town and Auerbach would have been out with it. Anytime Auerbach sits down and tries to tell you that Bird and Bill Russell are even, he's sick. Auerbach should have fifty pictures of Bill Russell in his office and he should kiss every one of them every day. Because Russell made him."

What does Auerbach say when confronted with the charge that "Russell made him"?

After a long pause, "In a way he did. What the hell. You got to be an idiot not to see that."

# 4

# RUSSELL

---

*We were all sitting down having lunch in Welling Hall, at George Washington. The team had just come back from the All-America College Tournament in Oklahoma City. San Francisco beat us and Russell blocked numerous shots. I was sitting at the table with Coach Reinhart and he turned to Red and said, "I just saw the greatest defensive player who ever lived—Bill Russell from San Francisco. Try to get this guy, no matter what you have to pay or who you have to trade."*

GENE GUARILIA, *former George Washington
and Celtic player*

BILL RUSSELL CHANGED THE FACE OF PRO BASKETBALL. MEASured by the most important yardstick of athletics—winning—Russell was the greatest player in the history of team sports. He was the starting center for a team that won eight consecutive championships and eleven world titles in thirteen seasons. Nobody else is close.

Red Auerbach rode side by side with Russell for each of those thirteen years. Auerbach and Russell were Huggins and Ruth, Lombardi and Starr, salt and pepper, brimstone and fire. Who made whom? Would Auerbach have been great without Russell? Would Russell have dominated if he'd played for a team other than the Celtics? It's one of the eternal arguments of sports.

Did Russell make Auerbach?

"People who say that are so full of shit," says Bobby Knight. "He made incredible use of Russell. In doing that, therein lies Red's greatness—just the mere fact that he recognized what can be done with Russell. I'm not sure how many other people would have recognized that. Prior to Russell, he'd utilized the break-and-run a lot. Now he ends up with the best defensive player ever. He turned it to his offensive advantage. He neutralized things at the defensive end. He used Russell to develop a game that probably at that point had never been played before—a game where a premium was placed on one guy capable of playing the basket. He made it tough for people to get to the bucket. He made a great use out of that. Red supplemented Russell with exactly the kind of players that could play the way Russell could play."

Tom "Satch" Sanders, a Russell teammate and a Celtic for thirteen years, says, "When it's said that Red only won because of Russell, that's like saying the only reason IBM wins is because they have a great company. People come up with all kinds of excuses and stories, but the only thing that counts is what is. The only reason why Joe Louis was what he was was because he had a great right hand. Without that great right hand, he never would have been champ, right? Think about it. Everybody says, 'If, if, if.' I understand why people have got to come up with those things, but the real deal is that even though the guy can play, as coach you've got to be able to get the guys to play together and keep 'em playing together, and keep that consistency of play. Make everybody happy. Well, Red believed that he ought to be happy. This was an interesting approach. 'If everybody keeps me happy, things will be good.' "

Auerbach's critics and rivals grant him this much: He knew enough to get Russell. Russell's abilities were not obvious to every fan, coach and scout. Selecting Russell out of the University of San Francisco was not at all like drafting Lew Alcindor (later to become Kareem Abdul-Jabbar) out of UCLA in 1969 or Shaquille O'Neal out of LSU in 1992. Russell wasn't particularly powerful and he didn't have the standard offensive moves of the average center. He lacked an outside shot. Wilt Chamberlain and Alcindor were obvious franchise players when they came out of college; Russell was not. He could have become Connie Dierking or Rick Robey. No one was sure—not even Red Auerbach, a ten-year coach who'd never won anything in the playoffs.

In 1956, Boston's needs were obvious, even to those novice fans Auerbach was so anxious to berate. The Celtics needed a rebounder. After the Celtics 1956 playoff loss to Syracuse, Auerbach told *The Globe*, "Damn it. With the talent we've got on this ball club, if we can just come up with one big man to get us the ball, we'll win everything in sight."

As was the case so many other times in his career, when Red Auerbach needed help and guidance, Bill Reinhart was there. In 1953, Reinhart's George Washington University team was crushed by the University of San Francisco in a tournament game at Oklahoma City. The San Francisco Dons that year were led by a skinny, 6-7 sophomore center named William Felton Russell. In Russell, Reinhart saw the perfect centerpiece for Auerbach's fast-break offense. Russell wasn't polished at the offensive end of the court, but he played great "help" defense, blocked shots while keeping possession of the ball and rebounded everything that came off the glass. He could whip the ball to the wings and run the floor all night.

Reinhart's glowing recommendation at Welling Hall put Russell into Auerbach's consciousness long before the Dons won fifty-five straight and two NCAA championships. This was an era without television. Auerbach didn't have ESPN, videocassettes or a raft of scouts equipped with air travel cards and portable telephones. Scouting was done via word of mouth. You needed guys in other parts of the country to tell you where the players were. You needed guys you could trust. For Auerbach, Reinhart had the best eye in the business. Russell became a player Red wanted. Getting in position to draft him would be another matter.

Russell became better known during the 1954–1955 and 1955–1956 seasons. He was the center on the two-time national champs, and San Francisco's winning streak was an NCAA record that would hold up until Bill Walton and UCLA broke it two decades later.

Few people in Boston or around the NBA knew that Auerbach had his eye on Russell. *Herald* sports editor Sammy Cohen knew Auerbach was tracking someone on the West Coast because when

Auerbach visited Sam Cohen's home, the coach would make late-night phone calls to USF coach Phil Woolpert and West Coast scouts. Butterball Freddie Scolari told Auerbach that Russell was the greatest thing he'd ever seen on a basketball court. Don Barksdale, another retired Auerbach alum living on the West Coast, reported that Russell could take NBA punishment under the basket. California coach Pete Newell forwarded another glowing recommendation. Reinhart, Scolari, Barksdale, Newell. These were Red's guys. These were people who knew basketball, people he trusted. Russell was the one.

"I played against Russell in college," says Tommy Heinsohn. "This guy was something else on defense, but as an offensive player, he was liable to throw the ball over the backboard. Nobody knew what this guy would be, because nobody ever played like he did."

"A lot of people were not that high on Russell," remembers Auerbach. "I could name you some top basketball people. Ike Ellis, the sports editor of the [New York] Post—he didn't think Russell would really make it. He'd compared him to Walter Dukes. He figured he couldn't shoot as well as Dukes, and Dukes is about two inches bigger, and he's just about making it. Why would Russell make it? he can't shoot."

Hall of Famer Eddie Gottlieb was in pro basketball for his entire life. One of the organizers of the NBA, he owned the Philadelphia Warriors when Auerbach set his sights on Russell in 1956. Gottlieb later said, "There's no question Red was the first to realize what Russell could mean. Red recognized a way he could take advantage of Russell's defense and rebounding and get big results which he couldn't get from him in any other way. He saw things in Russell that a lot of people didn't see. And he knew just how he planned to use him. So you've got to give the man credit. He was the first to spot Russell's real greatness."

When Auerbach attended a basketball luncheon and heard Harvard coach Floyd Wilson say that San Francisco's Russell would not make it in the professional ranks, Auerbach leaned over to Sam Cohen and said, "He's full of shit!"

Auerbach got his first look at Russell when he went to New York to watch USF in the 1955 Holiday Festival at Madison Square Gar-

den. Seeing the gangly shot-blocker for the first time, he thought of
Reinhart's words: *Russell could get you the ball.* As always, Red's old
coach was right.

The Celtics in 1955–1956 were going to finish nowhere near the
bottom, so a trade would have to be made if Auerbach was to get
into position to draft Russell. Though there were some doubts about
Russell, he'd have been selected by late in the first round. Auerbach
had to figure out a way to get in a position where he could draft
Russell.

Cousy says, "He used to share with his captain at that point, and
I would be privy to things occasionally if he thought he had a secret.
Sometime in December I remember him telling me that he had a
guy that he was going to draft that was going to change everything.
That's why when it's said that this happened by accident, that's a
bunch of crap. He knew that he wanted Russell, and he did whatever
he could to get him."

Auerbach set his sights on the St. Louis Hawks, owned by Ben
Kerner. Like Bill Reinhart, Kerner seemed to be there every time
something crucial happened during the early years of Auerbach's
career. Auerbach knew from his own bitter experience that Kerner
liked to make trades without consulting his coach, and Kerner was
holding the second pick in the 1956 draft.

Auerbach believed he had enough to offer to get Kerner's pick,
but it didn't make any sense to pursue a deal with St. Louis until
he was certain that Rochester would not select Russell with the No.
1 pick. Nothing could be left to chance. He needed to be certain.

At Auerbach's request, Walter Brown called Rochester owner
Lester Harrison. Brown was friendly with the Rochester owner, and
politely asked what the Royals planned to do with the top pick. The
Royals were fairly set in the frontcourt with Rookie of the Year
Maurice Stokes. Harrison knew that Russell was going to ask for
$25,000 and he knew that the Harlem Globetrotters were anxious
to meet the Californian's price.

Harold Furash, a Massachusetts insurance broker who attended
the first Celtic practice in franchise history, and who has been an
organization insider for forty-seven years, believes that Walter
Brown's ice show was used as barter for Russell. According to

Furash, "Brown made a deal. If Lester passed up Russell, he would arrange for Lester to get the Ice Capades for Rochester two weeks a year under Lester's promotion. It was then that Lester bravely announced that he didn't want to wait for Russell to make his [Melbourne] Olympic commitment. Of course, Lester made more money from the Ice Capades than he would have made with Russell."

Harrison's version of the story is different. An ex-coach, he said the decision to bypass Russell was a basketball decision. Prior to the draft, the only time he had seen Russell was at the collegiate East-West College All-Star Game at the 96th Street Armory in New York. In 1983 Harrison told *USA Today*, "Mr. Russell did not look good at all. Probably he didn't want to go to a small city. Anyway, he just looked bad. Stories were written that he might not even be able to make it in the NBA. It was just one of those things. The only way I can live with myself is that I made the decision on what I saw. If we had scouted him, there wouldn't have been a Boston dynasty."

Auerbach says, "What happened was this: Walter got him the Ice Capades, and he felt indebted to Walter. He said, 'Look, you gave me the Ice Capades, I'll give you my word that we won't take Russell.' "

Harrison admits that Brown delivered the Ice Capades, but denies that it had anything to do with the draft.

There is still another version. According to Auerbach and Russell, Harrison had tried to "recruit" Russell by getting Dolly King to lobby for Rochester. King was a black player, a former Long Island University star who was playing for Rochester in 1955. Russell didn't like the idea that Harrison would use another black player to help sign him, and raised his price.

In Terry Pluto's 1992 *Tall Tales*, Harrison told the author, "The real truth about this draft is that Auerbach and Russell set me up. You ever hear about a horse race where a three-to-five finishes dead last? That was what happened to me. I was cheated out of Russell, who played poorly at the All-Star Game because he didn't want to play in a small city like Rochester."

In any event, Auerbach was certain that Rochester was not going to select Russell with the top pick. With this knowledge in hand, Auerbach made his pitch to old pal Kerner. In his autobiography,

Russell wrote, "That must have been a phone call to listen to. Here were two guys who were really sharp, rough and tough. And really hated each other."

Auerbach offered Easy Ed Macauley for Kerner's No. 2 pick. Macauley was a seven-time All-Star and a St. Louis native who'd starred at St. Louis University. In an attempt to make Russell less desirable to Kerner, Auerbach noted that the USF star was committed to playing for the USA at the Melbourne Olympics, which would keep Russell out of NBA action until December. It might have been a moot point. There are those who believe Kerner would never have taken Russell because he didn't want a black star in St. Louis. Oscar Robertson later said, "St. Louis did not want black guys on their team, so they traded Russell. That was the difference. Red saw that."

Robertson might be paranoid, or he might be right. When rookie Russell played his first NBA game in St. Louis, he heard racial slurs from people in the crowd. He later wrote, "If one could query at what moment the string of world championships of the Boston Celtics was born, that would be the one moment that crystallizes in my memory."

Kerner didn't settle for Macauley. He asked for another player: Cliff Hagan of Kentucky. Hagan was a 6-5 All-American and Boston owned his rights. Auerbach wanted Russell badly. He agreed to include Hagan in the deal.

Walter Brown, ever loyal to his ballplayers, called Macauley to ask how he felt about being traded to St. Louis. In ordinary times, Macauley might have nixed the trade, but his year-old son, Patrick, had contracted spinal meningitis and needed constant care near specialists in St. Louis. Macauley welcomed the move. It was the best thing that could have happened to him. It was also the best thing that could have happened to Red Auerbach.

Seventy-three-year-old *Minneapolis Tribune* columnist Sid Hartman still claims he almost brought Russell to the Lakers. Hartman had been involved in personnel decisions with the Lakers in the early years of the NBA (it was not uncommon for reporters to moonlight, and nobody worried about conflicts of interest). Hartman says, "In 1956, before Russell came out, [George] Mikan had retired and I

made a deal with Walter Brown—and I'm sure Red okayed it; I've
got the paper somewhere. We were set to trade Vern Mikkelsen for
Magan, Tsioropoulos and Ramsey. What happened was, I called Pete
Newell, who was coach of California at the time. I told him we'll
give you a couple, three grand if you get Russell for us. I thought
he could get Russell to play for us. There were a lot of rumors that
Russell was going to play for the Globetrotters. If we had made the
Mikkelsen deal, we would have finished last and been able to draft
Russell.

"One day, one of the owners of the team came in and said, 'I
think we still can win the championship with Mikkelsen here.' At
that point, I said, 'If you call the deal off I quit.' He did. We called
the deal off and I called Walter Brown and Walter Brown sent me
a television set that I still have for calling the deal off. I've got it in
my basement. I guess they had second thoughts about making the
trade. Sure enough, then they made the trade for Russell. Red might
deny it, but I've got the papers from Podoloff on that deal. If we
make that deal, there's no Boston dynasty and we'd have been able
to keep the Lakers here because we'd have gotten a building built.
Later I was involved with Chicago, and the first year of existence
Walter played seven exhibition games for us, and one reason he did
it was because I called that deal off."

Auerbach says, "It might have been; I don't remember that. A
lot of people say that they had a trade going. They may have proposed that, but Walter never would have made that trade without
discussing it with me. He never discussed it with me, which means
there was no such trade, I don't care what Sid says."

Rochester finished last, two games behind St. Louis and Minneapolis, and on April 20, 1956, owner Lester Harrison selected
Duquesne guard Sihugo Green with the first pick of the NBA draft.
Si Green would play nine NBA seasons, averaging 9.2 points per
game in stints with Rochester, Cincinnati, St. Louis, Chicago, Baltimore and Boston. He retired in 1966 after playing ten games with
Bill Russell for Red Auerbach's Celtics. Harrison sold the team in
1958. He was inducted into the Basketball Hall of Fame in 1979
and will forever be tops in the hearts of historically minded Boston
sports fans.

After Rochester made its pick, the Celtics used the No. 2 to select Bill Russell from the University of San Francisco.

More work had to be done to sign Russell. The Celts feared a bidding war with the Globetrotters. It was rumored that the Trotters were willing to go as high as $50,000. Russell and his USF coach, Phil Woolpert, met with Globetrotter boss Abe Saperstein. Saperstein blundered by negotiating solely with the coach. Russell interpreted this as two white men haggling over the services of what they considered a dumb Negro boy who couldn't possibly keep up with the conversation. Saperstein had made the same mistake Harrison made: He had insulted Russell's intelligence. It was an error that Auerbach never made with Bill Russell.

The Trotters were out of the picture, but Russell's Olympic commitment prohibited Auerbach from negotiating with his franchise player. This made everybody in Boston a little uneasy, but their fears were assuaged when the 6-9 center invited Walter Brown to his wedding in San Francisco.

Prior to the Melbourne Games, Russell played in an Olympic fund-raiser with other college stars at the University of Maryland. Brown and Auerbach went to the game to get a firsthand look at their future. On this night, Russell played particularly poorly. Brown said little as he watched the disaster unfold, but he had to be thinking, "Macauley and Hagan for this?" It was awkward for Auerbach. Finally, he turned to his owner and said, "I don't believe what I'm seeing out there. Too many people have seen this guy too many times for him to be this bad. I know he was a lot better when I saw him in New York."

After the game, Russell and teammates K. C. Jones and Carl Cain went to Auerbach's Washington home for dinner. Russell apologized for his poor play. Brown and Auerbach were impressed.

"This kid showed me a lot of humility tonight," Brown told Auerbach after Russell left. "I just hope he doesn't think we're going to cut the price because of the way he looked in that game."

December of 1956 was a key month in the history of Red Auerbach and the Boston Celtics. On December 7, in French Lick, Indiana, Georgia Bird gave birth to her fourth child, a son, Larry Joe.

On Sunday night, December 16, Russell and his bride, Rose, arrived in Boston. Walter Brown picked them up at the airport and Bill Sharman presented them with a giant "Welcome to Boston" key.

He still had to sign his first contract. Auerbach knew that Russell was worried about his potential point totals, so he made a deal with the young player: He told Russell that as long as he played for the Celtics, personal statistics would never be discussed at contract time. Deal. Russell signed a one-year contract worth $19,500. Officially, his pay was $22,500, but he was docked $3,000 because of his Olympic commitment. This sounds cold, but Walter Brown made Russell feel he was giving him a break. A prorated portion of his time missed called for him to lose $6,000, but Brown felt that was unfair and split the difference with the gold medal winner. Thirty-seven years after Russell signed, No. 1 picked Chris Webber signed with the Golden State warriors for $74.4 million over fifteen years. Webber was given the option to tear up the pact and negotiate a bigger one after his first year of play. Nice. In 1956, Russell's advance went toward a loaded Chrysler Imperial worth about $8,000.

The 1956–1957 Celtics were already 16–8 when Russell arrived with his Chrysler Imperial and his Olympic medal. Boston's other draft prize, Holy Cross forward Tommy Heinsohn, was already establishing himself as an NBA star. A bruising cornerman with a deft hook, Heinsohn was a perfect player for the NBA game of the fifties and sixties. He was cocky, fearless and smart. No one had paid much attention to him on draft day because Russell was the story, but Heinsohn was an important piece of the jigsaw juggernaut Auerbach had assembled. In addition to rookies Russell and Heinsohn, thirty-four-year-old Andy Phillip had been brought in to strengthen the Celtic bench.

"What Red did that summer was fantastic," remembers Cousy. "He got exactly what he wanted, exactly what we needed. After six years of not winning a damned thing in the end, I went into that season believing we really had a shot at all the marbles. I felt that way before Russell joined us. I couldn't wait to get started."

On December 22, 1956, Russell made his NBA debut, scoring six points, grabbing 16 rebounds and blocking three Bob Pettit shots

in twenty-one minutes of a two-point victory over the St. Louis
Hawks. The NBA would never be the same. The Celtics had finally
arrived. Red Auerbach wasn't going to go home empty again.

Later in life, when Russell recalled his first NBA games, there
was one play that stood out in his mind. He remembered how Auerbach had argued in his behalf when he was slapped with the first
goaltending violation of his pro career.

"I learned what kind of a man Auerbach is," Russell told the
*Boston Record* in 1959. "The referee called goaltending on me.
Auerbach came storming out on the floor and argued like mad. The
ref called a technical foul on him. That's when I realized that here
was a guy who was 100 percent for me and the rest of the team.
You can't help liking a coach like that."

Bill Russell was born in Monroe, Louisiana, the second son of a
paper factory worker. The family moved to Oakland when Bill was
nine. Race relations in northern California were much more progressive than conditions in Louisiana, but Russell never forgot the
way it was in Monroe. Awkward in sports, Russell didn't make the
starting lineup of his McClymonds High School basketball team until
his senior season.

He was good enough to earn a scholarship to the University of
San Francisco, where he roomed with K. C. Jones. Jones noticed
that Russell was a loner and a reader. He liked to make people
uncomfortable. He liked to intimidate. He would not sign auto-
graphs (this led to a heated intramural argument in the Madison
Square Garden locker room one night when Russell refused to give
Heinsohn an autograph for Heinsohn's uncle). He had anger in him.
When he was a freshman at USF, the school sent him to St. Louis
to compete in the AAU meet as a high jumper. USF officials made
a reservation for him at the Chase Hotel, but the Chase didn't know
that young Mr. Russell was a Negro. Russell was turned away and
spent the night in his car. So much for St. Louis.

A superior intellect, Russell no doubt was intrigued and amused
by the player-coach relationship that existed when he joined the
Boston Celtics. Auerbach was a dictator, but he was benevolent. The
coach didn't mind being feared, but he preferred to be respected.

The coach was white, but had a good understanding of the plight of blacks in the NBA in the mid-1950s. Russell could spot a phony in a second. He still can. He was suspicious of all white people and was quick to anger at the condescending attitudes and efforts of Harrison and Saperstein.

Early in his career, Russell told *Sports Illustrated*, "I don't like most white people because they are white. Conversely, I like most Negroes because they are black. Show me the lowest, most downtrodden Negro and I will say to you, 'That man is my brother.' "

There were only six black players in the NBA the season before Russell joined the league. Ten years later, forty-seven of the ninety-nine NBA players were black, including fourteen of the league's All-Stars. Auerbach was right for his time. He wasn't afraid to draft a black player. Years later, he'd be first to start five black players and first to hire a black head coach. Auerbach hired three black coaches (Russell, Tom Sanders and K. C. Jones) before many NBA teams had hired even one.

In his 1977 autobiography, Auerbach admitted this about his dealings with Russell: "Russell just hated to practice [but] we knew he was going to give us forty-eight minutes of playing his guts out during the games. But every once in a while I'd really get on him. 'You big shvartzeh sonofabitch! All the plays revolve around you. When the rest of these guys see you loafing, they want to loaf, too. You're ruining it for everybody. Now start moving.' He'd stand there and give me the famous Russell look, but in all of our years together, he never once answered back."

Could anyone other than Red Auerbach get away with calling Bill Russell a "shvartzeh?"

Auerbach admitted that the term—a Yiddish word for "black"—is generally considered an insult. "It's a German derivative," he says. "It means black. It's an insult according to who says it. The players knew I was Jewish, and I'd call Russell a dumb shvartzeh. Later, when he started coaching, he used the same expression. I asked him one time. I said, 'Russell, what do we call you guys? I can use colored, or Negro, or African-American. Is it black, or what?' He said he preferred 'black.' That's all. And that was the only time in all the years I've been associated with Russell that we ever discussed black or white. I just wanted to know where we were at, because I didn't want to insult anybody."

"Red's strength in terms of dealing with the black players was that he treated everybody the same," says Cousy. "He screamed at everybody and he called them shvartzehs, so it was out in the open, and I think that's what everybody wants."

Heinsohn says, "I think what he did was treat the black guys as human beings, and they respected that. He went to bat for them over a lot of things. Red certainly did not treat them like they used to treat the Globetrotters. A lot of the other teams didn't treat the black players nicely. Society was having a problem with it, but Red treated everybody as a human being. And he wasn't afraid to tell everybody what Russell's impact was."

Sanders, one of Russell's black teammates, says, "The race issue became an issue for people that had to deal with it on a daily basis, but we didn't have to deal with it on that team. Red confined his world and his efforts to basketball, and with the players that were there, race was never an issue. It blossomed when it came to a situation in Kentucky where the black players wouldn't play because of a situation we had at the hotel. It was an exhibition game in Lexington. Red just said, 'You guys do whatever you have to do.' The feeling you got was that it was your choice. That's the important thing. It doesn't matter whether he believed in it or didn't believe in it. The ball was in our court. Clearly he preferred for us to play; no doubt about that. We were down there. He's coach. He's management, that's to be expected. But he also recognized the gravity of the issues that were involved."

Sanders, Russell and the other black Celtics went home, but the game was played. Whites only. The stands were integrated—a first for Lexington. The year was 1961.

Clif Keane admits, "He was great with black guys. In the dressing room, he'd sit a black next to a white—Cousy, Satch, then Heinsohn. And he'd talk to them all. Other teams had all the black guys over in a corner snickering, not paying attention. Auerbach paid attention to everybody. Down in the hotel lobbies, he'd send 'em off in cabs. Two black guys and a white guy. He'd say, 'You three go.' He never let three black guys go together, or three white guys. I don't think it was a game he played, that's just the way he was. He was great at it, I'll say that for him."

"I never looked at it that way," says Auerbach. "To me, a player is a player, and still is. I mean that sincerely. To me, a guy was a guy. Every once in a while a guy would say, 'How do you understand this type of situation?' I'd say, 'Hey, I'm Jewish. I went through some shit, too.' I don't' talk about it. I didn't tell anybody about it. When I was a kid you either had to fight and run or run and fight. So what? The club team I played on in high school had a Polish guy, an Irishman, an Italian and a couple of Jews. And my whole life has been that way. I got the first award given in Boston from the NAACP. And I got mad. Russell didn't even attend. I said, 'What the hell is going on?' "

Dick O'Connell, the brilliant general manager of the historically racist Red Sox organization, spoke at a brotherhood breakfast in Boston and said, "Gentlemen, here we are in a sports environment, talking about brotherhood: On the great battlefields of war, kids fought side by side with no regard for the other fellow's race or religion. That's fine, but may I suggest that the best example of what we're talking about can be found right down the street. There you'll find a team of blacks and whites, Catholics and Protestants, who are coached by a Jew, and they've been champions for a long time now. Everyone's running around looking for theories, looking for things that happened in the past which might shed light on problems we face today. But the best illustration of all is right in front of our eyes. Just look at the Celtics."

By the time Russell came along, Auerbach had coached ten seasons in the pros. At this stage of his career, he was both coach and parent to his ballplayers. He was gruff on the court, but sometimes soft when he was away from the hardwood. Still in his thirties, he was not that much older than many of his players. He made it a point not to get close to them but didn't mind having some fun at their expense. He'd devised a clever way to make them opt for the top bunks on sleeper cars. He told his tall players that the bunks on top were four inches longer. Instead of fighting like children, the taller guys requested the upper bunks. It took a while before they realized the coach had fabricated the bunk-bed theory.

"They weren't animals, they were men," Auerbach wrote of his players. "And without getting too sloppy about it, they were also a family. My job was to be the head of that family. Sometimes it called for disciplining them. Sometimes it meant they weren't going to like me. I couldn't be their buddy and be their coach, too. I don't care what anybody says, that won't work. But I loved that family, and there wasn't a single day when I wasn't proud of every member of it."

Auerbach rarely fined his players. Early one morning on the road, he found two of his players in a hotel coffee shop in the company of a couple of local lovelies. He asked what they were up to. The unshaven, red-eyed ballplayers told their coach that the girls were their cousins and they were all getting ready to go to Sunday Mass. Auerbach excused himself from the group. A few days later, back in Boston, he fined the players $25 each. He told them they were fined not for breaking curfew, but for "insulting my intelligence."

The travel was hardly exotic. Here's Heinsohn (in his book *Give 'em the Hook*), writing about the experience of getting from Rochester to Fort Wayne: "We'd take a sleeper train out of Rochester, then at about five in the morning they'd wake us up to make a special stop in the middle of this cornfield located on the outskirts of the nearest town to Fort Wayne. They wouldn't stop in the town, just near it, and just long enough to unload our baggage, which we'd then have to carry as we walked two miles to a place they called the Green Parrot Inn. I'll never forget that name. We'd get to the Green Parrot Inn at about six in the morning, which meant we now were within fifteen miles of our ultimate destination. Then we'd have to bribe some high school kids to drive us the rest of the way."

On a train or airplane, the coach would sit in the front, away from the players. Occasionally, he'd play cards with the guys.

"He was scared of flying and always took Dramamine," remembers Brannum. "Then he'd try to play cards and he'd fall asleep in the middle of the game. He'd wake up and say, 'What are you guys doing?' He spoiled a lot of bridge games that way."

"Usually, he got one of the rookies to sit in for him," says Conley. "He'd stake 'em, give 'em ten bucks or something and tell 'em to play for him. Red found out that Gene Guarilia was a good card player, so he would give him ten or twenty dollars and share the winnings, and I think Gene won some money for him. Red never had to play a hand. He didn't want to take anybody's money or vice versa. If somebody had beaten him at cards, it might give 'em a little power, you know, and he didn't want to do that.

"He wanted to be in complete control, and what helped the power of those guys in those days was the purse strings. That helped coaching. These guys could take your money. There was no players association. The coach could tell you, 'Put out the next game or you go home.' You'd get two weeks' pay. He could just say, 'We don't need you.' That's a terrible feeling. When somebody tells you at halftime that there's no more pay if you don't hustle, that's enough to make a guy dive for a ball."

He didn't have bed checks or secret agent security sleuths.

"I said, 'Whatever you do, I don't want to see you,' " Auerbach recalls. " 'I don't want to see you with a drink in your hand. I don't want to see you doing anything that's really out of line. So now if you're smart, do whatever you want to do, but make sure I don't see you. I got no spies. But if you're dumb enough to get caught, then it's your tail.' "

"Avoid confrontation," says Cousy. "Which makes sense. Why do you want to catch your star quarterback coming in at one o'clock in the morning the night before the big game? It causes you to take a stand. Make 'em think there are all these rules, but don't go looking to enforce them."

Celtic players couldn't drink beer in the team hotel, but they were on their own elsewhere in the city. Hard liquor was never allowed. Auerbach believed that whiskey cut into your stamina. If he thought some of his boys had been partying overtime the night before, he'd get them at practice the next day. They'd hear him chuckle and say, "There's an awful lot of sweat under the basket, hey, hey." They knew he knew.

The same rules applied at home. "I worked at a candy store when I was fifteen," says Randy Auerbach. "I went to a wedding and got drunk for the first time. Whiskey sours. I was very sick and I had to go to work the next day. I got the lecture from him—'You have a responsibility and this is why you can't do these things.' But he never yelled. I wasn't grounded or punished. It was more like, 'You're going to have to suffer.' "

*An awful lot of sweat under the basket, hey, hey.*

The coach had an odd rule about no pancakes before games. He felt that pancakes would lay in the belly and make the player slow. Sam Jones hated this rule. Auerbach also wouldn't let his ballplayers drink cold water, because he thought it sizzled in the stomach, like an ice cube on a hot stove. Later in life, he admitted he was wrong about the pancakes and the cold water.

He wouldn't take any guff in the huddle or on the court. This never changed. Players rarely challenged him, and then only once, or they were gone. He made all the decisions and there were no questions asked, but he often solicited input from the troops. It wasn't unusual for Auerbach to call time-out, duck his head into the team huddle and say, "Anybody got anything?"

He often is asked about how to "handle" employees. *Handle* is a buzzword for Red.

"They are not animals," he says. "You do not *handle* them. You develop a chemistry, and chemistry is developed through respect. Primarily, you develop an ability to communicate. To me, that's the number one thing in being a good coach. There's a lot of people that know their Xs and Os. A lot of people tell people to do things, but then the players go on the court and forget them. I prided myself on having the ability to communicate to a point where they would absorb what I was saying. Contrary to the opinion of most people, I never ranted and raved—well, I won't say never. Once in a while, to show a change of pace, in the locker room I would raise holy hell, but I would try to do it after a win or before a game that we should win.

"You'd be a liar if you said you treated everybody equally," he says. "You don't. It doesn't work. For example, I never balled out Cousy. I never balled out K. C. Jones. I used to get on Russell, Ramsey, Heinsohn, Loscutoff. I never balled out a sub. I'd get on those guys I mentioned. That's one way of keeping great chemistry. They knew they were not immune to criticism. Anybody can get on a sub. What the hell kind of balls does that take?"

In 1956, Auerbach was smart enough to exclude Russell from the routine rookie-hazing that had been part of all his Celtic teams. Typically, the first-year players were required to carry veterans' luggage, fetch snacks and pay for group cab rides. Veterans annually would "set up" a kid during pregame introductions. The Celtics would give their proud, naive rookie the "honor" of leading the team onto the court for warm-ups. Full of adrenaline, the innocent rook would snatch the ball from some veteran and charge onto the court after the public address announcement of "the Boston Celtics." When the poor kid turned around, the rest of the team would be backstage laughing at him. The dignified Russell was never mocked in this fashion.

This special treatment was extended to the practice floor—quite a gamble for Auerbach to have taken. Bill Russell was into energy conservation long before the American fuel crisis of the early seventies. Russell's skills weren't the kind that could be improved by practice. So he was excused most of the time. Auerbach would try to get him to go hard for fifteen minutes of practice, and that was it. If Red felt like yelling at somebody, he usually would yell at favorite whipping boy Heinsohn.

Sanders, the other forward in the front court with Heinsohn and Russell, says, "Red was fortunate in knowing how to deal with each personality differently. What he would normally say, of course, is that he treated all of the players exactly the same. Well, he did, up to a certain point, and then he dealt with them as individual men. In game situations, dressing rooms and all the other things, everybody was treated the same. But if you had to talk to him about an individual situation, Red had a sympathetic ear. He dealt with us as individuals away from the court. When you have a guy like Russell—everybody knew he was going to play close to forty-eight minutes every night—I hardly ever expected him to play an entire practice. There's no way in the world you can play forty-eight minutes and an entire practice; it just doesn't work. So he dealt with the players and got the most out them, and it was easy because he dealt with everybody relatively fairly. That was the biggest thing he had to do, and it's difficult for a lot of coaches."

"They knew how to deal with each other," says former Celtic forward Willie Naulls. "Russell knew how far he could push Auerbach and Auerbach knew how to control the situation without ever embarrassing Bill. Those two were a lot alike."

"Red was Russell's John the Baptist," says Heinsohn. "Cousy was the white superstar from Holy Cross, and people covering the games really didn't know what Russell was. Red started to preach about rebounding and all that. Red really told the world how good Russell was, and that's what established their rapport. Red knew how to deal with Russell. He didn't yell at the black guys. He never spoke to Russell in front of anybody."

Looking back, Auerbach says, "I think he [Russell] liked me basically because I treated him as a person. I could say that I treated him no different than anybody else, but I shouldn't say that. Anytime you got a star, you always make a few concessions. Any coach is a liar if he says he doesn't make a few small concessions to the outstanding player. The main thing with Russell and myself, whenever something might come up, I'd talk to him."

Sometimes, he would ask Russell's permission to yell at him in practice. He figured it was something that might make the other players feel better. Russell would agree. A week later, Russell would ask for a day off. Auerbach would grant the request, tell his center "You owe me one," then call in the favor minutes before a big game against the Knicks.

Auerbach knew that most of the sportswriters were afraid of Russell. The big man was very intimidating and not a good quote. He did not get his due share of the credit, and Auerbach knew he was sensitive about it. Early in Russell's career, the Celtics went on a five-game road trip without Cousy, who was hurt. They won all five, thanks to Russell. When the team returned to Logan Airport, Auerbach noticed a Boston newspaper headline that read, "Will Cousy Play Tonight?" Sensing that this could hurt morale, Auerbach ordered his players to go directly to the Garden.

"I saw that headline and I went bananas inside," remembers

Auerbach. "I told all of them, I don't care who's picking you up, I want every one of you over at the Garden in fifteen minutes. I got them in the dressing room and told them to sit down. They knew it wasn't Cousy's fault, but they had to be told. They had to be convinced. I said, 'Are you gonna let one ass of a writer destroy the chemistry of this ball club?' Finally, it was done and they were okay and kind of laughing. In my mind, that was one of the crucial moments. I don't know what might have happened if I didn't call that meeting."

The game plan never changed. The Celtics were the best-conditioned team in the league. They didn't rely on one shooter to score all the points. They tried to beat you down the floor for easy baskets. They ran seven plays, with four options for each play. The plays were invented on the playgrounds of Washington, D.C. Auerbach would get an idea, stroll over to a court where he knew there were good players, then ask them to try it on for size. The Celtics fine-tuned the seven plays, and everybody else in the league knew them by heart. During a State Department tour of Turkey with an Auerbach-coached team of NBA All-Stars, Philadelphia's star forward, Tom Gola, would say, "Let's run the Number Six for them," or Oscar Robertson would say, "Never mind that, we'll run the Number One."

"Shit, yeah, we knew every play they had," says former Syracuse and Philadelphia center Red Kerr. "It was so stupid in those days. Guys would come down and yell 'Six' and we knew it was coming to Russell. 'Six' was Russell's number. But the execution was amazing, and they had some options."

Sharman once implored his coach to change the numbers of the plays. Auerbach resisted and told his players, "You're all too dumb.' Sharman kept asking, so finally Auerbach made a change. Number One because Two, Two became Three, and on to Seven, which became One. A few minutes into the next game, Cousy called out "Two" and two players ran Two while the other three ran Three. Auerbach called time, tapped each player on the head—like Moe bonking Larry and Curly in a Three Stooges episode—and said, "All right, it's wiped out of your minds. One is One. Two is Two." Seven was Seven. Forevermore.

"I still know those plays," says Gene Conley. "What I did like about Red was that he never overcoached. He didn't try to tell everybody what to do. He'd say something like, 'I want you to get the ball for me.' That would be it."

With Russell on board, the plays worked better, because Boston could always get the ball back. All of the Celtics were liberated by the presence of the new big man. They could take more chances on defense, because Russell was there to atone for mistakes. They could sneak downcourt for an easy fast-break lay-up. Russell's presence made the other team change its plans. The pre-Russell NBA was dominated by big white centers with heavy legs. These players became ineffective when Russell took over in the low post and started blocking their shots.

"Russell totally disrupted everything in the other team's offense," says Heinsohn. "He made teams change their style of play. He took the low post away by himself. Everybody was playing low-post basketball. He was quick enough to play the guy he was guarding, then he'd be there if you gambled on your guy, and he got by you."

At the other end, Celtic players would shoot with the knowledge that their misses probably would be snatched by Russell, that there would be another chance. Cousy was particularly gleeful about the addition of the big guy. He no longer had to be as careful.

Russell was the most active player anyone had seen. He didn't need to have the basketball in his hands. He got in position. He boxed out his man. He was the first to bring it to Auerbach's attention that 80 percent of all rebounds were snatched below the rim. When he blocked a shot, he did it softly, allowing him to retain possession of the ball. He didn't need to stroke his ego by swatting somebody's shot six rows into the loge; he'd rather get the ball back for his team. Russell never checked the stat sheet after a game.

These two men, a short Jew from Brooklyn and a tall black man from Oakland, shared a common purpose and uncommon respect. Their partnership would prove to be lethal for the rest of the National Basketball Association.

In his 1966 book, *Go Up for Glory*, Russell writes about his coach: "He knows exactly the right way to select a player—rookie or pro—and move him onto a squad without disrupting the fluidity

of the team. A tough kid who fought his way up from the streets of
Brooklyn, he never deluded himself. Auerbach has a reason for
everything—from yelling at a referee, to selling out Boston Garden
with a promotion, to bringing in a player who, on the surface, ap-
pears to be useless. Auerbach cannot stand the thought of losing.
Neither can I. Anyone who has ever come to the Celtics has immediately been instilled with this philosophy. If you don't play to
win, Auerbach has no place for you."

This is Russell again, writing about Auerbach in his autobiography, *Second Wind:* "Red would never let things get very far out of
focus. He thought about winning more than I thought about eating
when I was little. He ached when he didn't win; his whole body
would be thrown out of whack when we lost. He didn't care about
a player's statistics or reputation in the newspapers; all he thought
about was the final score and who had helped put it on the board.
He was our gyroscope, programmed solely for winning, and it was
difficult for any of us to deviate from the course he set for us."

Auerbach knew what he had in Russell—the kind of winner
coaches pray for.

"I was close to Russ, because we had an understanding," says
Auerbach. "He would do his thing and I would understand him. He
wasn't going to upstage me or challenge my job. We never had any
of that nonsense. I used to bawl him out. I used to get on him. But
I knew he cared. People don't understand him. That's the problem.
He's a brilliant guy. He's a very proud guy."

In the winter of 1956–1957, sixteen years after coaching his first
team at St. Alban's in Washington, Auerbach finally had the talent
to win it all. He had assembled the best basketball team in the world.
All he had to do now was take them where they were supposed to
go. This was the fun part. The Celtics would go to Syracuse, St.
Louis and Rochester and shove it down their throats. Never a gracious loser, Auerbach enjoyed the payback. This time he had the
horses. He was going to show everybody what kind of a team he had
and what kind of a coach he was. There would be no spring fold
this time. Red Auerbach had everything he needed.

Boston finished 44–28 and then met the hated Syracuse Nation-
als. Syracuse had eliminated the Celtics from the playoffs in each of

the previous three seasons. The first game of the Celtic-Nat series tells you everything you need to know about the next thirteen seasons of Auerbach-Russell basketball. The Celtics beat Syracuse, 108–90. Frank Ramsey scored 20, Tom Heinsohn 19, Bob Cousy 18, Bill Sharman 17 and Bill Russell 16, with 31 rebounds and 12 blocked shots. Find a way to beat that. The Celts swept the Nats.

The championship finals pitted Boston against St. Louis, a series ripe with subplots. St. Louis had Macauley and Hagan, the players traded for the rights to Bill Russell. St. Louis was owned by Kerner, a friend, foe and ex-boss of Red Auerbach.

Before the start of Game 3 in St. Louis, Celtic players complained that one of the baskets was not set at precisely ten feet. Cousy, a player with a pretty good eye, told Auerbach that the basket was low. Sharman and Russell agreed. Auerbach already was in a bad mood because he thought the hosts had supplied the Celtics with crummy basketballs for practice. He stepped onto the court to check it out and was confronted by Kerner. Since the beginning of the NBA, it's been an unspoken rule that you do not let a visiting coach or player take charge of anything in your building. It's a territorial issue, something Auerbach deeply believes: Never let the other guy call the shots in your building.

It was this belief that prompted Kerner to challenge Auerbach at midcourt. He swore at Auerbach. Unhappily for Ben Kerner, the insult brought back Auerbach's Brooklyn youth. Growing up, Arnold Auerbach learned never to let the other guy hit first. Confronted by Kerner on the Kiel Auditorium floor, Auerbach clocked his former boss with a roundhouse right. These were the good old pre-litigious days of America. Auerbach was not arrested, suspended or ejected. He didn't pick up a technical foul for coldcocking the home team's owner.

"I remember Red and Ben rolling around on the floor," says perennial St. Louis All-Star and Hall of Famer Bob Pettit. "It was just part of the intense rivalry you had between the Celtics and Hawks. In St. Louis, the fans were rabid; they hated the Celtics. I can remember people throwing things out of the stands in both places."

"He cussed me out and said it was another one of my dirty

tricks," Auerbach remembers. "Then when he took a half step toward me, I popped him, while he was ranting. You always hit first."

A writer asked Kerner if he would have Auerbach arrested. Kerner, lip bleeding, replied, "That would be the worst thing. I'd rather have him on the bench. We have a better chance to win with him on the bench."

Fighting words, indeed.

Referees Sid Borgia and Arnie Heft measured the basket and found it to be a regulation ten feet from the floor.

In 1957, the going rate for punching an owner was $300. Walter Brown's letter to Commissioner Podoloff read, "I'm ashamed of Auerbach, but I'm also ashamed of Kerner and of Maurice Podoloff for not fining Kerner as well as Auerbach. Throwing punches belongs in the Blackstone Valley League, not the NBA, but from all I hear Auerbach had some provocation."

This would not be Auerbach's only NBA duke-out. Earlier in the fifties, coming to the defense of Cooper, the first black player drafted by an NBA team, Auerbach was coldcocked by St. Louis coach Doxie Moore.

"It was the only time I ever saw Red get whacked and not know it was coming," says Brannum.

Auerbach's daughter Nancy understands. Now in her late forties, with a grown daughter of her own, Nancy Auerbach remembers the day she made her old man proud:

"It was during one of the summers when we were in the Catskills. I got in a fight with a girl and she called me a name. So I turned around and I punched her. I gave her a black eye. It was a lucky shot. I told my parents about it and my mother said, 'How could you do that?' But Dad thought that was the best thing I've ever done. It doesn't matter what else I ever did. That was the best."

Hit first, ask questions later. It is the Auerbach way.

During the dynasty years, Auerbach poked an abusive fan (a gas station attendant named Edward Finke) in Cincinnati. The fan had Auerbach arrested later that night at the Celtics' hotel and trainer Buddy LeRoux had to put up $100 to bail out the coach. (Cousy went with LeRoux and told the jailer, "You can't put that man in jail, because you don't have Chinese food.") The fan eventually dropped the charges, Auerbach started leaving him tickets when the Celts played in Cincinnati and they became friends.

In Philadelphia, Auerbach punched Warrior coach Neil Johnston after an argument with the Philadelphia timekeeper. "Red was on their timekeeper," says Conley. "Neil Johnston came down and said, 'What's the problem? Nobody's cheating anybody.' Next thing I knew, Red took a punch at him. And I don't even know how he could reach him. Johnston was about 6-8 and led the league in scoring one year. They kicked Red out of the game; I think he wanted to get kicked out. He came over to the bench and said, 'Cooz, you and Russ, don't let 'em do this to me. This isn't' right.' You could see what was happening. You could read Red pretty good, really, but even though you could read him, it was so good that you just did it anyway. So all of a sudden we came back and won the ball game and he was sitting up there in a little room with his cigar. And you could just tell he was thinking, 'The things I have to do to get you guys to run.' He was so proud. He took a fine, just to motivate you."

The 1956 Kerner bout didn't turn out very well. The Celtics lost Game 3 to St. Louis, and Auerbach was ripped by Ben Kerner's mother. "I'm through with him,' said Mrs. Kerner. "He's no good. I used to like him, but to do a thing like that after Ben helped him out—he's no good."

Thirty years after the episode, a young St. Louis sportscaster named Bob Costas got Auerbach and Kerner together on a radio show.

"We were doing a series on great confrontations," remembers Costas. "We'd had Bob Gibson and Hank Aaron and a lot of others. I called Kerner to set up a show with him and Auerbach. They had this feud going. Kerner hadn't spoken to Auerbach since he'd sold the Hawks. Kerner agrees to do it, but says he doesn't know how Auerbach will react. I call Red and he's gruff with me on the phone, but says he'll do it. So we wound up with Kerner in the studio and Auerbach on the phone, and this thing was great. It started out with Red in his gruff exterior, but after about ten minutes he started to warm to this and he and Kerner had this very almost sentimental visit on the air. Red inquired about Kerner's health and all the great times they'd had. It was almost touching between the two. They literally had not spoken for a decade."

In 1957 NBA Finals stood at 3–3 after six games. On Saturday afternoon, April 13, 1957, the St. Louis Hawks and the Celtics met in the Boston Garden to determine the world championship of professional basketball. It took four quarters and two overtimes to produce a winner. Russell scored 19 points with 23 rebounds and 5 blocked shots. Fellow rookie Heinsohn scored 37 before fouling out and the Celtics won it, 125–123, in double OT. To this day, Heinsohn says that the greatest single play he has ever seen was Russell's come-from-behind block of a Jack Coleman lay-up in the final minute of regulation. After Pettit's final shot clanged off the rim, Russell and Jungle Jim Loscutoff carried Auerbach off the court. Winners' playoff shares were $1,681 per man.

It was a great day for Boston. The Red Sox hadn't won a World Series since 1918 and the Bruins had last won a Stanley Cup in 1941. Auerbach gave the city its first championship in sixteen years. He was thirty-nine years old, had been coaching in the pros for eleven years and never had won anything, but with this championship on his resume, he would never again be second-guessed in Boston. There would be no more slings and arrows from those who had thumbed their noses at professional basketball. The city was thirsty for a winner, and the "arrogant Jew" had delivered something that all the Joe Cronins, Joe McCarthys and Milt Schmidts had failed to deliver: He had made Boston a championship city. Boston was No. 1. It had been a long drought for the Hub of the Universe. The Celtics were about to make sports history, and Auerbach was about to become a local legend in a town he would never call home.

His players tossed him into the showers (fortunately for Red, there were no Gatorade buckets in 1957). New at the championship game, Auerbach hadn't brought a change of clothes. He put on some dry sweatpants and a Celtic practice shirt. He put his topcoat over the outfit and drove back to his room at the Lenox Hotel. He lit a cigar and called his home at 5243 Nebraska Ave. He told Dottie, "We won, baby. I'll be home tomorrow."

He wasn't home very long; he had to prepare for the draft. He called his former player Bones McKinney, who was coaching at

Wake Forest University. McKinney recommended a no-name guard
from North Carolina College.

"I was so damn busy," says Auerbach, "I didn't know who to
draft. I called Bones McKinney down in North Carolina. I asked
him if there was anybody down in that area who could play. Bones
told me this kid Sam Jones was fast as lightning."

On draft day 1957, Charles Tyra, Jim Krebs, Win Wilfong, Bren-
dan McCann, Len Rosenbluth and George Bon Salle were selected
before Auerbach picked Sam Jones. The reaction was, "Sam Who?"

The Celts were full of confidence at the start of the 1957–1958
season. "Once we won the first time," says Cousy, "we were so certain that nobody would beat us."

The Celtics did not repeat in 1957–1958. They went 14–0 at the
start and finished 49–23, tops in the NBA. Russell averaged 22.7
rebounds and was named MVP. All five starters averaged between
16 and 22 points per game and Cousy led the league in assists.
However, Russell went down with a twisted ankle in the playoffs,
and St. Louis won the finals, beating Boston in Game 6, 110–109,
on April 12.

Before the start of the 1959 playoffs, Auerbach told the *Globe*'s
Jerry Nason, "the prospect of any one club dominating our game,
as the Yankees have in baseball, is quite unlikely. The competition
among us now is rougher than in the days of the Minneapolis Lakers'
championship teams."

Was he being cute? Was he trying to lower expectations to make
himself look good? Or was the architect himself unable to foresee
what was coming?

We certainly know that he was incorrect. It would be nine years
before any team other than the Boston Celtics would win an NBA
championship. Children would come of age, America would go to
war, a president would be assassinated, and the happy days of the
fifties would yield to the long hair and short skirts of the revolutionary sixties. In the spring of 1959, Auerbach and the Celtics were
getting ready to retire the trophy.

# 5

# CIGARS

---

*I do stutter a bit. We were in the dressing room before a playoff game and I was trying to get Buddy LeRoux, our trainer, to work on my finger, which was jammed. I went over and said to Buddy, "Do you think you could fuh-fuh-fuh-fix, my fuh-fuh-fuh-finger?"*

*Red was right there, leaning against the wall, smoking his cigar, and he laughed and said, "What's the matter, Ramsey, little nervous? Having trouble with your Fs again?"*

*I said, "Fuck you, Red. How's that?"*

FRANK RAMSEY

LIGHT IT UP. FROM 1959 TO 1966, THE BOSTON CELTICS WON the NBA championship eight straight times. There's nothing like it in professional sport. The Celtics beat the Minneapolis Lakers in four in 1959 to win the championship; then the St. Louis Hawks in seven in 1960, the Hawks in five in 1961, the Los Angeles Lakers in seven in 1962, the Lakers in six in 1963, the San Francisco Warriors in five in 1964, the Lakers in five in 1965, and, finally, the Lakers in seven in 1966. Russell, Sam Jones, K. C. Jones and Auerbach were the only constants. Sharman, Cousy, Ramsey and Heinsohn retired, but they were replaced by Sanders, Havlicek, Naulls and (Larry) Siegfried. The team was so good that some of the sport was extracted from victory. Citing the 1965 finals, when the Celts ripped off twenty consecutive points against the Lakers in the clinching blowout, Russell wrote, "We were not just beating this team. We were destroying it . . . It was my worst moment in sports. There was the horror of destruction, not the joy of winning . . . We knew—and did not know—we sensed, and did not completely comprehend, that we had taken sports out of the realm of the game."

Did another professional team experience this? Ever? Doubtful. The 1959–1966 Celtics reached a plateau that no other team has found. It was the outer limit of team excellence. This is why the Celtics today are still important. This is why we still write books about Arnold "Red" Auerbach.

Red lit the cigar. The Celtics won. The victory cigar remains one of the great symbols of American sports. There was a time when men gave cigars to other men after the birth of a son or daughter; in the National Basketball Association of the fifties and sixties, the cigar meant the ball game had been won by the Boston Celtics. It was an American tradition. Johnny Carson had the golf swing at the end of his monologue, Bob Hope had "Thanks for the Memory" at the end of his Christmas show, and Red Auerbach had the Hoyo de Monterrey at the end of a ball game.

When Red Sox left fielder Carl Yastrzemski capped his Triple Crown/MVP season with the 1967 Red Sox, he clenched a cigar between his teeth, looked into a television camera and said, "Light it up, Red Auerbach."

"People know that cigar all over the world," says Auerbach. "I remember one of the astronauts once lit one and said, 'Just like Red.' People from all over the world send me cigars. Every time I used to see Joe Cronin, he'd give me a box of cigars. He smoked those two-for-twenty-seven-cent Robert Burns. When I started out I smoked Robert Burns, Antonio Cleopatra, and you went up."

Auerbach has never smoked a cigarette. He smoked a pipe when he got out of college, then switched to an occasional cigar when he was in the navy in 1943. He started smoking on the bench when he coached the Washington Capitols.

Former Cap guard Freddie Scolari remembers, "Talk about rubbing it in! He'd sit there with that big grin and he'd stretch his legs out in front of the bench. Then, very slowly, he'd remove the cigar from his pocket, take off the cellophane and twirl it around, light up with a big flourish, then sit back and laugh. He never changed the act over the years. But later on he did buy more expensive cigars."

Cigars relaxed Auerbach. When he felt a game was won, he lit up and started thinking about the next game. He's always scoffed at the sight of coaches who keep standing, stomping and barking orders once a game is decided. The cigar was a message to Auerbach's players that the game was won and the coach wasn't worrying about it anymore.

Johnny "Red" Kerr broke into the NBA with the Syracuse Nats in 1954–1955. The Celtics and Nats regularly bloodied their knuckles on each other's faces and Syracuse usually beat Boston in the play-offs. "I don't think anybody liked Red," says Kerr. "All the fights we had during the years. Guys would be swinging and hitting cops. One time a guy hit a big Irish cop and the cop got his club out and started chasing us. There was one game when we were lining up for the opening tap and I turned around and [Paul] Seymour and Sharman already were in a fight. The ball hasn't gone up and they're swinging and whaling at each other. The one big thing that crushed everybody was when you'd see Red light that cigar up. That was a murderous thing. We just couldn't touch them in the Garden."

"The cigar made all of us uncomfortable," remembers Cousy. "It was more offensive to us and everyone else on the road. When he did this, it got everyone's attention. And hell, we had enough hostility focused on us as it was. This was another trigger point. The fans were already pissed off because then it looked like they'd lose the game. And they did. This was an irritant. He sat benignly and comfortably on the bench, smoking away, with a guard behind him. Meanwhile, we were out on the floor taking all this abuse. The fans would get more belligerent and hostile toward us, and we had to bust our tails to keep the lead because once he went for the cigar, the other team's intensity went up a hundred percent. I hated that thing. Paul Seymour told me that his ambition in life was not to win an NBA championship as much as it was to have Arnold light up prematurely, lose in a game that they were involved in so he could go down and just stuff that cigar in his face."

When NBA games finally started to be televised, Commissioner Maurice Podoloff sent Auerbach a memo asking him to cease smoking cigars on the bench. Auerbach's reply was, "I'll stop smoking cigars when the other coaches stop smoking cigarettes on the bench." When it became apparent that the cigar was a signal of victory, some rival coaches protested. Red mollified them by telling them that he had a commercial deal with the Blackstone cigar company. Coaches bought that. These were the hungry years for the NBA, and nobody wanted to deny anybody else a chance to make a buck.

Walter Kennedy, a former mayor of Stamford, Connecticut, and an associate with the Harlem Globetrotters, succeeded Podoloff in 1963. "Arnold didn't just smoke the cigar," he says. "He actually glowed."

"I thought it was funny," says Russell. "It was part of what made us what we were. Ungracious? What's that got to do with it? Red never was gracious . . . Who cared about that? We certainly didn't."

Laker coach Fred Schaus says, "The success of the Celtics was not due to Auerbach, but to Number Six—Bill Russell. I respect Red's ability to coach and judge talent, but not his attitude. Not too many people in the NBA liked it when he lit up the cigar, and when you play and lose to him in the finals four times, as I did, it can get to you, because the cigar wasn't necessary. I didn't admire some of the things Red said and did. It would have been nice to make him choke on that cigar."

Don Nelson, who played for the Lakers under Schaus, then for the Celtics under Auerbach, says, "Poor Freddie. He hated Red for lighting that victory cigar in his face. I can remember many times we'd be in that locker room listening to Fred go on for five or ten minutes about Auerbach; all of a sudden it would be time to go out, and we hadn't even discussed our assignments. That's what Red did to his head."

Former Laker great Elgin Baylor added, "It would have been nice to beat him, take it out of his mouth and puff on it just once . . . Yeah, I just wish I could have done that once."

"Of course he was hated," says Sanders. "He won all the time. It's like in business if one guy gets all the contracts. You respected him, you understood what happened, but there's not gonna be much love lost. And Red would rub it in. Blow that smoke."

"It probably would have made me mad if I'd been on the other end of it," admits Auerbach. "I didn't think of it that way when I did it. I felt, the game is over. It's garbage time. And I'd sit there. And after a while I said to myself, 'Jesus Christ. Lapchick is smoking. Other guys are smoking.' So I lit up a cigar. And it happened to catch. It was one of those crazy things that caught on."

Heinsohn once had a cigar—a gift from Red—explode in his face. Auerbach knew there would be retaliation, so for months he had Heinsohn test-smoke most of his cigars. The patient Heinsohn finally wore down the old coach. In the middle of one of his pep talks, Auerbach's cigar blew up in his face, and Heinsohn had his revenge.

On February 8, 1966, Auerbach's final year on the bench, he was honored as Man of the Year by the Boston Humidor Chapter of the Cigar Smokers of America. Smoking was outlawed inside the Boston Garden one year later. Perhaps this step would have been taken even if Red had stayed on as coach; perhaps.

The champion Celtics played in Boston Garden, a dirty old gym, built in 1928 and located atop the North Station, across Causeway Street from the elevated tracks of the MBTA Green Line. (The Celtics are scheduled to move into the "new" Boston Garden in the fall of 1995.) Inside and out, the Garden looks like a set for an old Edward G. Robinson movie. Senses are bombarded by rumbling rails, dark passageways and the smell and grime of sticky, stale beer under your feet. In its time the garden has housed the Ringling Brothers circus, the Ice Capades, a Notre Dame football game, Calvin Coolidge, the Bruins, FDR, ski-jump competition, Joe Louis, Judy Garland, Sugar Ray Robinson, Elvis Presley, Jake LaMotta, John F. Kennedy, the Beatles, Muhammad Ali, high school hockey and basketball, that Beanpot college hockey tourney, the Rolling Stones and the Boston Celtics. After all these events and all these years, it turns out that JFK, Elvis, the Beatles, the Bruins and Ali were just camping out: Bruin owner Jeremy Jacobs has his name on the deed, but the Garden is Red's building. Ask any sports fan.

The Celtics became professional basketball's showcase team once television finally caught up with the NBA. Two generations of American sports fans grew up watching games televised from the Boston Garden. Sitting in front of the tube at home in La Jolla, Las Vegas

or Sioux Falls, one always knew when a game was being televised
from Boston. Only the Celtics played on a parquet floor. It became
part of American sports folklore, like the Detroit Lions playing on
television on Thanksgiving.

The Garden's parquet floor was built in 1946 by the DiNatale
family of Brookline. Hardwood was in short supply at the end of
World War II, but the DiNatales had some oak scraps cut from a
Tennessee forest. Cut against the grain, the inch-and-a-half-thick
boards are strong and durable. The Celtics' home court had to be
portable, because the Bruins needed the same space for their ice.
Craftsmen put the wood together in 264 five-by-five-foot panels and
arranged it in an alternating fashion to form the distinct parquet
effect. For forty years, basketball fans have associated the Celtics
with the parquet floor. An entire "Cheers" episode was devoted to
finding out the exact number of bolts needed to assemble the Celtic
home court.

The checkered pattern reflects the era in which the floor was
built; workers took their time and added details to give it a distinct
look. New houses rarely have the detail and craftsmanship that we
see in houses built in the old days. The Boston Garden court is an
antique Victorian with wainscoting; all other NBA floors (even those
intended to imitate the parquet) are high-rise condominiums. When
the new Boston Garden opens in the fall of 1995, the old floor is
scheduled to go with the Celtics—it is, after all, portable.

There were other elements that were unique to the Celtics. Boston's players wore black sneakers. Always. Scan old pictures of the
early days of the NBA and you'll see that players' dark footwear
gradually changed to white for every NBA team except one. As always, there was a practical reason. Auerbach was annoyed when he
found out that some teams were getting free sneakers. The Converse
company had an outlet in greater Boston and the Celtics had to pay
for their shoes. Auerbach figured that if his team wore black sneakers, the dirt wouldn't show and they'd last longer. So the Celtics
wore black Converse footwear. Today, it is dark green, almost black.

The dark sneakers look particularly cloddish on the feet of white
basketball players; they definitely made Larry Bird look even slower
than he was. The shoes have contributed to the image of the Celtics

as a team of slow white guys. In an era of high-tech sneakers that are heavier than ski boots and designed by NASA, the Celtics continue to go with old-timey dark basketball shoes. Nike, Reebok and the other companies have stocked the Celts with special orders of dark green shoes. In 1994, even the coltish Dee Brown looks like an aging Y. A. Tittle when he clomps around the backcourt. Auerbach hates high-tops. He thinks today's shoes weigh too much and contribute to injuries. His ideal uniform has no extra weight—no knee pads, no elbow pads and no heavy high-top shoes.

The championship Celtics developed some in-house customs. They wore jackets and ties on road trips. They were not allowed to drink hard liquor, and there was Auerbach's odd no-pancake rule. Players drank coffee before games (except Sharman, who preferred tea, then a chocolate bar) and each player had a mug with his number on it. Before the game, in the grimy locker room, Auerbach smoked his cigar, Heinsohn lit a cigarette and Sharman drank his tea. If it was a really big game, they waited for Russell to lose his lunch. When Russell vomited, they were ready to take the court. Havlicek remembers Auerbach calling the team back to the locker room before a seventh game against Philadelphia. Russell had not yet thrown up and Auerbach felt it was bad luck. He told the players they were not going back out to the court until Russell tossed his cookies. On cue, Russell threw up, and the Celtics took the court. They won, of course.

They always started their lay-up lines from the left side, and at the conclusion of warm-ups, a senior player (Jim Loscutoff, Frank Ramsey and later John Havlicek) was designated to put a final couple of shots through the hoop. They kept their jerseys tucked into their pants and they never sat down during time-outs. ("He wanted everybody around him," remembers Sanders.) They broke the huddle and got back out to the court before the other team. Auerbach didn't have a lot to say during time-outs. Plus, he felt it was a psychological ploy to send his team back out first—make it look like you're in control, never tired.

Celtic players did not talk to players on the other team when they were on the court. A brutish frontcourt player (Brannum, Loscutoff, Clyde Lovellette, Wayne Embry, M. L. Carr, Greg Kite) was kept around to make a statement if opponents tried to strong-arm any of the Celtic stars. Black players roomed with white players. A talented player (Ramsey, Havlicek, McHale) was kept on the side-lines at the start of the game. The "sixth man" would come in and take over when everybody else was tired. Havlicek always made it a point to sit next to Auerbach on the bench; he thought it improved his chances of getting into the game. Rookies carried the ball bags, paid for the cabs (Auerbach would reimburse them) and showered after everybody else; there was only one shower at that time in the Celtic locker room at the Garden, so this might keep a rookie around an hour after games.

The Celtics never had a scoring champ. After NBA games, a pile of postgame statistic sheets is placed somewhere in the middle of the locker room. Players who came to the Celtics noticed that the stat sheets didn't get much attention in the Boston clubhouse. Carl Braun, who'd played for the Knicks, remembered wrestling matches over the stat sheet in New York. In Boston, the pile of papers just sat there. Nobody cared.

"You know what I think about stats?" says K. C. Jones. "I once heard that a man drowned in three feet of water. That's what I think of stats."

Their games were broadcast by Johnny Most, the most loyal, biased, unadulterated homer in the history of radio. Sitting "high above courtside," Johnny nightly narrated a morality play in which every Celtic was an honorable gladiator and every opponent an ax murder who "just crawled out of a sewer." Most bragged that he gargled with Sani-Flush. Only seasoned Celtic listeners could track his escalating voice range, which topped out at what became known as Johnny's dog-whistle voice. Probably every New England sports fan who came of age in the 1960s has at one time or another tried an imitation of Most. Auerbach loves loyalty, and Johnny was the most loyal announcer in the history of sports broadcasting. He died in 1993. Along with three handfuls of Celtic numbers, Johnny Most's microphone has been retired.

On the bench, presiding over all this tradition and success, was a man wearing a jacket and tie and holding a rolled-up program in his left hand. He sat hunched forward, watching intently. There were

no assistant coaches cluttering up the bench. Auerbach could remember exactly how many fouls had been slapped on every man on
the court. He would often stand and holler at the referees. He'd
cup his right hand to his mouth and bark his protests. Auerbach was
the NBA's first star coach. It was fun to watch him battle the refs.
Sometimes he was mad at them, but sometimes he did it for show,
using the zebras to light a fire under his team.

Boston's coach ran up more than $17,000 worth of fines during
his years on the Celtic bench. (Owner Walter Brown paid most of
the fine money.) Between 1952 (when records were first kept) and
1960, Auerbach was fined forty-two times. He was fined for telling
writers that official Arnie Heft was "stupid and incompetent." For
good measure, Red added, "And I told the son of a bitch that to his
face." He was fined $150 for running onto the court and giving ref
Richie Powers the choke sign. He was fined $350 for calling officials
Norm Drucker and Mendy Rudolph "a couple of *chokers.*" He believed that Drucker was hired by the league specifically to get him.
He was suspended for three games for pushing referee Joe Gushue.
He was fined $500 for pulling the Celtics off the court two minutes
before the end of an exhibition game in Oceanside, Long Island.
After the Celtics were pelted with eggs in St. Louis, he said, "I hope
Boston fans give them a taste of their own medicine." Of course,
when the Hawks came to Boston, they were pelted with eggs.

"I didn't get ulcers," says Auerbach. "I *gave* them."

Auerbach vs. Sid Borgia was almost as heralded as Russell vs.
Wilt Chamberlain.

Borgia: "Red rarely came after me on the rules. It was usually a
matter of questioning my judgment. If he did come after you on a
rule, you knew you'd have a lot of answering to do, because he knew
every rule in the book. Hell, he helped write most of them."

There. What official could argue with a man who wrote the rule-
book?

Drucker: "A coach tries to get into the referees' heads. They all
read the papers, and it has to make some impression. The original
artist at that was Red Auerbach. Every time he lost a playoff game,
he claimed that it was because his team was so good they didn't get
any calls. I know when I was refereeing, whenever we heard Auer-

bach crying, we let him cry. But I think it works on the weaker officials."

In Charles Salzberg's *From Set Shot to Slam Dunk*, (E. P. Dutton, 1987), Drucker says, "Red Auerbach never impressed me with his mode of behavior. He tried to portray the image of being brighter and more intelligent than the other coaches in the league. I was more impressed with the other coaches who did their job and didn't blow their own horn but were recognized by their peers. Red has said the reason he carried on during the game was to intimidate the officials and get the calls at the end of the game. He has told stories of how he used this weapon. Most of this is his imagination."

Former referee Charley Eckman remembers it this way: "Piss and moan, scream and yell, then piss and moan some more—that was all an official heard from Auerbach. Then he'd get in your face with that awful garlic breath of his . . . it was just awful. A lot of people are afraid to tell the truth about Auerbach because he's been a big shot in the NBA for so long, but he has bullied too many people, and he was the luckiest man alive to end up with Bill Russell."

"We always thought that Boston had the edge," admits former Syracuse player Al Bianchi. "We always said K. C. Jones got called for six fouls, but got away with twelve. That was Boston. They did it. They're the champs. But you've got to be ten points better to beat them at home."

"I battled the referees all these years because I believed the NBA desperately needed more uniformity in the officiating," says Auerbach. "Let them all call all of the infractions or one of the infractions, but play it one way, night after night."

The explanation is rational and unemotional—nothing like the manner in which Auerbach voiced his protests from the sidelines for twenty years. He was relentless. He didn't like the men with the whistles. He felt the refs were out to get him. If the Celtics lost, he often felt his team had somehow been cheated by the officials. He'd point to the stat sheet and show everybody how the other team went to the foul line more than the Celtics. There were nights when he was certain he was going to lose just because of the identity of the officials.

"He used to send two guys out into the lobby to find out who was reffing the game," remembers the *Globe*'s Clif Keane. "He'd find out it was Willie Smith and Borgia and say, 'Why can't we get somebody else? Why are they here?' "

Gene Conley says, "He'd spit at them. They'd be walking by him before or after the game and he'd turn and spit on the floor."

Darrell Garretson never worked as an official during Auerbach's reign on the bench, but when Garretson went to Japan with one of Auerbach's State Department tours, he got the cold shoulder.

"Red said, 'Hello, Darrell,' on the first day of the trip," recalls Garretson. "Twenty-six days later, at the end, he said, 'If we do it again, I'll talk to you again.' Twenty-six days. That was it."

It's the Auerbach way. On the field of battle, you don't trust anybody who's not in your foxhole. Everybody on the outside is a threat. Opponents, fans, writers, referees: You've got to fight them all or they'll take what they want. Baseball had Leo Durocher and later Billy Martin and Earl Weaver. Basketball had Auerbach—nose-to-nose with Sid Borgia and Mendy Rudolph.

Johnny Kerr remembers, "He was more into the refs than any-body, and probably got away with more. It was the intimidation factor. Eastern Conference guys ran the league."

This is what Milt Gross, an Auerbach friend, wrote in his syndicated column: "Red Auerbach is a quick-tempered party who has made professional basketball respectable in staid Boston by being thoroughly unrespectable as coach of the Celtics. No coach is so violently disliked by other coaches in the NBA. No coach has been slapped so consistently with fines so large by Maurice Podoloff. No coach has cast himself as such a general nuisance to the league's head man. None beefs more with the referees, tangles with spectators or ignores propriety more by shouting instructions louder from a seat in the stands after he has been banished from the floor. And none is appreciated more by his players than Auerbach."

Quick-tempered? Unrespectable? Disliked? Nuisance? Small wonder Auerbach liked this writer.

Most of the time, the Celtics were in better shape than the rest of the teams.

"The key to Red's success was training camp," says Sharman.

"When he coached, there were no rules about when you could start training camp, so he started earlier than most teams and he played a lot of exhibition games. By opening night, we were the best-conditioned team in the league, and Red believed that we'd steal three or four games early—especially on the road—because we were in better shape than anybody else."

One of Auerbach's torturous drills required players to put their hands behind their head, then jump forward and reach out at the same time. Players had to do this for the length of the court, then do it backward. The first player to drop out was designated for sprints. They ran long fast-break drills. Two-on-two breaks. No breathers. No time to come up for air.

Sanders recalls: "I clearly understood that it was necessary. I was just angry that I had to do it. It's like coming to camp and your name was [Wayne] Embry and you had to lose so much weight. Being forced. You're not going to like the guy that's forcing you. Loscutoff was coming back from a disk operation and he made him dive on the floor after a ball to prove that he was ready to play. I had to go through a similar-type thing after a knee operation. It was, 'Do you have the nerve? Are you really up to playing the contact game? Could you really dive for the ball if you have to, or are you afraid of injury?' That kind of stuff did not endear him to the rest of us. Those things did not make you want to love him. There was never any question in our minds what we had to do, we just didn't like doing it. Just push until guys got sick. Believe me, we all talked about it and laughed about it later, but the record speaks for itself."

If there was a fight in practice, that was okay, too. During one fistfight, Bob Brannum broke the nose of teammate Jack Nichols. Auerbach did not object. His troops were in shape and battle-ready. The starts were impressive: The Celtics started 34–4 in 1960, 29–5 in 1962, 25–5 in 1964 and 31–7 in 1965. And the finishes were even better.

He didn't have much time to bask in the afterglow of victory—he was always in the process of maintaining and strengthening his roster. Twenty years on the bench hid some of his front-office talent, but it was there. He'd carved his first unit out of old military buddies

Red, when he was really a redhead, as a starting guard for George Washington University in 1938. (*Courtesy George Washington University*)

In action, on the bench, probably hollering at nemesis referee Mendy Rudolph. (*Courtesy Boston Celtics*)

Dorothy, Red, and young Nancy in the family den in the early 1950s. (*Auerbach family collection*)

Red, the general manager, with star player and coach Bill Russell in November 1967. (Boston Globe *photo by Dan Goshtigian*)

The 1962–1963 world champion Celtics: (front row, left to right) K. C. Jones, Bill Russell, owner Walter Brown, Auerbach, treasurer Lou Pieri, Bob Cousy, Sam Jones; (standing) Frank Ramsey, Gene Gaurilia, Tom Sanders, Tommy Heinsohn, Clyde Lovellette, John Havlicek, Jim Loscutoff, Dan Swartz, and trainer Buddy LeRoux. There are nine NBA Hall of Famers in this team photo. Every man in the front row—except Pieri, who helped bring Auerbach to Boston—is in the Hall of Fame, along with Ramsey, Heinsohn, and Havlicek from the back row. Trainer LeRoux went on to become an owner of the Boston Red Sox. (*Jerry Buckley photo*)

The Auerbachs—Nancy, Red, Randy, and Dorothy—relax on Cape Cod after a championship season in the early 1960s. *(Auerbach family collection)*

A family gathering in the early 1960s. Red and Dorothy are in the top right corner. Red's parents, Mary and Hymie, are seated on the far right. Red's brother Zang is fourth from left in the back row, and brother Victor stands next to Dorothy. Red's sister, Florence, sits next to her mother in the second row. *(Auerbach family collection)*

Arm-in-arm, Dorothy and Red. (*Auerbach family collection*)

In Houston, after winning the championship in 1981. Larry Bird, a second-year player, has taken the cigar from Red's mouth and enjoys a victory salute. (Boston Globe *photo by Frank O'Brien*)

The Auerbach offices, in Washington and as shown here in Boston, are mini-sports museums. (*Courtesy Boston Celtics*)

The 1985–1986 world champion Celtics: (seated, left to right) Danny Ainge, Scott Wedman, Alan Cohen, Jan Volk, Auerbach, K. C. Jones, Don Gaston, Larry Bird, Dennis Johnson; (back row) Wayne Lebeaux, Dr. Thomas Silva, Jimmy Rodgers, Sam Vincent, Rick Carlisle, Greg Kite, Robert Parish, Bill Walton, Kevin McHale, David Thirdkill, Jerry Sichting, Chris Ford, Ray Melchiorre. This is the last Celtic team to win a championship. Draft pick Len Bias died a few months after this photo was taken, and the franchise has endured many years of bad fortune. (*Steve Lipofsky photo*)

Red, face-to-face with his statue, at the dedication in 1985. The Auerbach statue is in Boston's historic Faneuil Hall Marketplace. (Boston Globe *photo by Janet Knott*)

Dave Gavitt, Auerbach, and Jan Volk as the Celtics prepare to draft.
(*Courtesy Boston Celtics*)

Dozens of Red's "guys" celebrate his 75th birthday in the fall of 1992. Everybody's got a tuxedo and a cigar. (*Steve Lipofsky photo*)

Dorothy, making a rare trip to Boston, celebrates Red's 75th at the Copley Marriott in front of a live television audience. *(Steve Lipofsky photo)*

Red at home in Washington with the latest in a long line of boxer dogs, C. P., which stands for Celtic Pride. *(Auerbach family collection)*

and college pals. In Boston, he'd built the greatest dynasty in sports while doing the scouting, trading, free agent singing and drafting in his spare time. It was a tour de force.

Russell, Heinsohn and K. C. Jones were the mother lode of the 1956 draft. Boston picked dead last almost every year after that, and it took skill, luck and innovation to stay afloat when the last-place teams each spring got the top draftees. There was nobody out there scouting the colleges while Auerbach went about the business of winning championships. The coach had to keep a finger on every pulse. He had the telephone. And at the other end of those phone lines, he had his trusty guys telling him where the players were. And so Sam Jones was ready to step in for Sharman and John Havlicek was there to fill in for Ramsey. And Willie Naulls was brought on board when Heinsohn retired. And Don Nelson was acquired when Russell needed help up front in the final days of pro sports' longest reign.

"He built a dynasty by picking complementary players who had a job to do, and that was to fill a role," says K. C. Jones. "The other thing he did was he motivated us. Only losers accept losing."

"I kept in touch with a lot of guys that used to play for me," says Auerbach. "Bones McKinney covered the whole South. Bill Reinhart, my old coach, saw players out West. Guys like Matt Zunic, Feerick and Scolari. I'd call em. I was friendly with college coaches. In those days, I was the only pro coach—with the exception of Joe Lapchick, who didn't do many clinics—who was invited to conduct clinics for college and high school coaches. I made a lot of contact with these guys, and I'd call them up. I'd always ask, 'What kind of a kid is he?' Then I'd call a rival coach and compare. I was so damn busy."

McKinney delivered Sam Jones in the weak draft of 1957. In 1959 Auerbach could have plucked Dartmouth's Rudy LaRusso (a teammate of Celtic CEO Dave Gavitt), but selected John Richter, who didn't make it. In 1960, Auerbach landed NYU's Tom "Satch" Sanders, a nonscorer. Two years later, NBA teams were looking for height and eight big men were selected before Auerbach snatched up 6-5 John Havlicek with the final pick of the draft.

"Don't let anyone make you think he wanted LeRoy Ellis or any of those guys," says Tom Heinsohn. "Red had his eye on Havlicek. I remember hearing his name a lot before that draft."

Red passed on Willis Reed in 1964, but that was minor compared with his bonehead stunt in the spring of 1965. When he could have had Gus Johnson, Auerbach picked Bill Green, a 6-8 forward from Colorado State. Green came to Boston overweight and informed Auerbach that he did not fly. Red bought the kid a train ticket home and chalked it up to experience.

There were other bad drafts, including the forgettable Ollie Johnson, Jim Barnett, Mal Graham and Clarence Glover (drafted because ownership in 1971 could not pay UCLA's Curtis Rowe). But Boston always was picking at or near the bottom of the barrel.

Auerbach's success with trades and waiver-wire rejects bordered on criminal.

In the summer of 1964 he saw Naulls at the Kutsher's Country Club summer basketball camp in Monticello, New York, and talked him out of retirement. After Cincinnati waived Larry Siegfried, Auerbach picked up the former Ohio State guard for the $1,000 waiver price. He got Nelson for $100. He traded some cash and a draft pick for backup center Embry. He traded Mel Counts for Bailey Howell. He didn't have a lot of money to spend, but he did what he had to do to keep winning.

"You don't take it for granted," he says. "What happened was, when we were winning these championships, we didn't have any money. When the Yankees were winning championships, come August or September they'd buy somebody. I could never do that, 'cuz I didn't have a dime to do that. Theoretically, if I were in New York with their money in those days, lord knows, instead of eight in a row, we could have gone a lot higher 'cuz I'd buy a key player from a team that needed money. In all the years that I coached, we bought one player—six thousand dollars for Wayne Embry. But I got the money back by selling another player."

"The big thing was that his job was never in question," says Sanders. "In a lot of cases, the coach depends on the general manager or the player personnel guy. But when you are The Man, it's a lot easier. And as players, we were under the impression that Red was there forever. And what you have to deal with is the reality of dealing with Red. He would tell us, 'If you don't like what the coach is doing, go complain to the GM.' That was a favorite statement of Red's, and that was the truth of the issue."

Today's NBA commissioner, David Stern, grew up in New York City, where Auerbach and the Celtics were loathed. Before he succeeded Podoloff, Walter Kennedy and Larry O'Brien, Stern was a fan. He says, "When you said the Celtics, you knew that the most famous, most successful sports team in the world was being described. I think that gave the league probably its single identification in difficult times. And I think that Red Auerbach was the most famous coach on a global basis. In this country, someone could say Paul Brown or Casey Stengel or Walter Alston, but on a global basis, the Celtics and Red Auerbach were the Number One sports team."

Global. It's a 1990s word. We have a global economy, global environment and global understanding. Basketball is the global game. Soccer, of course, remains the world's most popular sport, but basketball has more big-name stars and continues to grow in major markets outside of North America. Basketball in the last decades has made remarkable strides worldwide, and much of this can be attributed to aggressive marketing of such superstars as Magic Johnson, Larry Bird and Michael Jordan. The USA's 1992 Olympic basketball Dream Team was the first internationally famous, "global" team. But before Magic, Larry and Michael, there was "Red on Roundball."

In the early years of the NBA, Auerbach was basketball's door-to-door salesman. At the lowest, most elementary level, he spread the gospel of hoop wherever he coached. When he came to the Celtics in the 1950s, he took the team all over the main streets and back roads of New England. In 1958–1959, for example, the Celtics and Cincinnati Royals played seventeen exhibitions in eighteen nights. They started in Houghton, Maine, and worked their way down. Heinsohn claims the Celtics dedicated every New England high school gym built between 1956 and 1966. "By the time we finished, we really hated each other," remembers Cousy. "I mean, you can't spend that much time with your *wife*. That's one of the reasons I started the Players Association. Less exhibitions."

On the long drives, the fellows found ways to pass the time.

There was a car-to-car apple fight that ended when Auerbach was pulled over for driving on the wrong side of the road. When Auerbach wasn't speeding, swerving across the road to fling an apple or narrowly missing guardrails in the dark, he was looking for dogs. It was part of a game they played. The dog game was called Zit, and it had a very specific point system. Spotting a dog was worth one point. If the dog was urinating, you got five points, A dog defecating was worth ten points, and if you saw two dogs humping, you won. Auerbach liked to win—even at Zit.

This crude, shrewd man who scoured the New England countryside in search of copulating bowsers also served as an unofficial United States diplomat, representing America throughout the world as an ambassador of basketball. Well connected in the nation's capital, for twenty years Auerbach captained tours for the U.S. Information Agency of the State Department. In no particular order, he brought American basketball teams to Morocco, Turkey, Iran, Austria, Germany, France, Italy, Yugoslavia, Poland, Czechoslovakia, Egypt, Romania, French West Africa, New Zealand, Taiwan, Malaysia, Hong Kong and Burma. The tours started in 1955 when Auerbach and Cousy joined Kentucky coach Adolph Rupp, and referees Sid Borgia and John Nucatola for a trip to Landsberg, Germany, where they conducted basketball clinics for U.S. servicemen. Three years later, Auerbach and Cousy toured France, Austria, Belgium, Denmark and Turkey for the State Department. In 1959 it was off to Morocco, the United Arab Republic and French Territorial Africa.

Red Auerbach and Cooz in Casablanca. No doubt they strolled the airport tarmac in the fog and Cooz said to Red, "Arnold, I think this is the beginning of a beautiful friendship."

In 1964, an ill-prepared American amateur team had been soundly defeated in games played behind the Iron Curtain. According to Auerbach, "All kinds of second-rate commercial and industrial teams, wearing USA on their red, white and blue uniforms, had gone over there and had their ears pinned back."

At the request of Nick Rodis, of the State Department's Inter-Agency on International Athletics, Auerbach led an NBA All-Star team on a tour of Yugoslavia, Poland, Romania and Egypt. His players were Bob Pettit, Oscar Robertson, Jerry Lucas, Tom Gola, Russell, Cousy (who had retired from NBA play), Heinsohn and K. C. Jones. They got a White House send-off from President Lyndon Johnson, and Secretary of State Dean Rusk accompanied the team to the airport. Auerbach's Dream Team arrived in Zagreb, Yugoslavia, and found sixteen thousand hostile fans, many of whom believed American's basketball supremacy was something of a myth. Auerbach was angry when he found no U.S. flag hanging from the rafters of the host arena. When he was told that raising American colors was not permitted, he threatened to call off the game. Officials finally told him that there was no available flag, but they'd raise one for the next night's game.

Before Game 1, Auerbach told Russell that he did not want the Yugo high scorer to get a point. He told Russell to devote all of his attention to the home team's star. Russell blocked the poor kid's first six shots. The frustrated player eventually was thrown out for unsportsmanlike conduct. The USA won by thirty-two points. The next night the Yugoslavians came out playing rough. Auerbach summoned the Yugo team officials and told them to make the home team knock it off or "we'll beat you so goddamned badly in front of this crowd that you'll want to give up the sport!"

The Yugos backed off. Buoyed by the presence of Old Glory, the USA won the second game by fifty-two points. Luckily for the Yugoslavians, Auerbach had ordered leniency.

The tour was not without further incident. When the U.S. team arrived in Cairo, there was no official greeting from the U.S. Ambassador or anyone in his office. Seven months later, back in the USA addressing the faculty and students of the prestigious Fletcher School of Law and Diplomacy at Tufts University, Auerbach said, "Pardon my colloquialism, gentlemen, but I'd like to report that our ambassador to Egypt is bush . . . The guy is stupid . . . I have to say we've got some real phonies in the diplomatic service."

Small wonder Lyndon Johnson considered Red his kind of diplomat.

"I never really knew Red until that tour," remembers Pettit. "In those months we traveled, losing money to him daily in gin rummy, I came to appreciate him even more."

Auerbach loved the trips. He loved to shop. Walk through his

Washington apartment and he will show you hundreds (and we mean hundreds) of knickknacks from around the world. Each little statuette has a story, and the best part of the story comes when Red smiles and says, "I got this for only six bucks. Who knows what it's worth."

His collection of letter openers runs well into the thousands.

"I never like to use my fingers opening mail," he says. "The first letter opener I bought was in Turkey. It's legitimate ivory."

He knew the world. The world knew Red Auerbach. In Tokyo he was known as "NBA Icheban Honcho-San" ("The Big Boss of the NBA").

What the Celtics did between 1959 and 1966 forever changed the image of the franchise and of Auerbach. If not for this long, glorious run, the Celtics would be just another good team and Auerbach just another good coach. They would be like the Oakland Athletics under Tony LaRussa, the Oakland Raiders under John Madden, the New York Knicks under Red Holzman. Instead, they become synonymous with their sport, and synonymous with winning.

Photographs of all the Boston teams line the walls of the waiting area of the Celtic offices on the fifth floor of 151 Merrimack Street in downtown Boston. The 1960–1961 team photo features nine Hall of Famers—four starters, three bench players (three guys on the *bench* who made the Hall of Fame?), Auerbach and Walter Brown.

Part-time contributor Gene Conley says, "You got a club like that and if a team had you down by eight or ten points by the third period, you didn't worry about it. It was just a matter of 'In the next four or five minutes, let's put a kill on 'em.' "

"There were a lot of factors, including the dress code, that played a role in it," Auerbach says. "We looked like champions, we acted like champions, we felt like champions. All that is a psychological move to have a little competitive edge. We got inside their heads. Some of these coaches, they would try everything. I would try certain things. I remember one particular game. We're playing the Warriors. And they start Chamberlain, [Nate] Thurmond and [Tom] Meschery. So here's what I did. Instead of Loscutoff or somebody, I put in Ramsey, Heinsohn and Russell. Normally, you'd put Ramsey on Meschery, Heinsohn against Thurmond and Russell against Chamberlain. I didn't do that. I put Russell against Chamberlain, Ramsey against Thurmond and Heinsohn against Meschery. Now Thurmond's got Ramsey by nine inches, but Ramsey's very smart and he'll get help from Russell. Where is Thurmond going to go in the pivot, and at the same time he's got to guard Ramsey, and Ramsey is very quick and can go by him. So we start off and we're ahead by something like 15–0 and they took one of 'em out. And we did the same thing when the Lakers got cute and put Baylor in the backcourt.

"You've got to change. You've got to be very, very flexible. You gotta be sarcastic, humorous, loud, soft. Every game is different. Sometimes you come in and say nothing. I did something that I think very few coaches have done. Sometimes, when we'd lose a ball game, I'd be in there after a game and I'd say, 'Hey, keep your head up. You guys played pretty damn good. Two things happened: The ball didn't go in for you, and I was horseshit on the bench. I did a lousy job. I'm human, just like you guys.' Most coaches, they're not human. They never make a fuckin' mistake. I treated my players, most of 'em, as people of intelligence. I would ask them what they think. They're thirty years of age, they're college graduates. A lot of people that age are running big corporations. What do you treat 'em like, a kid? That if they're five minutes late, they're fined five hundred dollars? No. That's why I don't believe in fines."

Sanders says, "Because Red forced you to do things you didn't like to do, you sort of disliked him. Always temporarily. It's like a parent when they whip you. For the long run, you certainly love them. But at that moment when they're laying that strap on your ass, I don't think you're definitely in love with your mother or your father. That was the kind of authority figure that Red represented, and during those times you hated him. But there was never any question in anybody's mind that we all liked him, because Red was a lot of fun to work for.

"Make no mistake about it: It was a lot of fun. The fun was his sense of humor. You could mess with him. He would get back at you in practice—make no mistake about that—because he didn't want to feel that his authority was being threatened. So he'd let us know. 'All right, you guys, it was a good joke, but I'm gonna have the last laugh.' What was he going to do, run us to death? He wasn't going to kill us, shoot us or beat us. We had fun. He has a great sense of humor. He was a character. He *is* a character."

Always, there was something to win for, someone to win for. They wanted to win it in Sharman's last year, and in Cousy's last year. They wanted to win it the year Wilt Chamberlain first came into the league. They wanted to win it the year Walter Brown died. And, of course, they had to win it the year Auerbach announced he was retiring from the bench. Russell wrote, "For a few years in there we couldn't think of anything special, so we won those on general principal."

"One thing we always had was a healthy respect for everybody that we played," says Heinsohn. "The Lakers probably wouldn't believe that, because they have such animosity for the fact that we beat them so much. There was no cockiness. We knew we had to do certain things to beat the teams. And we respected everybody we played, unlike some of the guys I coached. When I coached, it was the era of 'cool.' You played just hard enough so that in the end you could beat them. That was the macho thing, and it drove me crazy.

"Red was a great listener. If somebody came up with an idea, he knew that the guy would make a commitment to make it work. It was a little management trick. We always had these unbelievable, mysterious comebacks at the end of games. That would come after his time-outs, when he'd say, 'Has anybody got anything?' Everybody would say, 'I can do this on this.' Everybody always had their head in the game, and as a player, you had pride of authorship. That's what made it work. He got the extra commitment from everybody. I call the Celtics basketball's La Cosa Nostra. Because La Cosa Nostra means 'Our Thing,' and he made us all believe it was Our Thing."

Eight straight. Which was the best? Auerbach admits, "I don't know one from the other. I have to look it up if anybody asks me. I had no 'best team.' They would change from year to year. When I had Cousy, Sharman, Ramsey and Phillip, it was a great backcourt; then I had Cousy, Sharman, the Jones boys and Ramsey, which was a great, great team. But then, when Cousy retired, Sharman retired, I had the Jones boys and Havlicek instead of Ramsey."

The championships run together like so many Beatles albums, each one a work of artistry and brilliance:

**1. 1958–1959. Something to Prove.** Auerbach and his boys were on a mission. The Celtics wanted to prove that 1957–1958, when the Hawks had ended their one-year championship reign, was an aberration. Going into the season, they knew they'd had the best team two years in a row, but they had only one ring to show for it. Nothing could be taken for granted; nothing could be left to chance. This had to be a wire-to-wire effort. Auerbach had known for a long time that anything could happen once the playoffs started, and now his team knew it as well.

The Celtics bolted to a 23–9 start and finished with a league-record fifty-two victories. Sharman, Cousy, Heinsohn and Russell were ranked among the league's top fifteen scorers. They charged into the playoffs and almost let it get away in a seven-game conference final with Syracuse. Boston trailed by sixteen in Game 7 and Russell fouled out in the final quarter, but the C's won it by five. (Coach Red Auerbach would never lose a seventh game of a playoff series.)

Boston demolished the Minneapolis Lakers in four straight games in the finals. It was the first four-game sweep in the history of the NBA Finals, and Auerbach incorrectly said it would never be done again. Impossible as it now seems, the 1959 Celtics drew only 8,195 for Game 1 of the championship series. Game 4 was in Minneapolis, and Auerbach was carried off the floor by Heinsohn, Loscutoff and K. C. Jones.

**2. 1959–1960. Wilt.** The big kid from the University of Kansas was going to change basketball. It was assumed that Wilt Chamberlain would lead the next dynasty. After winning a couple of championships in his first three seasons, Russell was finally going to meet his match. A good number of rival fans, coaches and players were anxious to see Auerbach and his boys take a fall.

In later years, Lew Alcindor [Kareem Abdul-Jabbar], Bill Walton and Shaquille O'Neal would arrive with huge credentials and expectations, but their arrivals pale in comparison with that of Chamberlain. Wilt was so big and strong that there was actually fear he would strip the sport of its competitive edge. It was as if Nolan Ryan were coming in to pitch against Little Leaguers.

The introduction of Chamberlain was the great challenge to the Auerbach-Russell dynasty, but decades later Wilt the Stilt merely serves as affirmation of Boston's dominance. One of the fundamental elements of sports is competition, and the arrival of Chamberlain elevated the level of competition in the NBA. Able to respond to the challenge, the Celtics found out how good they truly were. Great sprinters run their fastest times when they race against other great sprinters. We will never be able to measure the true collective talent of the 1992 USA Olympic Dream Team basketball squad, because there simply was no competition for Messrs. Jordan, Johnson, Barkley and Bird. Auerbach and his Celtics have no such frustration. Their deeds are enhanced because of the high level of competition they faced—particularly after the arrival of the man-child who threatened to make a mockery of the game.

Naturally, Auerbach knew a lot about Wilt before the big kid splashed down in the NBA. Every summer, Red was a coach and counselor at the Kutsher's Country Club basketball camp in New York's Catskill Mountains. As a teenager, John Thompson, now coach of the Georgetown Hoyas, worked as a bellhop at Kutsher's and sometimes commuted to the mountains with the famous Celtic coach. It was at Kutsher's that Auerbach first noticed the nifty game of a busboy from Kentucky named Frank Ramsey. Young Wilt already was tossing opponents aside when Auerbach first coached him at Kutsher's. Auerbach worked with Wilt, but he could tell the Philadelphia high schooler wasn't listening. Chamberlain was going to do it his way.

In his rookie season with the Philadelphia Warriors, Chamberlain averaged 37 points and 26 rebounds and was named the league's Most Valuable Player. Undaunted, the Celtics won fifty-nine games and averaged a league-record 124.5 points per game. When the Celtics played Philadelphia in the playoffs, Chamberlain got his points, but Boston won the series in six games. It was the beginning of a pattern that would haunt Chamberlain for all of his days. To this day, Auerbach has tremendous regard for Chamberlain's skills (he considers Chamberlain far superior to Shaquille O'Neal—the behemoth of the 1990s), but believes the Stilt was a player who played for statistics. Chamberlain says he thinks he would have won many more championships if he had played for Red Auerbach.

In the 1960 finals, the Celtics beat the Hawks handily, 122–103, in a seventh game. As the clock wound down toward 0:00, Auerbach removed his coat, loosened his tie and lit a cigar. He knew he was headed for the showers.

**3. 1960–1961. Best-Ever I.** The 1966–1967 Philadelphia 76ers later staked a claim to the title of best-ever. A couple of 1980s Kareem-Magic Laker teams are in the running, and of course the Frazier-Bradley-Reed Knicks of the early 1970s are favorites of every New Yorker. The 1971–1972 Lakers won thirty-three in a row and finished with a league-record sixty-nine victories. The 1982–1983 Philadelphia 76ers went 65–17 and took the playoffs 4–0, 4–1 and 4–0. The 1985–1986 Celtics went 40–1 at home and 67–15 overall and had a frontcourt of Larry Bird, Robert Parish, Kevin McHale, Bill Walton and Scott Wedman. In sports it's easy to believe that now is better, because the players are bigger, faster and stronger. That said, one can make a case for the 1960–1961 Celtics as the best-ever in the NBA. They are the 1927 Yankees of basketball.

This was Auerbach's team at its peak. All the parts from the fifties were still there, now meshing with the stars of the sixties. He still had Cousy and Sharman in the backcourt, Russell in the middle and a host of help in Heinsohn, Loscutoff, Ramsey, Sanders and the Jones boys. Sam Jones, K.C. Jones and Frank Ramsey were three Hall of Famers who came off the bench. The Celts went 57–22, beat Syracuse in five, then took St. Louis in five to win the championship. Auerbach was pelted with eggs in St. Louis. It didn't ruin his day.

After the final victory, Auerbach crowed. "This is the greatest team ever assembled. And there are two reasons for it. One is the way these guys get along together and play as a unit. On some teams the players get into each other's hair over a long schedule. That doesn't happen here. And the other reason we're so damned good is the quality of the people. We've always got somebody ready to explode. Any one of them can tear you apart. With most teams, you can win if you stop one man. But you can't stop the Celtics that way. That's why we're the best."

Six players averaged 15 or more points. Nine of them had their numbers retired by the Celtics. Four players on this team (Russell, Heinsohn, Sanders and K. C. Jones) later went on to coach the Celtics. There are eleven players in the 1960–1961 team picture— and all of them eventually became either a pro or college coach. Great ballplayers became good coaches and teachers. And they all took something from the man with the cigar.

Sharman retired at the end of the 1961 season, and at the end Auerbach felt some bitterness for his All-Star guard. Cousy remembers, "I think it was Arnold's insecurity that popped up. We went on the road to the West Coast and Billy was hurt and didn't play. He was thinking about hanging 'em up, or going into the other league, or whatever, and he simply went to Walter Brown and asked what his chances were of eventually becoming coach. Red saw this as a threat and took exception. Maybe there was some justification. Willie was the nicest guy in the world. I'm sure he did it without being devious. But Willie also was then, and is now, the most unsophisticated guy in the world. I think it just didn't occur to him what it might look like to the coach. When Red found out, he blew his top. But certainly at that point, it shouldn't have been a threat to him."

Auerbach remembered star player Bob Feerick going to owner Mike Uline in Washington in 1949. Anyone could be a threat, even when you were on top. Sharman did eventually become coach, and later general manager, of the Los Angeles Lakers.

Today, Auerbach says, "I wasn't mad, but I was a little disappointed." He says he can't remember why, that it had nothing to do with Sharman going to Walter Brown.

**4. 1961–1962. Appearance of the Leprechaun.** Luck is an ingredient of any championship team. The Celtics were good, but they were also lucky. Most of their good fortune was their uncanny ability to avoid injuries. Auerbach had the same players, year after year, and it seemed that nobody ever got hurt. Russell turned his ankle in the 1958 playoffs, but that was it. In addition to good health, the Celtics in the spring of 1962 benefited from an uncanny bounce of the basketball, Bob Dylan's simple twist of fate.

The string was almost snapped at three. On April 18, 1962, at the Boston Garden, Game 7 of the NBA Finals was knotted, 100–100, with two seconds left in regulation time when Laker sharpshooter Frank Selvy lined up for a medium-range jumper from the left baseline. Selvy's shot hit the front rim, skipped over the basket, popped up off the back of the rim and fell into the hands of Russell as the buzzer sounded. Of course, the Celtics won in overtime. Russell played all fifty-three minutes, scoring 30, with 40 rebounds.

According to Auerbach, Boston's winning wasn't a result of luck as much as of justice. "We were cheated," says Red. "The timer froze. There were three seconds to go. They took it out at midcourt and threw it to a guy at midcourt. He took a bounce, and he threw it all the way into the corner. Now that goddamn thing is three seconds there. Selvy takes the ball and goes up for a jump shot and misses it. The rebound goes in the air, and the clock still hadn't gone off."

This was the year that Wilt Chamberlain averaged 50.4 points per game and scored 100 in a single contest.

"He was a phenomenal scorer, and you saw Russell struggling with him, trying to hold him," remembers Sanders. "He was a monster. But you got to remember one thing—Chamberlain was only a man. That's all he was. When you ran him down the court, he got tired like everybody else did. He missed free throws and wasn't the greatest passer or shot blocker in the world. But there's no question he could do a little of everything very well."

It didn't matter: Russell still won the MVP and the Celtics still won the championship. Nothing could stop them now. They were even getting the lucky bounces. They had four titles in a row, halfway to eight.

In the spring of 1962, NBC dumped the NBA because of woeful ratings. First broadcast on the DuMont network, the NBA had been picked up by NBC, which had enjoyed success with a Saturday afternoon "Game of the Week." The game stopped selling in the early 1960s, a fact that sounds impossible in the light of its popularity today. It's said that the league today is attractive because it has marquee stars, but the 1962 NBA had one player who averaged 50 points a game and another, the MVP, who did nothing but win (NCAA, Olympic and NBA) championships. The league of the 1990s could sell Michael Jordan vs. Charles Barkley, but thirty years earlier a ripping rivalry between Chamberlain and Russell wasn't enough to keep a mediocre television contract alive.

**5. 1962–1963. Farewell to the Cooz.** Time has not been particularly kind to Bob Cousy. There simply aren't enough people around who saw him play. NBA insiders talk about John Stockton and Kevin Johnson as breakthrough players—6-1 guards who're able to dominate a game from the backcourt. Before them, there was Magic Johnson redefining the position as a 6-9 point guard. In some ways, Magic destroyed the position for all those who will come after him, and for those great ones who preceded him.

When Kevin McHale retired from the Celtics in the spring of 1993, WEEI's Dale Arnold went on the radio and spoke of McHale as the fourth-greatest Celtic—trailing only Bill Russell, Larry Bird and John Havlicek. There was no mention of Cousy. This is remarkable, given that for more than a decade Bob Cousy was the NBA's "Mr. Basketball."

"I've never seen anybody pass like Cousy," says Heinsohn. "They talk about Magic Johnson today and all these other guys. Christ, nobody ran an offense like Cousy. That's all I got to say. You had a half step on your man, you got the ball."

On March 17, 1963, they gathered at the Garden to say goodbye to the Cooz. Auerbach read a letter from John F. Kennedy, then told the crowd, "That was from the president, but I've got something to say, too. I know you people here are here to honor Bob, are sorry to see him go. Well, how do you think I feel? . . . I want to thank all you people here for coming out, because that's Mr. Basketball."

A month and a half earlier, the Celtics had visited President Kennedy at the White House. This wasn't one of those phony "Let's give the commander in chief a team jacket" photo opportunities the day after the NBA Finals. Auerbach's boys went to Washington at the request of the president, a Boston-born sports fan.

Sanders: "We had some fun. President Kennedy had a marvelous sense of humor. He was a gracious host. We were sitting around talking in the Cabinet Room. We all took different seats and were making believe we were cabinet members."

Perfect. Red Auerbach as Dean Rusk. Russell wasn't there, but had he elected to attend, he no doubt would have wanted Robert McNamara's chair: secretary of defense.

Satch's farewell salutation to JFK was, "Take it easy, baby."

The 1962–1963 Celtics featured Cousy in his final season and Havlicek in his rookie year. Nice symmetry. This was the Auerbach way. Always, there was a young, capable player waiting to replace a retiring star. Havlicek was an Ohio State star who'd played in the long shadow of the great Jerry Lucas. Havlicek also was a football prospect who got a tryout with the Cleveland Browns. Broadcaster Curt Gowdy saw one of Havlicek's Ohio State games and told Auerbach, "There's this guy Havlicek who runs around like he's got a motor up his ass." Bones McKinney also came in with a hearty recommendation. Auerbach never saw Havlicek play a college game, but he knew the young man was a team player, a guy who didn't mind playing defense and a winner.

The final game of the 1963 NBA Finals was a 112–109 Celtic victory at the Los Angeles Sports Arena. Cousy was dribbling the basketball when the buzzer sounded. Cousy and Havlicek each scored 18 points. They were past perfect and future perfect, intersecting for one sweet season.

**6. 1963–1964. Period of Adjustment.** His image is that of an inflexible old-timer, but Auerbach has always been willing to tinker with the engine in order to keep the car running smoothly. With Cousy gone, the changing of the guard was completed. Sharman and Cousy had yielded the floor to Jones and Jones. K. C.'s presence in the starting lineup meant the Celts had to find a different way to win. The muscular guard had no offensive repertoire and couldn't be expected to make the passes that Cousy made.

"I changed the philosophy," says Auerbach. "My point production had to be lower, so I had to change and overemphasize the defense."

He went out and got players—Willie Naulls, Clyde Lovellette and Larry Siegfried. Siegfried was another Ohio State alum, a teammate of Havlicek and Lucas. He came from a winning program. Lovellette had played for NCAA and NBA champions. He fit in. Naulls was another story. He'd been a scorer his whole life. He needed the ball. He didn't worry about staying in shape. As a Hawk, a Knick and a Warrior, he'd been losing to the Celtics his whole life, and now here he was, one of Auerbach's troops. It was an adjustment. For both of them. Naulls threw up during his first Celtic workout. He couldn't believe how much running Auerbach wanted. Hanging over the toilet bowl, he finally realized why Boston got off to such a great start every year.

"Poor Willie Naulls," remembers Ramsey. "There was another practice where we were doing push-ups after lunch and Willie threw up. Russell thought it was hilarious, and he grabbed Willie's feet and pulled Willie off the court. Unfortunately for Willie, Russell dragged Willie's face through the vomit."

Even Russell had to stay in shape. Baseball's Johnny Pesky recalls this story: "Senator Ted Kennedy got in a plane wreck, and a group of us went to visit him. There was Auerbach, Russell, Heinsohn, Cousy, Milt Schmidt of the Bruins and myself. and I remember, here was Russell, Red's best player and a guy who had delivered all these championships, and the first thing Auerbach says to him is, 'You look like you're overweight.' Russell says, 'I bet you I ain't but three or four pounds over,' and they start yakking back and forth."

On April 26, 1964, the Celtics beat Wilt Chamberlain's San Francisco Warriors, 105–99, in the fifth and final game of the NBA championship series. This championship proved that the Celtics would win without Cousy, and it pushed Boston past the New York Yankees and the Montreal Canadiens. Auerbach's team had done something that had never been done in pro sports: It had won six consecutive championships. Naturally, Chamberlain was again the perfect foil. Wilt scored 30 points and pulled down 27 rebounds in the final game, but as always, he couldn't beat Russell or Auerbach. It was as if he had been placed on this earth just to give Boston's basketball dynasty a yardstick for greatness. Russell didn't win the MVP in 1963–1964 (Oscar Robertson did), for the only time in a five-season stretch between 1961 and 1965, but said he considered this his best season.

**7. 1964–1965. Havlicek Stole the Ball.** Russell inadvertently threw the basketball into a guide wire on an inbounds play in the closing seconds of the 1965 conference finals, and for a few tense moments it looked like the Celts' string was over. And then Havlicek stole the ball—a deed canonized by Celtic voice Johnny Most. Replays of Most's call can still be heard throughout New England. *Havlicek stole the ball! . . . Havlicek stole the ball! . . . It's all over! . . . It's all over! . . .* It's Boston's sports equivalent of "The British are coming!"

Again, Red was lucky. The guide wires were unique to the Boston Garden, running from the corners to the backboard to the balcony facing. They'd been lowered before Game 7 ("Somehow or other the goddamned basket was moving, and this was their way of tightening it"—Auerbach) and referees Richie Powers and Earl Strom met with Auerbach and 76er coach Dolph Schayes before the game. Schayes suggested that if a player hit the wire while inbounding, the ball be given back to that player's team. Auerbach disagreed. "The rule has always been that if the ball strikes the wire, the other team gets the ball out of bounds. Why change it now?"

Auerbach won the argument. And almost lost the game. Boston led, 110–103, with a minute to go when he lit the cigar. But Philadelphia roared back, and it was 110–109 with five seconds left when Russell turned the ball over.

In the spring of 1965, Johnny Kerr was nearing the end of his twelve-year career. He was on the court with the Sixers when Russell almost blew it, and Kerr has a memory that no one else shares.

"I saw Red put the cigar out," says the 6-9 Kerr, now a broadcaster for the Chicago Bulls. "He was all set. They were rolling. After Russell lost the ball and we got the ball back with five seconds left, I looked down at their bench, and I saw him grinding the cigar out with his shoe. It was a great thrill."

"He lies," says Auerbach. "I don't recall that. It happened one time in Providence. I lit up when we were ahead by three with ten seconds to go. I told my players, 'Let 'em shoot, let's get out of here.' So one of my players hits a guy as he shoots and the guy makes it and then he makes the foul shot and we're tied. I could have killed my guy."

Against the Sixers in 1965, there was no overtime. Havlicek stole the ball.

"Hal Greer was throwing the ball in," says Kerr. "He was going to throw it over the top of me to where Chet Walker was. Then I

was going to go in and close the door on Sam Jones and K. C., and
then Greer would have just stepped sideways and got the shot. He
threw the ball over the top and I heard thirteen thousand, nine
hundred and nine roaring and I was thinking, 'What the hell is going
on back there?' Then Red lit the cigar again."

The lucky No. 7 came with some sadness: Walter Brown had
died of a heart attack on September 7, 1964, just five weeks before
the start of the 1964–1965 season. Photos of this campaign are easily
identified because of the small black patch that adorned the left
shoulders of the Celtic jerseys. The driven C's won a league-record
sixty-two games. After surviving the scare against the 76ers (beating
yet another Chamberlain team), the Celts destroyed the Lakers in
five games in the finals. The clincher was played on the parquet
floor on April 25, and Red lit the cigar early in the fourth period.
After a few well-deserved puffs (the Celtics were en route to a 129–
96 blowout victory, opening the fourth quarter with a 20–0 run), he
wheeled around and flung a handful of his monogrammed cigars
into the crowd behind the Celtic bench. Nobody does anything like
that anymore.

Auerbach carried a St. Christopher medal throughout the playoffs. After winning the final game, he pressed the medal back into
the hand of the woman who'd given it to him: Walter Brown's wife,
Marjorie.

The winners' playoff shares were $5,000.

Auerbach was named NBA Coach of the Year. It was the only
time he was so honored, which surely says more about the award
than it does about Auerbach. The award was instituted in 1963, and
in the first two years of its existence Auerbach was beaten by Harry
Gallatin and Alex Hannum. Auerbach still has a chip on his shoulder
about this. He believes the Coach of the Year should be the coach
who wins the most games, not a guy who takes a team from fifth to
second place. In an ironic twist, the honor has been renamed the
Red Auerbach Award, and winners receive a mini-statue of Auerbach on the bench.

**8. 1965–1966. The Last Cigar.** Auerbach was tired of the sound
of his voice. He'd lost the edge. He couldn't generate the proper
anger at NBA officials. He wanted to spend more time in Washing-

ton with his wife and two daughters. He was astonished when he saw photos of himself. Only forty-eight years old, Red was gray and balding. He had heavy, dark bags under his deep-set eyes. There had been too many cigars, too much Chinese food, not enough sleep—and not enough time back at the Washington house. Nancy was twenty. Randy was fourteen. They'd grown up without the presence of a father, and their dad looked like a man who'd been working nine jobs at one time.

The 1965–1966 Celtics were without Heinsohn, who had retired at the age of thirty-one. Auerbach took 6-6 journeyman Don Nelson off the waiver wire. With Heinsohn gone, the Celts had a starting lineup of Russell, Sanders, Naulls and the Jones Boys. All five were black. The Celtics will forever be dodging racism charges, but the record is clear that Auerbach's last team featured the NBA's first all-black starting five.

The Celts got off to the usual good start, but Auerbach didn't feel he was at the top of his game. He told *The Globe,* "I haven't been getting myself up for games the way I should. I'm as guilty as anyone else for not playing better. In some of the practice sessions—and games, too, for that matter—I've been much too relaxed and casual. I've been taking things for granted, and when you do that you get beat."

In December, K. C. Jones and Nelson called a players-only meeting in Detroit and discussed some of the problems the team was facing. Through the years, Auerbach encouraged these meetings. He was secure enough not to worry about what the players might be saying about him. At this particular meeting, it was decided that nobody was doing his best, including the coach. Russell later told Auerbach about the meeting. The coach could see that his players were right. Auerbach wrote, "I'm convinced that we beat the worst enemy of any champion—complacency is the only word for it—in those few days in December."

In January 1966, Auerbach got together with his "friends" in the media and said, "I'm announcing it now so no one ever can say I quit while I was ahead. I'm telling everyone right now—Los Angeles, Philadelphia, everyone—that this will be my last season, so you've got one more shot at Auerbach!"

Typical. He announced his resignation in advance and peppered the pledge with proper historical perspective.

Was there any way these Celtics would be beaten? Could they possibly win seven consecutive championships for their crusty coach, then let down and lose in his final season on the bench? Doubtful.

NBA towns, most of them tortured by Auerbach's Celtics for a full decade, welcomed the chance to say good-bye to Red. The Cincinnati Royals' management handed out five thousand cigars to fans who attended Boston's last regular-season game in 1966. The promotion blew up in their faces. Red had the last laugh and the only cigar. The Celtics won again.

There was acknowledgment in Boston as well. In the winter of 1965, Mayor John F. Collins presented Auerbach with the Distinguished Achievement Medallion at a ceremony at the War Memorial Auditorium in Boston. Of the ten prominent citizens who were honored, six were Nobel laureates. Red's citation read, in part, "In the field of competitive sports he stands alone. In the major sport to which he has given most of his life, he has made the name Boston synonymous with success."

On Sunday, February 13, 1966, the Celtics celebrated Red Auerbach Day. It was one month after his thousandth career victory. It was early in the season for such festivities, but the Celts couldn't be sure that Auerbach would go out with another championship. The ceremony was held at halftime. Dorothy was there with Nancy and Randy. "I only wish my dad could have been here from Florida," said Auerbach.

There were numerous speeches and presentations. Cousy, one of the presenters, said, "I sweated out that whole first half, wondering what we'd do if you got kicked out early and couldn't come back to accept these gifts."

Making the day complete, referee John Vanak slapped Auerbach with the technical foul in the second half. The Lakers beat the Celtics, 120–110.

ABC television was broadcasting the NBA (three years after the sport was abandoned by NBC) and Frank Deford, a young writer with *Sports Illustrated* in 1966, remembers this vignette from Auerbach's final campaign:

"I was walking off the court with him after one of those rare television games. The game is over and we're walking off and he's talking to me and a little guy comes up to him and says, 'Red, Red, we need you on television right now upstairs.' These were the days when there were only two or three games on television all year. Red turns to this little guy and says, 'Where the fuck were you in February? I'm gonna be with my guys.' And then he put his arm around my shoulder. It's probably the last time that Red or anybody else in sports turned away television for print."

Winning consecutive title No. 8 wasn't easy. Boston's starting lineup had an average age of thirty-one, and the team finished second for the first time since 1955. In the first round of the playoffs, it fell behind the Royals, two games to one, in a best-of-five series, then rallied to win the final two games. The Celts crushed Chamberlain's 76ers in five sweet games, then lost Game 1 of the finals to the Lakers.

As with everything else, Auerbach used the announcement of his successor to help him win a championship. After the Game 1 loss to LA, he snatched all the headlines by naming Russell as the next coach of the Celtics. Ramsey was his first choice, but the Kentucky colonel had a booming construction business in Madisonville and was unavailable. Cousy and Heinsohn turned down the job after Ramsey was scratched from consideration. Cousy was committed to Boston College, and Heinsohn didn't think he could handle Russell. Heinsohn suggested that Auerbach have Russell serve as player-coach. Auerbach went to Russell and made the offer. The big center gave it a lot of thought, and by the time the playoffs rolled around, the only thing left was the announcement.

"We're like a family," said Auerbach. "It wouldn't have been easy bringing in someone from the outside and make him part of the family. Russ can do the job. He'll make a great coach."

The timing of Auerbach's announcement infuriated the Lakers and buoyed the Celtics. It was major news, not only because Russell would be replacing the most successful coach in the history of pro sports, but also because he would become the first black head coach in any major American sport. Newspaper coverage ignored LA's 1–0 lead and concentrated on the changing of the guard at the end of the Celtic bench.

The series went the full seven games. Auerbach had been suffering from strep throat before the finals. He slept well the night before Game 7, but was very anxious in the hours leading up to the ball game. He ate a salami sandwich for lunch and threw it up ten minutes later. He called Washington, and Dot offered to make a rare trip to Boston to watch the Celtics play. No. They wouldn't change anything now. It would end the way it started: Red coaching, Dot at home with the girls.

Before the game, played on a Thursday night in Boston, he gave the kind of pep talk that has become hideously obsolete in today's fat NBA. He appealed to his players' wallets.

"This one means seven hundred dollars apiece to you guys," he said. "That's the difference between winners' and losers' share. Show me another way you can make seven hundred dollars in forty-eight minutes . . . I want you to win this one for *you*, not for me."

The final cigar almost blew up in Red's face. Beating the Lakers on the Garden parquet, Red kept his cigar in his pocket until victory was assured. Governor John Volpe of Massachusetts, a front-running publicity hound of the highest order, had stationed himself right next to the Celtic bench and was prepared with a cigarette lighter. Russell dunked with thirty seconds left to give the Celts a 95–85 lead. With victory secure, Red went for the stogie, Governor Volpe for the lighter. Meanwhile, fans lined the perimeter of the court, overflowing onto the playing area. While the Celtics and Lakers tried to finish the game, there were fans on the basket supports and fans standing on the court next to the players.

Bad things started to happen. The Celtics committed four consecutive turnovers and the Lakers cut Boston's lead to 95–93. Finally, K. C. Jones dribbled out the clock and threw the ball to Havlicek, and Auerbach was carried through the crowd on the shoulders of his players. After the obligatory fully clothed shower—another Russell dunk—Auerbach emerged, cigar still lit, and said, "I never came closer to disaster. I feel drunk, and I haven't even had a drink."

Russell finished with 25 points and 32 rebounds, playing the full forty-eight minutes. He was the only active Celtic who'd been part of Auerbach's first championship in 1957.

Dripping wet, Auerbach went to the equipment room to call home. The line was busy. Dot was talking to Red's brother Zang. When he finally got through, his long-distance bride said, "When are you coming home, Arnold?"

"Well, everyone had their last shot at me," he later wrote. "Everyone had their chance. And when it was over—the longest year of my life—there was a lump in my throat as I walked out of the locker room after that last game."

Outside the Garden, there was a parking ticket attached to the window of his car. A true Boston experience. Auerbach went back to his room at the Lenox, ordered Chinese food, made himself some french fries and had dinner with a pal, New York columnist Milton Gross. He had coached 1,585 NBA games and won 1,037 of them. He had missed only one game in twenty years—the night his father suffered a stroke. He was forty-eight years old and he was through coaching. He was prepared to enter the next phase of life in the NBA. He had been the best coach there ever was, and now he was going to be the best general manager.

"Cry?" he said to Gross on the ninth floor of the Lenox. "I may cry later—by myself, you know? The emotion will catch up with me. I'm not supposed to be superstitious, but I've worn the same pair of shoes all through the seven games of this series. All through my coaching career, I've carried this same wallet. You think it's time to get rid of it? . . . How about that cop tagging my car on a day like this? What the heck. A guy so lucky has to have some bad luck. Look what I got—success, a nice family, money, friends."

There was one last bit of business to deal with before he went home for the summer. On his desk was a note from NBA Commissioner Walter Kennedy: "For your public criticism of officiating during championship series as carried by the wire services and local press particularly following game played on April 10 you are hereby fined $150."

It would be Auerbach's last fine as a head coach. It would not be his last fine.

The Celtics had their annual breakup dinner at the Lenox Hotel the next night. Russell, as always, was most eloquent, and said this about his one and only pro basketball coach: "Personally, I think that you're the greatest basketball coach that ever lived. I think that you have contributed as much to basketball as any man alive. I think you've contributed more to the Celtics as a team than anybody realizes. You know, over the years it's been funny to me: I heard a lot of coaches and a lot of writers around the country say that the only thing that made you a great coach was Bill Russell. It helped, yeah, but that's not what did it. This is Red's team. He picked every guy here. He had different reasons for picking guys. An attitude, desire, fundamental ability . . . I can't imagine ever playing for a greater coach . . . We'll be friends until one of us dies."

When Russell was through, Auerbach spoke briefly, then sat down, buried his head in his hands and sobbed. In his autobiography, he recalled the moment: "Hell, let's face it. I finally choked. But I was off the bench by then."

There would be plenty of offers and opportunities in the years ahead, but Auerbach never returned to the bench. He did not succumb to the temptation that tainted the illustrious careers of Vince Lombardi, Casey Stengel and Earl Weaver. Red Auerbach never came back.

The end of his coaching career coincided with the death of his father. Hymie Auerbach died in the summer of 1966.

# 6

# SMOKE-FILLED ROOMS

*The best contract signing was when Red signed Larry Siegfried. Siegfried was sitting in a whirlpool and Red was sitting next to him, outside the pool, and it was about a hundred fifty degrees in the room and Red was sweating to death. Siegfried didn't have much leverage and he knew he wasn't going to do any better than what Red was offering, but he couldn't just take it. He had to get something more. So he asked if he could have a case of Coke anytime he wanted it. Red said that would be fine. He put that right in there. So he signed him by promising him a case of Coke.*

JEFF COHEN, *former Celtic assistant GM*

CELTIC FANS ASSUMED AUERBACH WOULD FADE AWAY AFTER he retired from the bench. High-profile general managers in 1966 were not the order of the day. You either were on the bench in the middle of the action or you were out of sight. Fans thought that Auerbach's "retirement" meant the end of his day-to-day impact on the Celtics. It never happened. Auerbach has retired more times than Frank Sinatra and Sugar Ray Leonard. But he's never ceased being a presence and a force at every Boston Celtic game.

Free of his whistle and clipboard, Auerbach in 1966–1967 confronted a pair of obstacles far more imposing than Wilt Chamberlain and Jerry West. He was facing the challenge of keeping his franchise on top despite continuous ownership instability . . . and he was going to have to do it while battling what he considered to be the single greatest plague to strike professional sports: player agents.

Auerbach dealt with ownership instability and/or fiscal peril throughout his first three decades in Boston. The Celtics' money problems in the 1950s were well documented. The team didn't draw very well (the average regular-season crowd during the run of eight consecutive titles was 7,803) and Walter Brown sometimes had to ask players to cut him a break when checks were late. Despite the shallow pockets, Brown was generous with his players. Ramsey was famous for sending Brown a blank contract; he played for whatever management thought was fair. Russell was always paid $1 more than Chamberlain. Players always tried to negotiate with Brown instead of Auerbach. "I'd leave town for a few days and they'd all go running to Walter," remembers Auerbach.

"Everybody loved Walt Brown," remembers Heinsohn. "He was like your father. He didn't make any money. He savored the life at the Garden. You went in to talk contract with Walter Brown. You'd walk into the men's room and he'd say, 'What do you want?' And you'd say, 'What do you want to give me?' And it would be back and forth, and by the time you zipped up, you had a deal."

Auerbach was much more stingy with the owner's money. He would have a player in his office for two hours, but when asked how long the contract talks had gone, both Auerbach and the player would say "five or ten minutes." They weren't lying. Auerbach would change the subject every time money came up. A player would come into his office and spend an hour or so looking at Red's latest letter openers or some gift watches that were part of an upcoming team promotion. On those rare occasions when a player would get Auerbach to agree to a guaranteed contract, the GM made it official by turning the contract over and writing "This contract is guaranteed" on the blank backside. That was enough for Red. He gave you his word—he even wrote it down in longhand. It should, he felt, be enough.

Jeff Cohen, who joined the Celtics in 1965 and eventually became assistant GM, remembers, "We would judge how well he had done in a contract negotiation by how many key chains and hats they walked out of his office with. If they walked out loaded, we knew we got a good deal."

The practice of players representing themselves was on the wane when Auerbach moved behind the desk full-time. Most of the sports world was grudgingly accepting of the role of player agents. Not Auerbach. In June of 1967 he said, "I have always dealt with my players directly and I have always treated them fairly. I see no reason to change my way of operating now. I will not deal through agents, and I want no agents sitting in when I'm negotiating with my players. If these players want an agent, that's their business. But I draft *them*, and they're the ones I'm going to talk with."

This was Hymie's son talking. Born in Brooklyn in 1917, Auerbach could not fathom a world in which middlemen were needed to negotiate a price for services. There were no agents in the deli business or the cleaning business. Roosevelt High School teachers didn't have agents, and twenty-eight-year-old Arnold Auerbach didn't have anyone representing him when he persuaded Mike Uline to hire him to coach the Washington Capitols. As coach and contract negotiator, he rarely had problems with money. One thing he demanded from the owners he worked for was that he would control the players' salaries. He told his players that the money never was attached to statistics. He knew what they were worth. And he knew that they knew he was fair.

All of this, of course, was changing in the 1960s. The NFL in the summer of 1967 found itself competing with the AFL, and the NBA was losing players to the newly formed American Basketball Association—the league with the three-point shot and the red, white and blue basketball.

The late Larry Fleisher was an NBA agent in the early days of player agents. This is how he remembered his first dealings with Auerbach: "I was on guard. His initial hysterical position—allowing nobody to represent his players—suggested to me that he had a desire to take advantage of the people he was dealing with. Prohibiting a player from using an attorney is wrong, and very few industries in the world—if any—would allow that kind of nonsense to go on."

In the summer of 1977, Auerbach and Fleisher hammered out a deal for Sidney Wicks. After one negotiating session, Auerbach told the press, "We had our Chinese lunch and I presented an offer. Larry's going back with it, and I'll be in contact with him. Everything was very nice, the whole process." Later, Red confided, "Hey, how much ass can you kiss? Then the guy owns you. I'm not crazy."

Paul Westphal was drafted by the Celtics in 1972. His agent was the notorious Howard Slusher.

Westphal's story: "At that time, you found out you got drafted by reading the paper. It certainly wasn't on ESPN. There wasn't all the buildup. The Celtics sent my telegram to the wrong school— Southern California College instead of USC—so I didn't find out until the next day when I read it in the paper. Things were a little more low-key then. I certainly was well aware of Red Auerbach. I grew up in Los Angeles and watched all the basketball I could, so I got to see them kick the Lakers' butts every year. I was excited to be drafted by such a historic franchise, and Red Auerbach was a big part of the mystique they had and I couldn't wait to meet him. He hated my agent, Howard Slusher. I was Howard's first client, and this was in the days when they didn't have agents. We introduced Howard as my friend who was helping me with my contract. And that was okay. Red would talk to him then. If I had introduced him as my agent, Red wouldn't have talked to him."

As years passed, it became obvious that Auerbach would have to deal with player representatives. He relented. But he never liked or trusted the men who came to his office to represent ballplayers. He hated guaranteed, long-term contracts and said they were the primary contributor to the decay of American sports. These positions served to further solidify Auerbach as a man of the everyday people. Red Auerbach aired the grievances of Joe Six-Pack.

David Halberstam, author of *The Breaks of the Game*, says, "Auerbach was smart when nobody else was smart. He understood always that it was about lines of authority, and that's why I compared him to Mayor Richard Daley. He understood that the agent was the challenge to him, and the way he did it, more than anything else. So he was always fighting the clock of contemporary sport."

"As far as agents go, I finally had to give in on that," Auerbach admits. "Even though my personal view of them never changed. Sometimes you've got to bend with the times."

One of the lasting misconceptions about Auerbach is that he is inflexible. Not so. He's too smart to dig in. Those who've worked with, and against, him know that Auerbach has always been willing to bend (albeit grudgingly, in some cases) when it served his purposes. It's the same reason he never had ironclad rules. If a player broke a sacred rule and the penalty called for him to be benched for a game, it might cost the team a victory. No rule was *that* important.

"I never like fining players for something like missing a plane," he says. "If he's a good kid and you don't fine him, he'll feel like he owes you one; he's going to kill himself that night in the game. But if you take a guy making all that money and you fine him three hundred dollars, what the hell good is it? This way, he thinks you're a helluva guy and the players play harder for you. But nine out of ten coaches don't look at it that way. They say, 'We got rules. You broke the rule.' That's crap."

Auerbach's ethics have always been those of expediency. It was the same with agents. After holding off for a while, he saw that it might cost him some good ballplayers. His disdain for money-hungry agents was overruled by his love of a victory cigar.

His reputation as a shrewd negotiator sometimes hurt him in his own house. Players on other teams told Celtic players that they were underpaid (this sounds strikingly like the kind of psych tactic Auerbach suggested in his coach-player-fan handbook of the fifties). Auerbach's posture was that he could only spend what his owners could afford, and until the 1980s there was never an abundance of cash.

Jan Volk came to work for the Celtics after graduating from Columbia Law School and passing the Massachusetts bar exam in the spring of 1971. Volk remembers this story about young Jo Jo White sitting outside Auerbach's office:

"Jo's contract was up and he came in to see Red in the middle of the summer. I remember he went into Red's office and in ten or fifteen minutes he was out, and he sat outside the office muttering to himself. I said, 'What's wrong, Jo?' and he said, 'I think I made a big mistake.' I said, 'What do you mean?' He said, 'I went in to see Red and he asked me what I wanted and I told him and he said okay. So I think I made a big mistake.' "

Good instincts, Jo Jo. If Auerbach jumped on your first offer, you probably were low.

For many years after the death of Brown, it was unclear exactly who was signing the checks. Auerbach deftly sidestepped ownership chaos for his entire term of office. After Brown, there were eight ownership changes in ten years. None of the owners were basketball men. Some were meddlers. Most left Red alone. Until John Y. Brown came along in 1978, Auerbach was loyal to all of the owners. He was smart enough to stay on the good side of whoever was writing the checks. He'd put the picture of the owner du jour on the wall of his office. Every time there was a change, Red would simply remove one picture and pledge allegiance to a new guy. This required patience and smarts. Besides, they all wanted to learn basketball from the great Red Auerbach.

Auerbach owned approximately 11.6 percent of the Celtics after Walter Brown died. He became a minority partner with Lou Pieri and Walter Brown's widow, Marjorie. At the end of the 1965 playoffs, they sold the team for $3 million to Marvin Kratter and Jack Waldron. Auerbach sold all of his stock in the club, a hefty take of more than $300,000. Kratter was head of National Equities, a major conglomerate with offices in the Pan-Am Building in New York City. He installed a hot-line telephone in Auerbach's Boston Garden office. Auerbach refused to pick up the phone. He didn't need to be talking with a meddling owner six times a day. In 1968, just before Kratter sold the Celtics to Ballantine Brewery, he summoned Auerbach to the Pan-Am Building to talk about whom to protect in the expansion draft. Several directors of National Equities gave their opinions, and then a smoldering Auerbach said, "Listening to you guys discussing the skills and future abilities of ballplayers is like letting civilians run a war. It's a joke. Would I pick out a piece of real estate and tell you people how much it's worth and what you should do with it? If this is how you plan to run things, then you can take your ball club and shove it."

In 1969 Ballantine sold to Trans-National Communications,

which resulted in more headaches for the man in the corner office. TNC, like National Equities, was based in New York. According to Auerbach, "They took all of our money and then never bothered to pay our bills. We owed money to hotels in every city. So the Celtics had to travel COD all over the league. They wouldn't let us stay unless we paid in advance. One time I had to lay out nine thousand dollars of my own money before our guys could board an airplane . . . There were people on the payroll who I never heard of. It was just awful . . . One day we were notified that our office telephones would be shut off if we didn't pay our phone bill. On top of that, the phone company insisted on a two-thousand-dollar deposit, just to make sure we didn't default again."

It was embarrassing, and in today's NBA, unthinkable. Auerbach was general manager of a team that had won eleven world championships in thirteen seasons, and he was digging into his own pockets to pay for travel and begging Ma Bell to keep the lines open. When Trans-National couldn't come up with a $7,424.69 premium, Travelers canceled the Celts' accident insurance policy.

Trans-National went bankrupt, and the Celts were taken over by the anonymous Investors Funding Corporation, a custodian group of Ballantine. The team had only 860 season-ticket holders. In 1972, the franchise was purchased for $5 million by Bob Schmertz and Leisure Technology. Schmertz had made a fortune developing retirement companies, and he had a little Walter Brown in him. He owned the new England Whaler hockey team. He loved ballplayers. He liked to take trips with the team and hobnob in the locker room. He liked Auerbach and Auerbach liked him. Schmertz brought West Coast businessman Irv Levin in as a partner before the 1974 season. Levin is the man who brought John Y. Brown into the Celtic ownership, and Brown is the man who nearly drove Auerbach out of Boston.

While owners and agents were necessary nuisances, trading and drafting was the fun part for the full-time general manager. For the first time in his twenty-year NBA career, Auerbach had the time to employ his skills as a horse trader and judge of talent. He had been a good basketball player and a great basketball coach. But he was born to be a deal-maker. He was born to be a general manager. As a GM, his eyes, instincts and street smarts were utilized to the max. He knew what it took to assemble a team. Starting in the summer of 1966, he could devote all his attention to keeping the Celtics on top.

Phoenix Sun GM Jerry Colangelo grew up in Chicago Heights and broke into the NBA with the Chicago Bulls in 1966, the same year Auerbach went behind the desk. Colangelo was twenty-six.

"My first recollection of Red is that he made a special deal to protect K. C. Jones [in the expansion draft] with Dick Kleine, my boss in Chicago. He pulled a Red Auerbachism. It's like with the salary cap today. There's always ways to circumvent the cap. I don't remember what we received, but we received some compensation for not taking K. C. Jones in the draft.

"We got the franchise; two weeks later I was out on the road scouting. I went to Kansas City for a tournament. I met Marty Blake, general manager of St. Louis; Pepper Wilson of Cincinnati; Buddy Jeannette of Baltimore; and the scout for the Knicks, Red Holzman. For three days we watched basketball for ten hours a day. And every night we went to the Italian Garden in Kansas City and had a meal. On the third night, Red turns to me and says, 'Kid, I want to tell you something. You're going to do pretty well in this league.' I said, 'Why is that, Red?' He said, 'Because you keep your mouth shut. You don't know anything.' "

Auerbach knew he had work to do. His 1966 champions had a starting lineup with an average age of thirty-one and the Philadelphia 76ers were peaking with a unit that included Chamberlain, Chet Walker, Hal Greer, Luke Jackson, Billy Cunningham and Wali Jones. Auerbach's first deal as a full-time GM was a trade that sent 7-foot center Mel Counts to Baltimore for a supposedly washed-up forward named Bailey Howell. Two weeks later, he acquired Wayne Embry from Cincinnati for cash and a draft pick. These were spare parts for coach Bill Russell.

In his first few weeks on the job, Russell gained new respect for his old coach. As a player under Auerbach, Russell felt the coach was too tough on Sanders and Nelson; the constant bench-jockeying seemed cruel and unnecessary. Russell told himself that he would be nice to these capable veterans, that he would treat them like the professionals they were. Early in the season, Russell noticed something. He'd be on the court and think to himself that he only had four players on his side. Then he'd realize that it seemed like five-on-four because Nelson was daydreaming. Other times, it was Sanders who'd be in a trance. He started to yell at them. They started to produce. Russell understood. Red was right.

Auerbach came back to coach one game in 1966–1967. He agreed to coach the East squad in the annual All-Star Game, and he was ejected by referee Willie Smith. It was the first time in the seventeen-year history of the All-Star Game that a coach had been ejected. "The whole thing is stupid and irrational," he said. "Something like this happens and you're glad you retired."

The 1966–1967 Celtics won sixty games, but were no match for the 76ers. Philly won a league-record sixty-eight games and wiped out the Celtics in five games to snap Boston's championship streak. The clincher was a twenty-four-point beating in the Spectrum, where fans chanted "Boston is dead, Boston is dead" as the sand ran out.

No one would say it then or now, but there may have been some significance in the timing of this first Celtic playoff loss in nine years. Auerbach was not on the bench and the Celtics were finally beaten. It fit. Sure, the 76ers were better, but the Celts had overcome tough odds many times. They'd never lost to a Chamberlain team. Maybe Auerbach was not simply lucky, a guy who rolled the ball on the court and told his talented players to "go get 'em." Maybe the Redhead had had something to do with all those championships.

Auerbach and Cousy went on a memorable State Department tour of the Far East after the 1966–1967 season. Cousy was coaching Boston College at the time. They departed in early May and made stops in Taipei, Taiwan; Hong Kong; Kuala Lumpur, Malaysia; and Tokyo.

"You know what a finicky eater Arnold is," says Cousy. "The State Department used to wire ahead to their state department and tell them what we like and so forth, so they would try to a small degree to cater to that. So we flew endlessly to Taiwan.

"We got in at midnight [the first night]. We got geisha girls to come up and stomp on our backs. I was asleep before they got through. Then we had a luncheon the next day. All the government,

military and federation people were there. We were the guests of
honor and we were kicking off this tour. They had a huge lazy Susan
in the middle of the table. Arnold didn't drink to speak of, and they
also had this saki. Most of the stuff in those damn dishes was moving.
I'm nudging him, saying, 'Arnold, it's not going to look good, these
people get offended if you don't eat,' and he's saying, 'Fuck 'em.'
And then each guy makes a toast and we've got to drink the saki.

   "So we go through that whole week and he hardly ate anything,
because the food was strange for us. We go from there to Kuala
Lumpur. Now, we get to the hotel in Malaysia and the food is
equally bad. The next morning, I had to have something done to my
passport. I go down to the State Department offices. There's this
huge square downtown. It's very beautiful, with marble and everything. And I see a sign down the other end that looks like it says,
'A & W.' I get closer to it and, Jesus, if it isn't some little Jewish
guy from Brooklyn who's going to put A & W stands all over Malaysia. I find this guy and he's serving hot dogs and hamburgs. I get
on the phone and I call Arnold. Christ, we ate breakfast, lunch and
dinner there all the time we were in Malaysia. The little guy saved
our lives.

   "We went from there to Hong Kong, and they were having the
riots. [Communist-led rioters in the spring of 1967 demonstrated in
opposition to use of Hong Kong harbor by U.S. warships.] At this
point I remember Red getting a wire saying he'd better come home
because the IRS was going to put Russell in jail—Russ had a peculiar
habit of getting behind on his taxes. But anyway, we get to Hong
Kong and the whole city is closed down. They had to cancel our
clinics because of the riots. We just sat around. They told us to stay
in the hotel, but we got little berets and shit and we used to sneak
out. If nothing else, Arnold wanted to go shop. There was a tax-free
PX store. That's all he did was shop for three days, and we also
followed the riots around. We were trying to make out like we
weren't westerners. We figured we could outrun them, I suppose."

   They made it back safely. Auerbach had a couple of dozen new
letter openers and stories to last him into the next century. It was
time to get back to the work of winning NBA championships. The
1966–1967 season proved to be nothing more than an interruption—

one of two aberrations in the thirteen-year reign of Russell. With Russell as coach, the Celtics came back to win championships in the next two seasons. Havlicek emerged as a starter, captain and star of the team.

The 1968 Celtics trailed the Sixers, three games to one, before winning the conference finals in seven games, becoming the first team in NBA history to bounce back from a 3–1 deficit. It was special for Auerbach, Coach Russell and every other member of the green team. Celtic fans had the additional treat of hearing Auerbach as a television commentator during this campaign. "I told [Boston's Channel 56] that I might set television back ten years," Auerbach admitted. "But nobody seems to be turning off the sound at Celtic games."

Flag No. 10 in 1968 was very satisfying, but the 1969 crown, the last stand for the old guard, was perhaps the sweetest of them all. Auerbach owns sixteen championship rings, but the one he wears on his hand is from 1969. He says it's because it's lighter than most of the others. Maybe.

In the spring of 1969, Russell was thirty-five, Sam Jones thirty-six, Howell thirty-two and Sanders thirty. No announcement had been made, but Russell and Sam had made up their minds that this was it. The Celtics staggered to a 48–34 record, finishing fourth, their lowest placing in twenty years. They would be without the home-court advantage throughout the playoffs.

They beat the Pistons and the Knicks. New York, a team on the rise, featured Walt Frazier, Willis Reed, Dave DeBusschere and Bill Bradley. The Knicks were a year away from being champions. The Celtics were a year away from Palookaville. But Russell's geezers took the New York kids to school and won the series in six games.

Los Angeles again provided the opposition in the finals. This time, the Lakers were ready. They had added Wilt Chamberlain to a cast that already included Elgin Baylor and Jerry West. In the spring of 1969, you could argue that the Lakers had the best center, forward and guard in the history of basketball all playing on the same team. Ever defiant, Auerbach said, "You still play this game with only one basketball."

The series was 3–3 when Laker owner Jack Kent Cooke made

the mistake of preparing a postgame victory celebration for Game 7 in Los Angeles. Cooke had the USC band on hand to play "Happy Days Are Here Again," and five thousand balloons were suspended from the ceiling above the LA Forum court. Auerbach had all the weaponry he needed. At the end of the night, the Celtics again were champions and Auerbach was pointing to the sky and shouting about "all those goddammed balloons." No doubt he'd have liked to have popped them one by one with his cigar. Since Russell had arrived in 1956, the Celtics had been faced with twelve "must-win" (Game 5 of a best-of-five series, Game 7 of a best-of-seven) situations. The Celtics in those games were 12–0.

In the postgame madness, ABC broadcaster Jack Twyman (a former Cincinnati forward) interviewed Sam Jones on the Forum floor. In the middle of the nationally televised interview, Auerbach interrupted, chortling, "What a way to go out. What are they going to do with all those balloons up there? They'll eat 'em! Ha, ha."

"That seventh game will always be one of my favorites," Auerbach said later. "Not only was most everything in the Lakers' favor, but Jack Kent Cooke got stuck with a lot of balloons in his rafters. And Russ and Sam went out winners."

The year of the eleventh championship, 1969, was an active one back home in Washington. Auerbach's only grandchild, Julie, was born in March. Julie is the daughter of Nancy Auerbach and Steve First, a graduate of George Washington Medical School. The proud grandfather cradled Julie and noted, "She weighs less than a basketball." He also said, "Well, she's okay, but she'll need a nose job." Nancy was mortified, until her mom told her that he had made the same remark about his own infant daughter—Nancy herself—when she was born in 1946. Nancy and Steve divorced fifteen months after Julie was born. Nancy and Julie moved in with Arnold and Dorothy, and lived there for the next four years.

Red Auerbach had not tried to talk his daughter into working things out. "When things don't work out, you're better off cutting it and looking in different directions," Auerbach says. "I saw some of the things the guy did, and I didn't like it. When she said she wanted to get a divorce, I said, 'Great.'"

Grandfather Red, known to Julie as "Goomp," because a surrogate father of sorts. "In some ways, she got to do more with him than we ever did," says Nancy, who is now married to CNN anchorman Reid Collins. "He took her to see *Mary Poppins*, things like that. They've always had a very special relationship." It was so special that Julie, when she was ten, had her last name legally changed to Auerbach.

"She thinks he's her father," says Dorothy. "She says he's the only father she ever knew."

'I watched her grow up as much as I could," says Auerbach. "I wasn't exactly a workaholic, but I was a thinkaholic. I used to think all the time. You try to do things with the kids, but you know, she's got her mother."

Auerbach was able to get home more than he had as head coach. Second daughter Randy was in her teen years, always on the telephone. The general manager took comfort in his attic study atop the unpretentious brick colonial on Legation Street. The third-floor dormer had sloped ceilings that were covered with plaques and framed photographs. Most of his six hundred letter openers were also on display in the large attic. Auerbach called it "my egomania room."

Dorothy was coping well. She had her daughters, her new granddaughter, and a seventy-eight-pound boxer dog, Leroy.

"I'm a loner and a family girl," Dorothy said in 1969. "You just take the reins and that's it."

'I always had a guilty conscience about it," Auerbach says. "That's why I spoiled the girls so much."

He did. Both girls had television sets in their rooms. He bought Nancy a car while he was still coaching in 1965.

Longtime Celtic employee Tod Rosensweig went to Wilson High School with Randy Auerbach, and says, "If he'd had a son, I imagine an awful lot of people like me would have been hanging around his house. But somehow, having girls made sense for Red."

"I think everything would have been much more difficult on us if we'd been boys," admits Nancy.

In 1985 she told the *Boston Herald*: "Randy and I would bring these guys into the den, and there was Red, watching TV in his undershirt and drawers. He'd look up and say, 'Hi. Wanna salami sandwich?' . . . Dad never wanted to hear us swear. He'd say he lived with cussing all his life, so he didn't want to hear it at home. Then one day we were out in the car, just the two of us, and I really needed to talk with him. It was the first—and only—time I ever got aggravated over the Celtics, his traveling, that whole business. I guess he wasn't listening to what I was saying, because I blurted out, 'They're coming first and I need you now. Shit, they're more important than we are.' Wham. I felt a backhand across my lips. And I was twenty-six years old. I was so shocked. He had never hit me. He was the type who'd send you to your room if you were naughty at the table, then come up in five minutes to see if you were hungry."

He wanted his girls to be ladies. Women were women and men were men.

Arnold Auerbach was a little behind the curve in the area of gender equity. When there was news that a young woman had unofficially completed the Boston Marathon, Auerbach said, "It's hard to believe. I can't get these guys to run around the floor and a small broad goes out there and runs the Marathon. I don't know what the world is coming to."

His world was changing. There would be no more seventh games for a while. Russell was retiring and Auerbach was going to have to start over. It would be a little bit like taking over in Washington in 1946 or building the Celtics in 1950, except this time teams were lined up waiting to stick a fork in the Celtics. The NBA was bigger and better. There were more teams and more smart coaches and GMs. This wasn't going to be like the early days, when Auerbach assembled his Capitols from memory and military bases. And it wasn't going to be like 1956, when he used West Coast scouting, middle-America racial fears and an ice show commitment to land Bill Russell.

*Let's see how good you are now, Red.*

The first thing the general manager had to do was find a coach. Russell had been able to hold things together because he had a center named Russell. The new coach was not going to have Russell. The new coach was going to have to coach. The new coach was going to take his lumps.

Auerbach went to Cousy again. Cousy had finished at Boston

College and had received an offer to coach the Cincinnati Royals for $125,000.

"Red said, 'Forget about Cincinnati, I'll hold the job open for you,'" says Cousy. "He offered me about forty or fifty thousand dollars, and he knew I had the offer from Cincinnati, and I walked out of his office saying, 'What am I missing here?'"

Cousy said no thanks. Instead, the new coach would be Tommy Heinsohn, an odd choice, given his reputation as Auerbach's whipping boy.

When Russell coached, Auerbach was always around, but nobody worried about interference. Russell welcomed a degree of advice and knew he had the respect of his team because he was the best player. It was different for Heinsohn. He was young, had no coaching experience and many of the Celtic players hadn't been around when he played. Suddenly, Auerbach's presence was a little awkward. It didn't help when the ex-coach sat at the press table, one seat to the left of Heinsohn. Talk about having someone look over your shoulder.

"When I coached the team, Red would come to practice," remembers Heinsohn. "It was very difficult. Russell was Russell, but I was the first coach. It was tough for me to create my own identity, because Red had left such a big image, and at times there were problems. He liked to keep his relationship with the players, and they would go into his office and talk to him. I was like the father and he was like the grandfather. I'd say, 'Clean up your room, make your bed and rake up the leaves.' And they'd go in and say to Grandpa, 'Do I have to clean my room and rake the leaves and all that stuff?' and he'd say, 'I'll talk to your father.' Sometimes that caused problems."

Grooming a new coach was one thing; supplying him with talent was another altogether. Seeds for the second generation of Celtic success were planted by GM Auerbach in the spring of 1968 when he drafted Don Chaney out of the University of Houston. Chaney was a 6-5 guard, a nonshooter with long arms. He'd played in the shadow of Elvin Hayes. He'd played for a winner. He played great defense. His resume established him as a prototype Celtic.

One year after selecting Chaney, Auerbach again selected a guard with his first pick. This time he went for Jo Jo White, a flossy shooter from Kansas. White was a consensus All-American, clearly the second-best talent in the entire draft (behind UCLA's Lew Alcindor). Teams were reluctant to pick him because of what was believed to be a two-year military obligation. Auerbach used his pick on White, and suddenly Jo Jo was in the Marine Reserve program. Red's Washington connections were suspected in this matter, but Auerbach actually got a break from his baseball pal, Red Sox GM Dick O'Connell. (It was O'Connell who put Auerbach up for membership in Boston's Algonquin Club, allowing Auerbach to become the club's first Jewish member.) O'Connell had been through the military rigors with Sox players, and now he pulled some strings for his basketball blood brother. Small wonder Auerbach was despised by rival coaches and GMs.

At an Auerbach testimonial in September 1992, White said, "Red had a lot to do with the reason I was with the Celtics. I found out I had gotten in from an illegal standpoint, but I didn't find out until after I was in the service. I was fortunate I was drafted by the Celtics."

In the third round of the 1969 draft, Auerbach—on the recommendation of Nelson—picked Bradley forward Steve Kuberski. Kuberski was Nelson's Moline, Illinois, neighbor (the same Moline that's part of Tri-Cities). Assigned Celtic jersey No. 33, he was the last player to wear that number before Larry Bird.

Chaney, White and Kuberski were there when the bottom fell out in 1969–1970. With Hank Finkel playing center in place of Russell, and Heinsohn dealing with unhappy veterans, the Celtics failed to make the playoffs for the first time in twenty years. This was the season during which Auerbach pulled an unthinkable stunt: He got a ballplayer in exchange for somebody who'd been retired for six years. Cousy, in 1969–1970, was coaching the Cincinnati Royals. After a successful run as head coach at Boston College, the Cooz was struggling in the pro ranks and his team was sagging at the box office. Desperate to sell some tickets, management asked Cousy to come out of retirement. Cousy reluctantly agreed, but when the announcement was made, Auerbach came forth with his hand extended and said, "What about me?"

Cousy was forty-one years old. He hadn't played a game in seven seasons. But the Celtics owned his NBA rights—he was on Boston's "retired" list. Technically, he could not play for Cincinnati without Boston's permission. No sentimentality could be allowed to intrude here. Auerbach demanded compensation, and got 6-7 forward Bill Dinwiddie. Dinwiddie's Celtic career lasted only sixty-one games and he averaged only 4.9 points, but his name still symbolizes the competitive spirit of Arnold Auerbach: Yield nothing. Always look out for Number One. "How do we know he isn't better than ever at forty-one—like Gordie Howe and Pancho Gonzales?" reasoned the Redhead.

"I was upset at the time that Arnold was making this fuss,'" remembers Cousy. "It was purely a promotional gimmick, and I knew I wasn't going to have an impact, and I'm saying to myself, 'What the hell is he thinking? Thirteen years with this man? I go to Europe with him four times? My old coach and he's making a fuss? What is it with him?' so, I was upset at the time. Now, of course, hey, he did it just like he does everything else: He saw an opportunity there and he wasn't going to let it slip by."

Cousy and Auerbach have known one another for forty-five years and have never discussed this episode.

The Cooz was not the only old friend with whom Auerbach feuded in 1969. When the people at the Lenox raised his rent from $350 to $500 per month, Auerbach stormed out, and he took the weekly basketball luncheons with him. "After eighteen years here, you'd think I rate the decency of something more than a 'Dear John' letter," he said. He moved to the nearby Prudential apartments, where he has kept his Boston residence ever since.

During the 1969–1970 train-wreck season, knowing he was going to have a rare draft pick, Auerbach did something he had never been able to do: He scouted a lot of college games. The draft class of 1970 was loaded: Bob Lanier, Pete Maravich, Dan Issel, Charlie Scott, Calvin Murphy, Rick Mount, Tiny Archibald and Rudy Tomjanovich were in the talent pool. All were well-known high scorers. Auerbach would be in the running for all of them, but he had his eye on somebody else. There was a 6-8 redheaded center who could run, rebound and jump. Dave Cowens didn't get much ink, because his Florida State team was on NCAA probation. On the advice of scout Mal Graham, Auerbach went to a Florida State game. He stormed out at halftime, saying, "I've seen enough." He wanted to leave the impression that he wasn't impressed. In truth, he had seen the player he wanted, but didn't want to show his hand.

In many ways, Cowens was a white Russell. He didn't need the basketball to be effective. He could run all day. He could guard people taller than he was. He was a team player and a winner. And he marched to a different drummer.

The Celtics had the fourth pick in the 1970 draft. Cincinnati, coached by Cousy, was picking fifth.

Cousy says, "Right until the night before, they were saying they were gong to take Sam Lacey. They had no reason to lie—what could we do about it? We hated Lacey and loved Cowens. So we thought we were going to get Cowens. A year later, I played tennis with Ernie Barrett, the AD at Kansas State. He told me he never thought Lacey would be able to play in the NBA. He said that Auerbach had called him at eleven-thirty the night before the draft the year before and he'd told him that. I am convinced that's what changed Arnold's mind. Who the hell knows. Of course, it's not unlikely that Arnold would just lie to general managers for the sake of lying, to throw everything into confusion."

"Red knew who we were gonna pick," says Heinsohn. "He came back from a trip in the middle of the season and said, 'I know who we're gonna pick.' He saw Cowens play and left the game at halftime because he didn't want to show that he was interested. Cowens didn't have the good stats and his team was on probation."

Auerbach snatched Cowens in the first round. Later in the day, when few were listening, Boston's GM selected North Carolina's Charlie Scott, who already had committed to play for the upstart American Basketball Association. Red figured someday Scott might come back and it would be good to own his rights. Just in case.

Unlike Auerbach in 1970, Cowens was a true redhead. Asked what he thinks of when he hears the words "Red Auerbach," Cowens today says, "Frugal. Chinese food. Bad drivin'. Basketball man. Vince Lombardi . . . I was impressed when I first met him. I remember after they drafted me I came up here with my New York agent to work on a deal. I probably got screwed one way or another. If you're dealing with Red Auerbach and a lawyer from New York and a college senior, who's gonna get screwed in the deal? You don't have to be too smart to figure that one out."

Cowens impressed everybody when he arrived at training camp. He was a 6-8 Havlicek who never got tired.

"When we got him, we didn't know where we were gonna play him," says Heinsohn. "We thought we could play Garfield Smith at center and Dave at forward. Well, Garfield couldn't play and Dave got pissed off that he couldn't play center. We had to put Dave at center and improvise. I had to explain to Red what I was trying to do. He was committed to his number-six play. It was like working with your father in a business selling neckties. He'd say, 'Well, this is the way I used to sell neckties,' and then I'd have to say, 'Well, now we have marketing and there's discounting.' A whole new bunch of factors were coming into the game. This went on. He liked the type of situation where he could hark back to the way he used to do it. There was merit in all that. The toughest thing for me to do was to make the team I coached look like the one he coached."

*Globe* columnist Will McDonough, who started covering the Celtics in the 1960s, remembers, "When I started he treated me the same way he treated everybody else. The first time I asked a question, he said something like 'What kind of a question is that?' We became friendly when he got through coaching and I started playing tennis. He challenged me to play one day and I kicked his ass. He never beat me once in all the time we ever played. The reason we developed a friendship was that he didn't want to go to practice. He didn't want to look over Heinsohn's shoulder."

Cowens was the key to Heinsohn's new system. Giving away a lot of size, he consistently beat other NBA centers by making them conform to his game. He was quicker than the tall trees and he outran all of them. In one game his first year, Cowens scored 36 points in a head-to-chest matchup with Milwaukee second-year star Lew Alcindor.

Cotton Fitzsimmons remembers coming into the NBA as a head coach with the Phoenix Suns in 1970. His recollection of his introduction to Red Auerbach:

"Tommy Heinsohn was coaching the Celtics when I came in for the first time in 1970. They were having a board of governors meeting in Phoenix. We're playing the Celtics and we have a pretty good team—not as good as the Celtics overall, but we have a good ball club. Dick Van Arsdale, Clem Haskins, Neal Walk, Connie Hawkins and Paul Silas. It's not a great team, but a pretty good team. Boston had Chaney and Jo Jo and Cowens. We had a pretty good game going, and in the second half Chaney is pressuring Van Arsdale bringing the ball up, and all at once they just let the ball go and they start duking it out. The refs finally break up the fight. Heinsohn comes out and he gets kicked out.

"Here I'm a young coach. I'm standing in the background just observing all this. All at once I look up, and coming over the scorer's table is Arnold Auerbach. I have so much respect for him, like a dummy I just stand there and let him talk to the officials. He's talking this, he's talking that. He's going back and forth, doing this, doing that. And finally, after about ten minutes—and you've got to understand that the board of governors are all sitting in the front row watching all of this—I walk up there and get ready to say something. Immediately, Red turns to me and the officials and says, 'What's he doing up here?' That is Red Auerbach. And it's a true story. I had him in such high regard, I let him do it."

On February 24, 1971, in the middle of a charity free throw contest involving sportswriters prior to a Celtic-Laker game, Auerbach made an unscheduled appearance on the Garden floor. While the crowd roared its approval, he swished twenty-eight of thirty free throws, including twenty-three straight. He was fifty-three years old. A month later, he was voted the NBA's Silver Anniversary coach. Had there been any doubt? Bill Sharman sent him a telegram that read, "I DON'T KNOW WHY THEY'RE HOLDING THIS VOTING. IT CAN'T BE ANYBODY ELSE BUT YOU."

While Auerbach was rebuilding his franchise into a contender, he was learning what it was like to taste defeat at the hands of some of his pupils. All across the land, the Sons of Red Auerbach were getting coaching positions, and in Los Angeles, Sharman and assistant K. C. Jones were riding a wave of victory that has never been equaled in a single NBA season. The 1971–1972 Los Angeles Lakers, coached by Sharman, won thirty-three consecutive games and compiled a regular-season record of 69–13. Sharman brought another lasting gift to the NBA. While playing for the Celtics, he had made it a practice to go to the gym around noon on game days to practice his shooting. When he took over the Lakers, he brought this "shoot-around" to the NBA. The Lakers did it collectively on game days. Soon, every team was doing it. Now it is standard practice.

K. C. Jones went on to become head coach of the Washington Bullets, Celtics and Seattle SuperSonics. Every player on the 1961–1962 champion team later became a coach. Four members of Auerbach's 1964 starting lineup (Russell, K. C., Heinsohn and Sanders) eventually coached the Celtics. Sam Jones became an assistant coach with the Jazz. Don Nelson became a successful NBA head coach. Cousy coached the Royals/Kings. Ramsey coached the ABA Kentucky Colonels. Larry Siegfried coached the Rockets. Sanders coached Harvard before coming to the Celtics and Jim Loscutoff was at Boston State. Gene Conley ran a team in the Eastern League. By 1977, more than thirty Auerbach protégés were coaching in the pros or in college. Cowens and Chris Ford (the current coach) later became ex-Celtics who coached the Celtics. Don Chaney, Paul Westphal and Paul Silas were among those who took Auerbach's system and came back to Boston with a ball club intent on beating Red in his own building.

In 1972, when Sharman was scheduled to coach the NBA West All-Stars, he asked for film of Celtic All-Star representatives. The film was to be used for promotional purposes. Auerbach refused. Jeff Cohen, the Celts' assistant GM, could not believe it. "Red thought they were using it as a form of scouting. I couldn't believe he was serious. We hadn't done anything different since 1952. But he was serious about it." There was, of course, some ancient history at work. Auerbach was still mad at Sharman.

He could still be petty and he still sometimes played the bully. At the end of a close, nationally televised Boston Garden victory over the Knicks (there always seemed to be more emotion when the

Knicks were involved—probably he was still mad about the NIT's snub of George Washington in 1938), Auerbach fired longtime Garden timekeeper Tony Nota. The confrontation turned physical as Auerbach lunged at the mild-mannered Nota, a Garden employee since the earliest days of the old barn. In Auerbach's mind, Nota had been too fair with the clock at the end of the game. Auerbach wanted the hometown guy to shave seconds in favor of the hometown team. Everybody else does it, Auerbach reasoned. Nota told the press, "I don't make enough money to take the kind of abuse the Celtics give me."

Firing the timekeeper is an old NBA tradition, and Auerbach is in a large club of old-timey owners and general managers who've taken out their wrath on the little people. Nota was rehired a short time after the episode. No harm, no foul. Just let the clock run down if the Celtics are ahead with a few seconds to play.

John Thompson, another Auerbach protégé (he was Bill Russell's backup for two seasons—and for two rings), took on the Auerbach persona better than most. At Georgetown, Thompson adopted the distance and suspicion that Auerbach had: Take control, stay in control, put everybody else on the defensive.

Paul Westphal, coach of the 1993 Western Conference champion Phoenix Suns, says, "Red encouraged me a lot. I didn't play much my first year, and he would pull me aside and say maybe one thing that he had noticed that I did good or bad. He'd say, 'Hang in there. Your time's coming. Rookies never play here.' I learned a lot about him by hearing the other people talk about him. Havlicek, Sanders and Nelson would tell Red Auerbach stories, and it was like he was still coaching. He really influenced me a lot. I learned a lot about the NBA and what a coach should be."

Paul Silas's arrival in Boston was the harvest of another Auerbach scheme. In the autumn of 1972, ABA star guard Charlie Scott was set to sign with the Phoenix Suns. Not so fast. Phoenix and Scott had already come to terms on a multiyear contract, but they couldn't do anything without dealing with Auerbach. Because of Red's throwaway seventh-round pick in 1970, Boston owned the NBA rights to Scott. In exchange for the rights to Scott, Phoenix offered Silas, a strong rebounding forward. Done. Auerbach had done it again; he had gotten something for nothing. It was like getting Bill Dinwiddie for the rights to retire Bob Cousy. (In 1983, Auerbach got Quinn Buckner for the rights to the retired Dave Cowens.) The Silas acquisition was masterful. Auerbach had gotten a viable player for an invisible man.

"We wanted Scott," remembers Phoenix GM Jerry Colangelo. "We were not happy with the backcourt and thought Scott was a great talent. But we gave up a player, and it really hurt us. He helped Boston a great deal."

It hurt so much that Phoenix owner Dick Bloch attempted to purchase Silas from the Celtics. According to Auerbach, the Suns offered Boston's owners $150,000 to buy Silas back from Boston. When Boston said 'no, thanks,' Bloch raised his offer to $250,000. Steve Haymes, representing the Celtic ownership of the hour, wanted to take the money, but called Auerbach. Red said what he always said—you can't play dollar bills. The deal was rejected and Silas stayed with the Celtics, providing the kind of rebounding needed to complement the abilities of Messrs. Cowens, White and Havlicek.

Auerbach was on a roll. A man doing this well in Las Vegas is sometimes asked to leave the casino. This is the way it became for the Boston snake oil salesman. Auerbach made so many good deals, so many trades that swindled the other team, that opponents gradually stopped dealing with him. The fear still exists to this day. In 1994. Even though Auerbach is seventy-seven years old.

"People in the league are very wary," says Alan Cohen, a Celtic owner since 1983. "It exists. Look at the trades that he's made. There's great fear in dealing with Red. Just last year we were very close to a transaction and we got a call from the GM of the other team. He called back and said, 'My owner is absolutely against trading with Red.' And Red wasn't even involved."

"I was going to make a trade with him once," says Rod Thorn, NBA vice president in charge of operations and former GM of the Bulls. "Reggie Theus for Danny Ainge, I think it was. I always was a little skittish with him, because he made so many great deals. You're very skeptical about doing a deal with him, because you don't want to look bad. I can remember calling Bob Ferry about the trade possibility with the Celtics. He said, 'Don't do it, because the player you're going to trade to the Celtics will be even better for the Celtics than he is for you and you're going to look like an idiot when your player is playing in the finals.' "

By 1974, the Celtics were again ready to challenge for the NBA crown. Heinsohn was an innovative, assertive NBA coach and Auerbach had supplied Cowens, Silas, Chaney and White to go with the old nucleus of Havlicek and Nelson. Auerbach had assembled another mini-dynasty with Havlicek as the only Hall of Fame holdover from the golden days.

The Celtics won the championship in 1974, beating the Milwaukee Bucks in a seven-game final. Four of Boston's starters were Auerbach draft picks. The Celts were back. They'd won without Bill Russell. And Auerbach had won as a general manager. This cigar tasted pretty good.

Silas says, "The thing I remember most about Red is that after games he would come in and flip his ashes on you. Only after a win, though. He claimed he was never intending to hurt you. Coming to the Celtics was great for me. It afforded me the opportunity to show my skills to the world, because the Celtics were always on television. Becoming a rebounder for a championship ball club really aided my career, mostly because of Red.

"Prior to winning the championship, I didn't believe in all the Celtic pride and beliefs and little elf and all that kind of thing. That's my nature. I just thought they won because they had great teams, and I didn't believe in all the camaraderie and pride and all of that. But I became a believer. It was special. Guys that came from other organizations had to fall in line. Red was GM, but he was still around. When he came around, everything would like stop. I remember my first year at training camp, guys are saying, 'Red's coming down, Red's coming down.' Everybody had been kind of bullshitting in practice, but when they heard he was coming down, it was serious business. And I was saying to myself, 'Wait a minute, what is this? Who the hell is this guy?' But I found out it was the respect he brought. He started this whole thing, and without him, it just couldn't be."

Auerbach came back to the bench for a night in the fall of 1974.

Heinsohn was sick with the flu and assistant coach John Killilea was scouting on the West Coast as the Celtics prepared to play the Hawks in Atlanta. Auerbach left his D.C. home, caught a flight out of National Airport and arrived in Atlanta just after seven-thirty. He took a cab to the Omni and burst into the Celtic locker room minutes before the C's were about to take the floor. He gave a short pep talk, then sent the men out to battle. In the second half, Auerbach got into it with referee Richie Powers. This is the way Red remembers the exchange:

Auerbach: "That was a horseshit call!"

Powers: "That's enough out of you! Technical foul!"

Auerbach: "Richie, what for?"

Powers: "You cussed me out."

Auerbach: "Christ, haven't you been to the movies lately? Well, you've still got rabbit ears, I guess."

Powers: "Technical foul! You're out of here!"

Auerbach: "You're still an incompetent, pompous little son of a bitch! This is really outrageous!"

It was. Just like old times.

Auerbach also filled in for a home game against the Portland Trail Blazers. Before the Celtics took the floor, Killilea diagrammed ten Portland plays and gave a lengthy lecture on what it would take to beat the Blazers. When Killilea was through, Auerbach stood up and said, "That's all very nice. You want to win this game? Block out on the boards and play defense!"

They won.

Some things were not the same. Heinsohn, like Russell, had relaxed Auerbach's strict dress code. Red believes that champions always look like champions. Jackets. Ties. Socks. Haircuts. Shoeshines. Good grooming wasn't cool in the late sixties and seventies, and Auerbach sometimes had to bite his cigar when his rumpled players walked through an airport lobby.

"Times have changed, but I still prefer a necktie," he said at the time. "I still demand my players wear a suit or a sports jacket. I think it's terrible when I see players on other teams parade in public in T-shirts, leather jackets and dungarees."

The NBA started to become more marketing-conscious. The average salary in 1974 was up to $91,000, and only about six teams were making money. Intent on generating customers who might not be basketball junkies, owners promoted sideshows. Organ music bombarded the senses when action was taking place on the court. Scantily clad cheerleaders (Detroit's squad was the Classy Chassis) bounced around the perimeter of the court. Auerbach shook his head and scoffed. Couldn't the league sell good basketball? Even in the dark days of red ink, Auerbach never liked promotions that took eyes and minds off basketball.

Auerbach also bristled when he watched some of the trendy coaches of the seventies. Throughout the league, new-age coaches were standing for the full forty-eight minutes, calling out plays, delaying games with superfluous time-outs, wielding clipboards and overcoaching to the final seconds of blowout victories. Auerbach felt these coaches—Hubie Brown and Jack Ramsey, to name a couple—were calling attention to themselves.

Free of the bench, Auerbach was able to do more teaching. At the behest of CBS executive Clarence Cross, Auerbach starred in a series of NBA television shows entitled, "Red on Roundball." Auerbach taped twenty-eight segments of three and a half minutes each, and they are classics. Wearing his Celtic warm-up suit, appearing semihip with the long sideburns of the midseventies, Red looks at the camera and barks orders while the likes of "Pistol Pete" Maravich, Tiny Archibald, Rudy Tomjanovich and Doug Collins carry out his commands. Players were paid $300 to follow Red's instructions. Auerbach went deep into the well and coaxed Russell out of retirement for a couple of episodes on rebounding. "I told him to get his ass in uniform for two reasons," recalls Auerbach. "One, for the good of the game, and two, for me."

CBS ran the segments during halftimes of telecasts. These episodes would be dull if not for the depth of Auerbach's knowledge and the force of his personality. It is Red the Teacher at his best, and the instructions on rebounding, dribbling and the pick-and-roll remain true and timeless.

A *Sports Illustrated* review of "Red on Roundball": "He is a superior teacher with a booming voice and a latent talent for acting. And his knowledge of the game is unexcelled."

He wasn't afraid to flex his muscles. He'd earned his status as a local legend and he enjoyed playing the stately old coot who could get away with saying anything. He particularly liked poking fun at the Boston Bruin hockey team. The Bruins (owner of the Garden) were not kind to the Celtics in the early days, and Auerbach still tells stories about how Garden ticket sellers would challenge customers by saying "Basketball? Why would you want to buy tickets for pro basketball?" He enjoys mocking the Bruins' practice of hanging banners celebrating division titles. The Celtics would never hang a flag for anything other than a world championship.

"Red always hated the Bruins," admits Volk. "I think they deserved it. There was always uneven treatment between the Bruins and Celtics by the Garden. That's really why I came to work, because Red had determined that the Garden was sabotaging him. We needed to take the season-ticket portion of sales in-house."

The Bruins' president and general manager, Harry Sinden, knows the hatred. Sinden joined the Bruin organization in 1961. He took over as head coach in 1966, the year Auerbach left the bench. He has felt the cold chill of Auerbach for more than a quarter of a century.

Sinden: "He probably has some basis for the hatred, because at one time, I guess, I think some ownership here, prior to the present ownership, really didn't do anything for them—you know, made it tough for them. No question. But that hasn't been the case for the last fifteen, eighteen years. We've cooperated with practice times and board times. But he's never acknowledged that we exist.

"At the sixtieth anniversary of the Boston Garden, he got up at the party and knocked the Bruins. He said he hadn't turned on a hockey game since [Bobby] Orr left. He never could be bothered watching. Nobody west of Newton ever heard of the sport. Stuff like that. He's just totally unfriendly. I remember one time I went out and watched the Celtics practice. I used to love to play. I used to play with the ball boys. The Bruins would play Sunday nights. When I was coaching, we'd have a meeting at eleven in the morning. The ball boys and I would play a half-court game for an hour. I really got into it, and I really like the team. So they were practicing one day and I went out and sat, not on the bench, but awful close to the bench, and he threw me out of there. He didn't want me to watch.

"I loved basketball. I loved the athletes that play. Red had mocked our division pennants and all that stuff. I mean, the reason we have division pennants up there in the rafters is because we didn't win any championships. Sixteen championships apparently gives you the license to say whatever you want."

"Only Red can get away with certain things," admits Volk. "In 1974–1975, Cowens broke his foot in preseason and Red got Jim Ard off the waiver wire. Ard and Hank Finkel played center. Every two weeks or so, we'd have a tap-off luncheon at the Scotch 'n Sirloin. We'd have media people and fans, and Red would speak. On this particular day, most of the team is there, including Ard. A fan asked a question, something like, 'You're .500 after twenty games. Are you pleased with the job Jimmy Ard is doing in Dave Cowens's absence?' Red says, 'Look, you've got to understand one thing. If Jimmy Ard were any good, we wouldn't have been able to get him in the first place.' And he keeps on talking from there. Jimmy Ard is sitting right there in the front row and Red never skipped a beat. If Red thinks he's right, he absolutely doesn't care what anybody thinks."

This was the same Auerbach who was invited to address the Greater Boston Chamber of Commerce at a luncheon and started with, "Let me start by saying this is not quite an honor, my being here. I haven't had too much regard for the Chamber of Commerce over my years in Boston. When the Celtics won eleven championships in thirteen years in Boston, it was promptly ignored by their own town. The Bruins . . . a household word around greater Boston, but mention 'Bruins' fifty miles from the city and people immediately think of UCLA."

Here's Auerbach on the Boston Marathon: "What's their race prove? So you prove you can run a long time, so what? If you're running to keep in shape, run two miles maybe. Okay. But this! Twenty-six miles! You gotta be a nut. I used to stand there saying, 'What the hell is this?' All those bastards were running for nothing. They ran twenty-six miles for a cup of beef stew, a cupcake and a glass of milk. It didn't make sense. I followed them into the hotel once. I was curious to have a look, figuring they'd have some special chef behind the counter with a great pile of steaming stew. They were pouring it out of cans. It was goddammed canned beef stew! I couldn't believe it!"

Rod Thorn, now an NBA executive, knows what it feels like to be on the receiving end of an Auerbach dig. A 6-4 guard, Thorn came out of West Virginia in 1963 and Baltimore picked him with the second choice in the entire draft. Auerbach couldn't believe that the Bullets took Thorn over Bowling Green center Nate Thurmond.

"Red said, 'You can get two Rod Thorns for one Nate Thurmond.' " Thorn laughs. "And he was right."

Twenty-one years later, Thorn was GM of the Bulls and had the third pick in the land. He held his breath while Portland used the No. 2 pick on Sam Bowie. Then he took Michael Jordan. Whew. It must have been tempting to say that you could get two Sam Bowies for one Michael Jordan. Today, Thorn is the man who collects Auerbach's fines.

The Celtics did not repeat in 1975. They advanced to the conference finals, but were beaten in six games by the Washington Bullets. The Bullets were coached by K. C. Jones. Havlicek said that playing the Bullets was like looking in the mirror.

The reality of the ABA hit hard when Chaney left to take an offer from the St. Louis Spirits after the 1975 playoffs. It was a bitter defeat for Auerbach. Chaney was a prototype Celtic—a role player who put the team first. He played great defense and attacked the opposition. And now Auerbach could only view him as another greedy ballplayer, a puppet of changing times. In truth, Auerbach was the victim of the times. His Brooklyn-bred principles were being put to the test. He was being forced to adjust to a new marketplace filled with all the things he hated: agents, lawyers and long-term, no-cut contracts.

The departure of Chaney forced Auerbach to make a move for an experienced guard. In the summer of 1975, Boston and Phoenix made a startling swap, exchanging guards Charlie Scott and Paul Westphal. Fearful that the Celtics might lose Westphal without compensation (welcome to the wonderful world of arbitration), Auerbach dealt the promising guard for the talented Scott. Auerbach's last player-for-player swap had been made nine years earlier, when he'd traded Mel Counts for Bailey Howell.

Finally, Boston had gotten Scott, the player Auerbach drafted when he was ABA-bound—the player Boston used to acquire Paul Silas. Phoenix had decided that coach John MacLeod could not handle Scott.

"I went to ownership and said he [Scott] has got to go," remembers Colangelo. "And the only deal that was out there was Boston. We said it had to be Westphal because we were going for a young player with potential. And it was the kind of a deal that was a good deal for both teams. Charlie helped Boston and Westphal became a five-time All-Star."

Scott vaulted the Celtics back into the finals, Boston's second appearance in three years.

In the spring of 1976, Gerald Ford was in the White House, John Travolta was on the big screen, the Tall Ships were sailing toward Boston Harbor and America was sprucing up for its two hundredth birthday party when Boston made it to the finals for the fourteenth time in twenty years. Colangelo's "Sunderellas" (42–40 during the regular season) provided Boston's opposition in the 1976 finals.

"I have a very vivid recollection about that," Colangelo said when his Suns returned to the NBA finals in 1993. "I remember standing on the Boston Garden floor in 1976. I was on one corner of the floor being interviewed on CBS. Red was being interviewed at the other end by CBS. I was looking at the championship banners overhead and thinking, 'You know. I've only been here seven years and I'm in the finals. We're gonna be back here a lot.' And here it is seventeen years later. It took seventeen years to get back. And we had very good teams. That's how hard it is."

Boston won the first two at home, dropped a pair out West, then came back to the Garden for what might have been the greatest playoff game in the history of the NBA Finals. The Celtics won it, 128–126, in triple overtime. This game is remembered for its three overtimes, a collection of freeze-frame clutch shots and the sight of referee Richie Powers rolling on the court with a disgruntled Boston fan at the end of the second overtime. It's a tad ironic that Powers was attacked by a Celtic partisan, because there's evidence that a noncall by Powers might have delivered the game (and the series) to Boston. Late in the game, Silas called for a time-out that the Celtics did not have; Boston had already used its allotment of time-outs. When this infraction is called, the other team shoots a free throw. One foul shot would have sent the Suns back home with a 3–2 series lead. But no; Powers didn't make the call. Boston won Game 5, then wrapped it up a day later in Phoenix.

Al Bianchi, a Celtic-hater from way back, was an assistant coach with the Suns in 1976. Phoenix didn't win the championship, but Bianchi had a championship ring made for himself. The ring has a turquoise stone, and the engraved inscription reads, "Fuck You, Richie Powers."

Bianchi: "I had it made in Philadelphia. I told the guy what to put in there. I think Richie knows about it. At some point, they tried to call a time-out that they didn't have. There were three guys doing it, and he looked at them and walked away. Granted, we hated Boston when I was in Syracuse. We'd fight with them all the time. We'd walk into Boston Garden and the Irish cops would say, 'You boys gonna behave yourselves tonight?' And we had crazy people in Syracuse. After you get your ass beat so many times you start saying, 'Hey, I hate these fuckin' guys.' Red was Red. At the time, yeah, we'd say, 'That fuck, lightin' up the cigar.' You know. I hated Boston because they beat our ass every time. The seventh game would come and something crazy would happen—I call it the fucking ghost. Somebody would come in and tap the referee on the shoulder. It was crazy, but they did it.

"I don't think there's anybody out there now that really hates Red. It was at the time. I don't' think you hate people the rest of your life. After it was all done and you know Red, that's just Red. And the stuff he's done, no matter what you want to say about the guy—and there's people who love him and people who hate him— the fact is, he got it done. He got it done, goddammit."

The Celtics' lucky thirteenth was wildly cheered by the folks back home. This was a time when fans flocked to the Garden to see this new team built by Auerbach. Pro basketball was gaining in popularity and the Celts finally were embraced by Boston sports fans. A City Hall Plaza celebration honored the 1976 team. There were no such public displays of affection during the Russell years, and this has always fortified the argument that Boston is a racist sports town appreciative only of white (Cowens, Havlicek, Nelson) stars. Forced busing was coming to Boston, and race was on everybody's mind.

Auerbach, as always, was smoking his cigar, thinking about the next game, the next championship. He already had done it all. He'd won as a coach, moved into management, watched his team decompose, then built it from ashes and won again.

When he went home for the summer, it was to his new condominium at 4200 Massachusetts Avenue in Washington. The spacious house on Legation Street was sold in 1974. The girls were grown and on their own, and Red and Dorothy no longer needed the space and upkeep of a big house. Leroy, the boxer dog, was given away and Dorothy tried to find room for hundreds of plaques, trophies and letter openers.

"I didn't want to leave that house," says Dorothy. "But he never liked houses, because he grew up in New York with the apartments. I figured that he had let me have the two houses that I had found, so it was his turn."

After winning the 1976 championship, the proud Celtics went into free-fall. This dry spell was unexpected. It threatened to tarnish the Auerbach legacy and it quite nearly closed the book on his days in Boston. It was so bad that he actually almost went to work for the ever-hated New York Knicks.

# 7

# PLOTTING IN THE DARKNESS

*Red would have made a great spy. They would have shot him before he'd have given any secrets away. You could have tortured him and stuffed bamboo shoots under his fingernails and everything else. The only thing he ever really talked about was his dislike for John Y. Brown. And that was after the fact. He kept it to himself at the time.*

FRANK DEFORD, *writer*

IN THE 1950s AND 1960s, NBA FANS WANTED TO "BREAK UP THE Celtics." This was no problem in the years that followed the 1976 championship. The proud Boston Celtics dissolved under the watchful eye of Arnold "Red" Auerbach.

Nelson retired after the 1976 flag was won. This was expected. But the Celtics also lost the invaluable Silas when Auerbach was beaten in a game of contract hardball.

There was little warning for the hard times that lay in store for Auerbach and the Celtics. Larry O'Brien had succeeded Walter Kennedy as NBA commissioner. O'Brien grew up in Springfield, Massachusetts, where basketball was invented, and was a former aide to President Kennedy. He also served as Democratic national chairman, and it was his sixth-floor Watergate office that was burglarized by Richard Nixon's White House plumbers on June 17, 1972.

The NBA had eighteen teams when O'Brien took over, but before the start of the 1976–1977 season, the new commissioner consummated the merger of the NBA and ABA. ABA franchises in

Denver, New Jersey, Indiana and San Antonio paid $3.2 million apiece to join the National Basketball Association. The merger made the NBA a twenty-two-franchise league and ended the player bidding wars that had caused salaries to escalate. Professional basketball had grand plans to market itself as the sport of the eighties. Auerbach, meanwhile, was most happy to see the final days of the ABA.

"The league war destroyed the concept of good organization," he said when the merger was announced. "It brought salaries out of whack, long-term contracts, no-cut contracts, agents, lawyers and disloyalty into basketball. I'm hoping there'll be a settlement of ideals. The whole schmeer is law-oriented. Agents and lawyers start to guide these fellas to play toward the dollar, to go for certain statistics."

In the wake of the merger, star players changed teams. Moses Malone, Maurice Lucas, Artis Gilmore, Tiny Archibald and Gail Goodrich all found new homes. The Celtics were more than bystanders in this flurry. By the time the new season started, the defending champions had lost the self-sacrificing, team-oriented Silas and gained selfish scorer Sidney Wicks. The Celtics were gravely wounded by both the subtraction and the addition. These were uncharacteristic moves, and in these times of uncertainty, Auerbach was the man responsible for steering his team off the true, tested path.

This was an instance where Auerbach was stubborn and inflexible and it hurt the Celtics. After the 1976 finals, Havlicek and Silas were without contracts, and they informed Auerbach that they would not be in camp unless they had new pacts. Both were coming off four-year deals and had seen their compensation shrink while mediocre ballplayers made far more money in the signing frenzy set off by the merger. Havlicek and Silas were in good bargaining positions. They had honored their prior contracts, eschewing the nasty renegotiation ploy. They had said they would wait their turn. But when their turn came, Auerbach was stingy. It had something to do with the fact that both were represented by Larry Fleisher.

"Red has a personal vendetta against Fleisher, and we're caught in the middle," said Silas.

Indeed, it has been suggested that Auerbach had particular problems with Fleisher because the two men were too much alike. Fleisher was smart, connected and fearless. He was not easily intimidated. Yes, he was just like Auerbach, but his interests were in conflict with those of the Boston boss.

Auerbach acted illogically. He resisted change, let personalities get in the way, and it cost him. Havlicek and Silas did not have contracts, which gave them every reason to skip camp, yet the GM said, "John and Paul have violated their contract and will be fined accordingly. I don't care about negotiations, they should have reported."

Eventually, Havlicek came to terms, but Silas was dealt because Auerbach wouldn't give him a three-year $1 million contract. The proposed pact would have vaulted Silas ahead of Havlicek and Cowens, and Auerbach operated the Celtics on a strict merit-wage scale. The oldest, best players made the most money. Always. It was a star system, and it worked. It also meant that Auerbach really only had to negotiate with one player, the team superstar. Everybody else had to take less. This system had worked for decades, but in the mid-1970s, it was cracking. The power and authority of every GM was being threatened by outside forces of lawyers and free agency. Auerbach was one of the last to let go, and it cost him. Fearing that the Celtics might lose Silas without compensation (this type of contract complexity eventually led to the elevation of lawyer Jan Volk as full-time club legal counsel), Auerbach traded the rebounding forward in a three-way deal that brought former UCLA star Wicks to Boston.

"I wasn't bitter at all," says Silas. "I felt I deserved what I wanted and he said no and that was it. There wasn't any animosity about anything."

Years later, Auerbach told Silas, "If I had to do it over again, I probably would have done it differently. But at that time, I had to do what I had to do."

Eight games into the title-defense season, Cowens, one of the best players in all of basketball, a selfless Celtic winner in the finest tradition of Russell and Havlicek, walked into Auerbach's office and asked for a leave of absence. The star center said he was burned out. Everybody knew he missed playing alongside Silas. Cowens had begged Auerbach to give Silas the money. When the young redhead walked in and said he had to stop playing for a while, Auerbach did not debate with his star center. He gave him a break. This is the kind of front-office flexibility that kept Auerbach in the hearts of his ballplayers long after he stopped coaching.

"When I went in and told him I wasn't gong to play, he was a pretty reasonable fellow," remembers Cowens. "He absolutely was. He said, 'Hey, I can understand what you're talking about.' He figured, 'What am I gonna do—tell the guy he's got to stay?' That doesn't work. Right away he can access a situation. He has that kind of mentality."

"People sometimes think you're a hard guy, but you're not," Auerbach says. "When people's personal things are at stake, you've got to be very sympathetic and understanding and put yourself in their spot."

Randy Auerbach could have prepared Cowens for the surprising treatment. She remembers how her father reacted when she quit Boston University after only two days:

"I called him at the office and told him I was going to quit college and he said, 'You didn't start yet. Why don't you come down to the office and we'll talk about it.' So I went there and explained my reason and told him I'd take courses at night. And he said, 'Okay. As long as you're going to do *something*. I'm not going to force you.' He was great about it. I had no resistance at all. He trusted that I'd find my way."

When Cowens made up his mind to come back, Auerbach did something he says he did only once: He gave a reporter a scoop. Dave O'Hara, a longtime reporter for the Associated Press (O'Hara retired in 1992 after fifty years at the AP), was in trouble with his boss. "Dave needed some help, so I called him up and I gave him three hours to beat everyone else with the story," Auerbach says.

"It's true," admits O'Hara, one of the most popular newspapermen ever to work the Boston sports beat. "I had called him to tell him I was in trouble. Red felt he owed me one. He called me into his office and he was sitting in there with Cowens. He turned to Cowens and said, 'Dave, tell Dave what you just told me.' Then he asked me how much time I needed to get the story out. He would have held it for three hours, but I only needed ten or fifteen minutes."

Cowens came back to play, but the defending champs were not the same without Silas. Scott broke his wrist. The C's won forty-four regular-season games, then were eliminated by the Philadelphia 76ers in a second-round, seven-game series. Sixer coach Gene Shue said of the Celts, "There is no mystique."

Mystique, no. Mistakes, yes. The free-fall was about to continue. *Boston Globe* writer John Powers was assigned to cover the Celtics for the 1977–1978 season. Powers replaced Bob Ryan, a Boston College grad who reinvented basketball beat coverage during the early seventies. Ryan had strong opinions and had called Auerbach a liar in a column defending Silas's contract dispute. When Powers introduced himself to Auerbach, the godfather said, "Did you go to Boston College?"

"No," said Powers. "Harvard."

"That's worse," scoffed Auerbach.

On June 9, 1977, Auerbach drafted Cedric Maxwell from the University of North Carolina at Charlotte. He'd seen this odd player at the NIT finals at Madison Square Garden a year and a half earlier. Ernie Grunfeld, the player Auerbach wanted, was taken by the Bucks just before Boston picked. Max got the usual Boston introduction—dinner at a Chinese restaurant in Brookline and all the shoes, socks and T-shirts he could stuff into his suitcase. The Celtics were about to be reconstructed by Auerbach for a third time, and Maxwell was the first block in the foundation for the next Celtic powerhouse.

In October of 1977, Auerbach abruptly canceled a deal that would have brought forward J. J. Johnson from Houston. The transaction had allegedly been completed during the 1977 draft (Boston gave Houston its No. 2 pick), but the Celts had never seen Johnson's contract, and when Auerbach got a look at it in October, he called off the trade. Johnson had a two-year, no-cut, $75,000-per-year contract, and Auerbach thought it was outrageous.

"I feel sorry for a situation where you can't believe what people tell you," said Auerbach.

In the history of the Celtic franchise, this was a rather minor transgression, but it points out the archaic manner in which Auerbach still was doing business as late as 1977. He had a verbal deal, done over the phone, with Houston GM Ray Patterson. He never asked for, nor saw, paperwork on Johnson's contract. He gave his word and got the other guy's word. That was it. In Auerbach's day, nobody crossed anybody, because if word got out, you'd be done in the NBA.

"So much had changed," he said a few years later. "The game was what was fun, but they won't let you enjoy it anymore. They all bring lawyers to the league meetings, and then we have to have debates. We used to come by ourselves and talk basketball. But the last time, I even had to make an impassioned plea: 'Can't we talk about the game?' And the way these faces look at me—like I'm out to get 'em."

The rules had changed. Contracts were more complicated. Lawyers had to be involved. And there was modern technology (a telecopier in 1977, a fax today) that would allow you to swap papers before agreeing on a deal. In a new pro sports world of litigation, Auerbach the dinosaur still was trading in old-fashioned handshakes.

The 1977–1978 season, Havlicek's final campaign, was disastrous. The Celts were a dysfunctional unit. They had seven players who had played in an NBA All-Star Game. They had Wicks and Curtis Rowe, a pair of UCLA superstars who did not want to pay the price that's required to be great professional players. They went 32–50. The *Globe*'s Ryan, no stranger to exaggeration, wrote, "Auerbach abandoned his own principals . . . Resigning [Wicks] this season was an error which made Neville Chamberlain's 1938 analysis of Hitler's intentions look like a minor misjudgment . . . And please don't ask me what that John Johnson business was all about. Could more Auerbach arrogance have cost the Celtics the services of another potentially useful ballplayer?"

Longtime employee Rosensweig remembers one moment from this troubled era: "It was a game in Washington. Havlicek got thrown out of the game and we lost. After the game, we were hanging around and the crowd was thinning out and some drunk fan came up and said, 'Hey, Red, we really kicked your ass, and we're gonna kill you in the playoffs.' Red just flicked some ashes on the guy and said, 'Fuck off.' It just amazed me that Red Auerbach would say that to somebody."

It was a bad time. Silas was gone, Cowens' head was no longer in the game, White was unhappy with his contract. After a Boston Garden loss to the San Antonio Spurs, a horrible event that inspired a hail of boos from the Garden fandom, Auerbach addressed the team and called them quitters. He singled out Havlicek and the sensitive White. It was an unusually poor read by the veteran GM. He'd built a career by knowing which guys could take the gibes, and now he was hooting on one of his most vulnerable people. White quit for a couple of days, then came back, but it was never the same for him.

In December, the organization hosted its annual family Christmas party at the Garden. Havlicek and White were the only players who bothered to attend. There were unopened gifts strewn around the premises and it was pathetic to see the great Red Auerbach, head down, silently gathering them up. His ballplayers were part of his family no more. This was a new generation of selfishness. There was no pride, no mystique, just a collection of athletes with an attitude. It was Curtis Rowe who said, "Hey, man, there's no Ws and Ls on the paycheck."

Owner Irv Levin contributed to the malaise. He ordered Auerbach to coach a couple of practices. He made the GM take road trips, which Auerbach had vowed not to do anymore. The meddlesome owner asked Auerbach to return to the bench full-time, but Red said no. Levin took star players to dinner at Boston's Algonquin Club and let them air their gripes. The way Heinsohn saw it, Auerbach was in trouble, too. The owner didn't want to pay Auerbach's high salary plus the salary of a coach. Heinsohn believes there was a wild plan at work that would have landed former football New York Giant player Dick Lynch in Boston as coach and general manager of the Celtics. Heinsohn claims that when he asked Auerbach about this, Auerbach said, "I'm not getting along too well with these guys. I think I might leave. I've got an offer from Philadelphia."

Auerbach fired Heinsohn, and still says, "That was the hardest thing I ever did." Heinsohn was replaced by Sanders, his frontcourt

partner from the golden days. Boston feted Havlicek on the final
day of the 1978 season. The lowlight of the afternoon came when
Levin got hooted out of the old building as he presented Havlicek
with gifts at midcourt. Auerbach's handprints were all over the place.
He'd been the one to suggest that the owner make the presentation.
Auerbach knew that the owner would take a beating from the fans.
Celtic loyalists would never embrace a leisure-suited gentleman who
was attempting to leech off fame earned by Auerbach, Walter Brown
and generations of star Celtic players. After Levin was booed, Auerbach was cheered by the Garden legions.

In this quagmire of controversy and chaos, Auerbach pulled off
one of the shrewdest moves in basketball history. Boston's pitiful
finish gave the Celtics the sixth pick in the 1978 draft. In addition,
on December 27, 1977, Auerbach had traded Scott to the Lakers
for Don Chaney, Kermit Washington and LA's first-round pick in
1978. With two first-round selections, the Celtics could afford to
gamble a little. Celtic assistant coach John Killilea was touting an
Indiana State junior forward named Larry Joe Bird. Back from a
scouting mission, Killilea reported, "I think I found another Rick
Barry."

In the spring of 1978, Bird had completed his junior season at
Indiana State in Terre Haute. Because he had entered Indiana University in the fall of 1974 (Bird dropped out after twenty-four days),
he was eligible for the 1978 draft even though he still had one more
year of college eligibility. His original freshman class was graduating,
and that made him a candidate for selection when the NBA captains
convened on June 9, 1978. Prior to 1976, a team lost its rights to a
junior eligible if the player went back to school and played in an
NCAA game. Bird was on record as saying he'd play his senior year,
no matter what. Volk called the league office, and a young NBA
lawyer named David Stern said that the Celtics could draft a junior
eligible and would retain his rights until the next year's draft. Drafting Bird would be a gamble, because if a team picked him and failed
to sign him, Bird could reenter the pool in the spring of 1979. Nobody wanted to waste a first-round pick on a kid who could go back
in the draft a year later. Nobody except Red Auerbach.

"It didn't take much thinking," says Sanders. "We had two first-round draft choices, and Red knew that we could gamble one choice and still pick up another player that would be eligible right away. it was kind of an easy decision. There was no question that Bird was going to be a player, but there is no one that scouted him that thought he was going to be *that* kind of player. Red didn't think that either. Red thought that he could play ball, but great is another question. No one could foresee that."

And so on draft day, 1978, the Portland Trail Blazers selected Mychal Thompson, Kansas City took Phil Ford, Indiana picked Rick Robey, New York took Micheal Ray Richardson and Golden State selected Purvis Short. Why did all five pass on Bird? Portland needed a center to replace Bill Walton, and Thompson was a dominating college center at Minnesota. Portland GM Stu Inman had talked with Bird, but worried about Bird's beer-drinking reputation. Kansas City had been burned by David Thompson and Marvin Webster—first-rounders who never signed after they were drafted. Players did not want to play for the Kings. That's why there is no longer a team in Kansas City. The Pacers needed a player to replace Dan Roundfield, a free agent who'd signed with the Atlanta Hawks. When the Knicks had their chance, mighty Gulf & Western smothered GM Eddie Donovan's attempt to draft Bird. The Warriors, like everybody else, needed help immediately.

Thompson, Ford, Robey, Richardson and Short. None of these five players made a lasting impression in the NBA. Might Bird not have sold some tickets and won some games for the Indiana Pacers? And what if Larry Bird had played in New York? Willis Reed, coach of the Knicks in 1978, believes Auerbach really wanted Micheal Ray Richardson. Auerbach says it's rubbish. Auerbach says he never saw Richardson play college ball.

And so, at 12:14 EST on June 9, 1978, Auerbach smiled as he heard the announcement that Golden State had selected Purvis Short. He picked up the phone in the Celtic war room in Boston and called assistant GM Volk, who was at the draft in New York. The message was loud and clear: Take Larry Bird.

Auerbach had had some luck with junior eligibles (Frank Ramsey,

for instance), and he believed that the magnetic pull of the Boston
Celtics would induce Bird to forgo his right to take a second turn
in the draft.

"We're not stupid or ridiculous," Auerbach said on draft day. "If
there were any chance of him playing this year we couldn't get near
him. How many times do you get to sit at this table and get the
player with the No. 1 ability in the country?"

Years later, he said, "It was a gamble, but I had to do it. I've
always had the philosophy that you take the best kid that's available
in the draft. Worry later. I felt that the reputation of the Celtics was
such that every kid would want to play here."

With his second first-round pick, the No. 8 pick in the draft, the
Celtics took Freeman Williams, a shooting guard from Portland
State.

The annual NBA meetings were held in San Diego in the summer of 1978, and during those meetings Levin and Buffalo Brave
owner John Y. Brown concocted a bizarre trade. Levin and partner
Harold Lipton swapped franchises with Brown and Harry Mangurian. The sale transfer included player transactions. Boston gained
Tiny Archibald, Marvin Barnes and Billy Knight and lost Kermit
Washington, Kevin Kunnert and Williams. The pick used on Williams had enabled Auerbach to gamble on Bird. It was okay to wait
a year for Bird, because the Celts would still have something to show
for their first-round windfall. Now they had nothing to show for the
1978 draft, not for at least a year.

There had been rumors about a player trade, but prior to the
swap Auerbach said, "If there's a trade, any kind of a trade, I'll be
really aggravated. I don't care if it is part of this ownership deal,
apart from it or whatever. If there's a trade and I'm not consulted,
it will put me in a very difficult position. I'll have to ask myself, 'Can
I work for this new guy?' . . . I don't know Brown much at all, but
he's a flamboyant guy and that worries me. That stuff won't go in
Boston."

Auerbach and Volk were involved in the oddball swap without
knowing of their involvement.

Volk: "Red and I went down to Washington to meet with agents
representing Washington and Kunnert, both of whom were being

traded in this transaction. Red and I were not aware that this was happening at all. We went down and finalized the deal. The next morning, the franchise swap was announced. Apparently, the franchise swap was contingent on these contracts having been negotiated, finalized and signed. We were like the Japanese ambassador who was meeting with Roosevelt while Pearl Harbor was being bombed. We were absolutely in the dark."

Mangurian was Auerbach's kind of owner. He had a lot of money, knew nothing about basketball and stayed out of the way. John Y. Brown, meanwhile, was everything Auerbach detested. A future governor of Kentucky, a former owner of Kentucky Fried Chicken, Brown knew little about basketball, but he wanted to make moves. Brown was forty-four years old and had run the champion Kentucky Colonels in the American Basketball Association. He had folded the Colonels rather than pay the merger fee. Auerbach hated the ABA and all that the league had done to make life hard for NBA general managers. Brown was engaged to Phyllis George (a former Miss America who became Miss Information of CBS Sports), and he wanted to impress his fiancée, enjoy his toy and plot his political career. Auerbach was simply an employee, a functionary.

This is what Brown said about Auerbach when he acquired the Celtics: "Red is sixty-one years old. He's got a lot of good years to give and he's part of that Celtic tradition, but I don't think we're going to kid each other about hoping to put our arms around each other and get along . . . If he wants total control—which pretty much he's been given—I've got to ask myself, 'Why should I have a team?' "

Bob Cousy wrote, "For thirty-eight years, the essential duties of a Celtic owner have been to kiss Red's ring, sign the checks and be ready to accept the championship trophy."

John Y. wasn't gong to kiss anybody's ring.

Mangurian remembers, "John's a good friend of mine, but Red was unhappy because John was such an active participant. John had called all the shots when he was in the ABA with the Kentucky Colonels. When he bought the Buffalo team, before I came in, he was like Trader [Frank] Lane from baseball. So he stepped into the Celtics and, of course, Red wasn't informed by Levin as to what was happening, so it was almost like no matter who came in then, there were going to be some problems."

For the first time in his professional life, Auerbach was not in control of player transactions. In the winter of 1949–1950, Tri-Cities owner Ben Kerner had dealt John Mahnken to Boston for Gene Englund. The deal told Auerbach that it was time to get out of Tri-Cities. In 1978, a wholesale swap had been made without any consultation from Auerbach. And now there was a new, insufferable owner. Maybe it was time to move on again.

Auerbach's first (and almost final) duty for John Y. Brown was to introduce Brown and Mangurian to the Boston media at a July 11, 1978, press conference at the Garden.

Auerbach's contract was up August 1, 1978, and he went to New York to discuss a job with the Knicks. In a two-hour meeting at the Waldorf-Astoria, Knick CEO Sonny Werblin and Knick president Mike Burke offered Auerbach a four-year contract that would have made him at that time the highest-paid executive in league history.

Mangurian remembers, "Sonny Werblin had a contract for Red to sign, and for a few weeks he didn't know what he was going to do."

Dorothy said, "I told him if he was finished in Boston, I wanted him to come straight home to Washington. I didn't want him stopping in New York for a few years first. He was not a Knick, or anything else. He was a Celtic."

Boston folklore holds that Auerbach stayed in the Hub because of a series of pleas from cabdrivers who took him to and from Logan Airport when he was exploring his opportunity in New York. The pilot on the Eastern Shuttle aircraft reportedly ducked his head out of the cabin and begged Auerbach to stay in Boston. Havlicek called to say that if Auerbach went to New York, he would not allow the Celtics to retire his number. Jo Jo called. Cowens. Ramsey. There was speculation in newspapers in Hong Kong, in London and in the *International Herald Tribune:* "Auerbach leaving Celtics?"

"It's all so goddamn flattering," said Auerbach.

The anonymous cabbies may or may not have swayed Auerbach, but in the end, Red followed his heart back to 150 Causeway Street in Boston.

"I can't flatter myself and say it was going to crumble when I left," he told the *Globe*'s Powers. "But I'd be lying if I said it didn't enter my mind. And New York—working down there and living down there; that was what I was trying to envision. And I had a lot of misgivings. I thought about what it would be like to come back up to play the Celtics, to watch the ball game and look up at all the flags. And I didn't know what my reaction would be."

With the promise that he would be included in all personnel decisions, Auerbach stayed. He signed a three-year contract. "I just wanted to make sure we understood each other," he said. "We agreed our relationship is a partnership. He doesn't do anything without me."

They never clicked. The owner had little respect for the legend-in-residence. After a loss at the Garden, Cousy was present in the Celtic offices when Auerbach walked into one of John Y.'s postgame parties. "Well, well, well, here comes our great leader now," said Brown. "Say something intelligent, great leader."

Cousy wanted to fight. Auerbach let it go. He was meek in the shadow of this owner.

Weird events followed. Sanders was dismissed after only fourteen games and Cowens was named player-coach.

"I never really thought about who made that decision," says Sanders. "It was Red's job to convey to me that the organization had decided to make a coaching change. Red is a professional, so you wouldn't get him to say that it was somebody else's decision. We never discussed it after that. I never thought there was anything to discuss. I certainly didn't get a long enough run to effectively do anything, with Cowens being out and Jo Jo coming off a heel injury and a whole new group of players. But I'm a realist, and you have to deal with the bottom line."

Jo Jo White was traded to Golden State for a draft pick. This never would have happened in the old days. Loyal Celtics finished their careers in Boston; they were not dealt for draft picks. By mid-February the Celtics had made six trades and signed three free agents. Then came the coup de grace. On February 10, 1979, the Celtics played the Knicks at Madison Square Garden. After the game, Brown and fiancée Phyllis George had dinner at P. J. Clarke's with Sonny Werblin. Two days later, the Celtics shipped three first-round draft picks to the New York Knicks for Bob McAdoo. It is widely believed that Brown made this deal to impress George, who liked the way McAdoo played. Auerbach later said that Brown had made "one great big deal that could have destroyed the team, without even consulting me. He did ruin it. One guy can ruin it so fast your head will swim. John Y. Brown had an ego, like most people who are successful in what they do. He always felt he knew a lot about everything."

The McAdoo deal pushed Auerbach over the edge. He says he gave Brown an ultimatum: One of us must go. Within two months, Mangurian bought out John Y. Brown (for $4 million) and the nine-month Celtic siege was over.

"Nine months," says Auerbach. "But it was long enough to nearly destroy what we'd spent thirty years putting together."

Jeff Cohen, who served as assistant GM during the John Y. reign, says, "That was the worst experience I had with the Celtics, and it was the only time that Red seriously thought about leaving. We had gone through some guys that had literally been crooks. Trans-National. They were awful. We didn't have a dime to spend. These guys were taking every dime coming in to keep their other stuff going. The greatest thing Red did was keep the team together during that period, because the team could have folded.

"In comes John Y., who had money. Every conversation with John Y. was awful. The papers were beating him to death and he was the most PR-conscious man who ever lived. He and Red disagreed on everything. When he made the McAdoo trade, he asked me to set up a conference call, and I told him I didn't know how to do it. I was just making that up, of course, and I expected him to fire me right then."

After Brown sold his shares of the Celtics to Mangurian, he announced his candidacy for governor of Kentucky. Auerbach warned Kentucky citizens: "Watch out for that guy. He'll trade the Kentucky Derby for the Indianapolis 500."

In hindsight, it's interesting to note that Auerbach was careful not to rip John Y. Brown while Brown still owned the team. Auerbach is nothing if not pragmatic. He bit his tongue. He had survived other hideous owners and he would survive the playtime of John Y. Brown. Celtic owners come and go; Auerbach is forever.

"Everybody knew there was a mounting strain between us, but publicly I wouldn't knock him," says Auerbach. "I'd say something like, 'Well, he has his own ideas, and who knows, who's to say someone else's ideas might not be good ones, too? Let's give it a chance.' Ass-kissing? I'm sure it might have looked that way. God knows there were plenty of times I bit my tongue and said nothing. But it wasn't ass-kissing at all. I simply didn't want the players—or the fans, for that matter—to feel there was dissension in the front office. Because that stuff spreads down. Once players start believing there's insecurity in the front office they start playing for themselves and to hell with the team."

"The way it works up there," John Y. Brown said in the book *Selling of the Green,* "is that whatever goes right Red did. Whatever goes wrong, the owner did."

Auerbach's public neutrality toward Brown didn't fool his players. They quit. On March 9, 1979, the Detroit Pistons beat Boston, 160–117. M. L. Carr, who scored 20 for the Pistons that night but would soon become a Celtic, later admitted, "It looked to me like the guys were laying down on the job. They had just come off a West Coast trip. They were trying to send a message, I think . . . Guys really weren't playing. There just wasn't any effort at all. Our guys loved it. It was almost like going into the Garden and ripping down one of the flags."

Auerbach was torn up. His second, pocket dynasty had crumbled. The Celtics finished 29–53, last in the Atlantic Division. It was the second-worst record in the franchise history (the 1949–1950 team went 22–46 the year before Auerbach came on board). These Celtics were worse than the Celtics that were regularly throttled by Auerbach's Washington Capitols in the late 1940s.

Red Auerbach was sixty-two years old. Few believed that he could rebuild his team for a third time. The NBA game was changing. There were a lot more teams and high-tech coaching methods and sophisticated scouting. Perhaps the game had finally passed him by.

Not yet, said Red. He had an unsigned Bird in the hand. He had

a plan. And he had an owner who would let him run the show again.
No strings. Mangurian and Auerbach were good for one another.
Auerbach again was free to make all the basketball decisions. Mangurian wrote the checks, sat next to Auerbach at the games and
listened. Red liked owners who listened.

Mangurian says, "I loved it. I enjoyed Red Auerbach completely, and he and I became very good friends. He had a lot of
basic instincts about the game regarding players and how long
they could play and how big men should play and how they got
better. I thoroughly enjoyed Red, both my wife and I. Red had
some problems with John, but never with me. When John decided
to be governor and I took over, Red kind of settled everything.
Red was the team. He was very careful about money, and I think
that came from the years when he was coach and GM and there
was just one girl working in the office. He never really appreciated
spending a lot of money. As he saw things evolve, he'd kind of
shake his head."

Auerbach still bristles at the mention of John Y. Brown. Frank
Ramsey, an Auerbach favorite and now a successful businessman in
Kentucky, may be the only person who is friendly with both men.
"Red still says to me, 'How's your ex-governor doing, that expletive.' "

Bird was scheduled to be the savior, but he did not come cheap.
As ever, negotiations stalled because Auerbach hated the agent. The
Celtics had an entire year to sign Bird, but knew they couldn't do
anything official until Bird completed his senior season of competition. As Indiana State ripped off a 33–0 record (garnering more wins
than the 1978–1979 Celtics), Boston basketball fans wondered if the
C's might have trouble coming to terms with the quiet, blond forward.

To protect his investment (imagine the embarrassment if Bird
went back into the draft and the Celts got nothing for a No. 6 pick),
Auerbach made a couple of trips to the heartland of America. He
blundered his first meetings with Bird, because he tried to convince
him that it would be in his best interest to sign with Boston immediately after the Sycamores were bounced from the NCAA tournament. Red reasoned that Bird could be the first player in history

to play in the NCAA tournament and the NBA in the same season. Bird was insulted. Auerbach's implication was that Indiana State would be knocked out of the NCAA tournament very early. That wasn't Bird's plan.

Bird was right. He carried the Sycamores to the NCAA championship final—a summit meeting with a Michigan State team led by Magic Johnson, Greg Kelser and Jay Vincent. The game was televised by NBC and drew a rating of 24.1, a record that is expected to stand forever. Magic's Spartans were too strong for Bird's Sycamores, but the NBA was the big winner. A new generation of American sports fans came over to basketball during this Final Four, and all of them were waiting for Bird and Magic to take their game to the National Basketball Association.

When the tournament was over, a group of Terre Haute businessmen formed a committee to help Bird find an agent. Incredibly, the committee selected Boston-based agent Bob Woolf, a gladhanding carnival man who'd been dumped by scores of clients. Woolf was in a big-time slump when he landed Bird. He'd been Havlicek's agent when the Celtic great almost went to the ABA in 1970. Auerbach hated Woolf.

"They couldn't stand each other," Bird admitted a few months before Woolf died in November 1993. "Red was always a little pissed that I stayed with Woolf. It was funny as hell. If Red had one gripe with me, it was that I stayed with Bob Woolf. It was just a known fact: They didn't like each other."

Auerbach didn't hide his enthusiasm for Bird. He labeled the Sycamore "a big Cousy" after watching Bird score 49 against Wichita State. "Cousy was more spectacular, but that kid can do it all . . . He's the best passing big man I ever saw."

Woolf, no doubt, saved the clippings and used them as negotiation ammunition. The Celtics had to sign Bird before the draft on June 15 or lose him altogether.

A clear-thinking Cowens retired from coaching on the final night of the 1978–1979 season. Auerbach again needed a coach, and for the first time in history, he went outside the family. Since leaving the bench, Auerbach had entrusted his team to Bill Russell, Tom

Heinsohn, Tom Sanders and Dave Cowens. But there was a new
decade on deck. It was time to go outside.

Indiana's Bobby Knight was Auerbach's first choice. They met at
a Hall of Fame dinner, and when Knight turned down the position
he recommended Georgia coach Hugh Durham. Durham came to
Boston, met with Auerbach and called back two days later to say he
was going to stay at Georgia. Meanwhile, Bill Fitch had applied for
the position. Fitch, a tough ex-Marine, was coach and general manager of the Cleveland Cavaliers when he got his introduction to
Auerbach during a State Department tour of Japan. They were with
one another constantly for long periods of time, and Fitch impressed
Auerbach with his work ethic and his knowledge of the NBA. They'd
shop together as Auerbach searched for jade, ivory and more letter
openers, Fitch going along for the ride and impressing Auerbach
with his Irish humor.

Fitch says, "You have to know how to handle Red. I joined him
on a State Department tour a few years ago. None of the players
would room with him because he snored so loudly. So I got stuck.
We talked until he looked drowsy, then I walked over and kissed
him on the forehead and said, 'Good night, darling!' It worked fine.
Red didn't sleep all night."

Fitch was the right coach for the Celtics' changing situation. He
is an indefatigable worker who knows the NBA. Like Auerbach, he's
a terrific teacher, very good with young, impressionable players. Unlike Auerbach, he is a paranoid who demands total control of an
entire organization. This would create problems down the road, but
as the Celtics looked ahead to 1979–1980, Bill Fitch was the man
Auerbach needed. Fitch could do the job on the Celtic bench while
the NBA finally became major league, and while Auerbach rebuilt
the Celtics for a third and final time.

Fitch came on board during the two-month, highly acrimonious
Bird negotiations. The Celtics had invited Bird to town and
wanted to show him around the city, but Woolf insisted on total
control and ordered a "hands-off" policy. There would be no contact between the club and the ballplayer unless the agent was involved. This infuriated Auerbach. When they finally got to the
table, Woolf started by asking for $6 million for six years. The

agent set a target date of May 15. Auerbach countered with $3 million for six years. After a fourth meeting, on April 24, Auerbach broke off the talks, saying, "As as result of our meeting today, I consider the negotiations to be at an end at this time, We see no reason to continue." There was talk about trading Bird's draft rights. Woolf said Auerbach had made threats and that these might be taken to the players association.

"It was a mess," remembers Bird. "I couldn't believe it. I knew Red hated Bob Woolf from the word go, but Jesus Christ, with me standing there. I felt a little sorry for Mr. Woolf. Red was cursing him in front of all these people, embarrassing him. And I was with Woolf, and I felt about two inches tall. And here poor old Dinah [Bird's girlfriend, now his wife] was there and she didn't know what the hell was going on. I said, 'Let's get out of here. I'm going home. You guys can handle it.' "

Auerbach wouldn't budge. It went against his principles. Enabling everyone to save face, Mangurian stepped in and settled the dispute. Bird agreed to a five-year deal, averaging $650,000 per year, much closer to Auerbach's starting figure than Woolf's.

"Red never really appreciated spending a lot of money," Mangurian recalls with a laugh.

"It was ridiculous," says Auerbach. "The agent's telling me that if Larry Bird goes back to school, he wants the Celtics to pay the tuition. The guy's going to make eight hundred thousand dollars and now he wants me to pay fifteen hundred. Then he said that if Larry makes the All-Rookie team he should get another ten thousand dollars. I said, 'Do I look stupid? We're paying this guy the highest amount that any guy ever got coming out of college, and he won't make the All-Rookie team?' "

It went down to the wire. On June 8, 1979, one day shy of the one-year anniversary of the day Boston drafted him, Larry Bird signed a contract that made him the highest-paid rookie in the history of professional sports: five years, $3.25 million. In 1993, the year after Bird retired, the top four NBA draft picks signed for a combined $196 million. The Golden State Warriors locked up Michigan's Chris Webber for fifteen years, committing $74.4 million to a young man who hadn't yet played a day in the NBA.

With Bird, Fitch and Mangurian in place, there was one more deal to be done in the final dark days of the 1970s.

Bob McAdoo was still a Celtic. He'd played twenty games in the spring of 1979, averaging 20.6 points per game and shooting 50 percent from the floor. The smooth former scoring champ and MVP was twenty-eight years old and should have been at the height of his game, but he was difficult to motivate and cared only about his scoring average. Auerbach wanted no part of Bob McAdoo.

Auerbach wanted a 6-6 free agent swingman named Michael Leon Carr. A little-known college player from tiny Guilford in North Carolina, Carr first tried out with the Celtics in the fall of 1974. The C's that year were defending world champs, and Auerbach told M. L. there was no room at the end of the bench. But Auerbach liked him. He asked the kid to play in Israel for a year. Carr went to Israel for one season, then signed with the St. Louis Spirits of the ABA. Auerbach was angry with Carr's agent, Norm Blass, but by 1979, the Boston GM had cooled off enough to go after M. L. again. Carr led the NBA in steals in 1978–1979 and was the kind of old-timey player who had won championships for Auerbach. He didn't mind coming off the bench, he had great heart and he wasn't afraid to do whatever it took to win. M. L. would fight. He'd bend the rules a little. He was quick with a joke or with a match for your smoke, but he'd steal your lunch money if it would give him an edge over you.

On July 24, 1979, the Celtics announced that they'd signed Carr. The Pistons were entitled to compensation, and if the teams could not reach an agreement it would be settled by Commissioner Larry O'Brien. Auerbach went on record stating that the one player the Pistons could not get was McAdoo. Red knew when he had a pigeon, and Dick Vitale, coach of the Pistons, was a perfect fowl. Proposals went back and forth for several weeks. In late August, the Pistons buckled and proposed sending Carr and two 1980 first-round picks (their own and Washington's, which they had received for Kevin Porter) in exchange for McAdoo.

Done. In a little more than six weeks, Red Auerbach had made the moves necessary to win three more championships and assemble the greatest frontcourt in the history of basketball. It would take more dealing in the spring of 1980 to complete the maneuver, but his 1979 strategy gave him the pieces he needed to pull off the heist of heists. Bob McAdoo, obtained without the consent of Auerbach, eventually yielded M. L. Carr, Robert Parish and Kevin McHale. Auerbach took a shiny sports car with a bad engine and swapped it for a Mercedes and two Rolls-Royces. Thank you, Dick Vitale. And thank you, John Y. Brown.

# 8

# BIRD

———

*Red won't go nowhere. He is the Celtics, the special in-*
*gredient, and that's why he'll never say to hell with us. He'll*
*be part of the Celtics till he dies.*

LARRY BIRD

THE 1979–1980 SEASON MARKED THE BEGINNING OF RED AUER-
bach's fourth decade with the Boston Celtics. His teams had delivered
at least two world championships in each of the previous three decades. As the Celtics looked toward the eighties, there was no certainty
that the franchise would be able to deliver another pair of flags.

This was Auerbach's last chance to be Red. He was still current.
He could look at the college crop and beat everybody to the best
player. He could take advantage of franchises that were inept, disorganized or prone to panic. He could roll the dice and go for a
player who nobody else would take a chance on. He was like a party
boss, gearing up for one final convention in which he would wrestle
the nomination the old-fashioned way. He would call in favors, pay
off delegation leaders, deadlock the convention, then get the support
he needed behind closed doors . . . in a smoke-filled room.

In many ways these were the best days of Auerbach's life. He was
a national star, appearing in Miller Lite advertisements with Billy
Martin, John Madden, Brooks Robinson, Bubba Smith and other
famous members of the American Jockocracy. (In one ad, Auerbach's players are forced to say "please" in order to get their brew.)
He was on top, nationally respected, feared and revered. Life was

an endless sequence of plaid sport coats, cigars, late-night Chinese food and adulation. He was constantly reminded how great he was. There were honorary degrees and citations. He was lecturing at Harvard. He was honored during halftime at a New England Patriot football game.

Pulitzer Prize–winning journalist David Halberstam came to Boston during the 1979–1980 season while researching *The Breaks of the Game*. This is how he described Auerbach in the book: "For twenty-five years he had been smarter and shrewder, and more innovative and finally more concerned than anybody else in the league. He was brash, and crafty, and bullying, a man of equal parts character and con, high integrity and low craftiness. His ego was immense, but he used it as a force; he at once stepped on it and stumbled over it, but was never impaled by it."

The NBA in 1979 was teetering on the edge of financial instability, and the Celtics were still battling for their slice of the New England sports pie. Russell's dynasty teams only twice averaged as many as ten thousand spectators per game at the Boston Garden. The year the Celtics won their eighth straight championship, Auerbach's last season on the bench, the Celtics drew 7,941 per home game. There was a Boston basketball boom in the mid-1970s, and the Dave Cowens-led Celtics drew better than any of the Russell teams, but the Celtics had to win to draw fans, and when the winning stopped in the late seventies, fans stopped coming to the Garden. The Red Sox, Bruins and Patriots were hot. The Celtics were not.

Tod Rosensweig came to work in the Celtics' ticket sales department in 1974 (Auerbach flew to New York to have lunch with the young man—the son of Red's college pal Stanley Rosensweig—and offer him a job). He remembers the lean years of John Y. Brown and Bob McAdoo, and says, "Steve Riley and myself would go over to Fenway Park and put fliers on the windshields of the cars. We'd do anything to make a sale. We had a television ad on WBZ in which we told people they could buy a five-dollar ticket for three dollars. People would call by the thousands. Mark down anything and people will buy it. Red always helped us sell tickets. He'd stroll into the office and come in and sell for you."

Celtic GM Jan Volk on the impact of Auerbach with Celtic ticket buyers: "We were very service-oriented toward our season-ticket holders. We'd have a party for them. Red would come down to the ticket office all the time. He was great. He made a lot of sales. He'd come by and talk to the people and ask, 'Where are you looking?' And he'd say, 'Those are great seats. There's a great view from there.' And he'd point to a picture on the wall and say, 'Walter Brown used to sit right there.' "

In 1978–1979, Boston's attendance fell to 10,193 per game. Leaguewide, the NBA was struggling. There were too many teams and not enough talent. More was less. Drug scandals and highly publicized million-dollar salaries discouraged fans. TV stayed away from the league. The NBA championship finals were not broadcast nationally on prime-time television. The college game was gaining in popularity; the Monday night, prime-time NCAA championship final in 1979 between Michigan State and Indiana State (Magic vs. Bird) had established a rating record that will never be broken. The NFL, the official sport of bettors worldwide, still was fat with "Monday Night Football," huge television contracts and healthy rivalries between the Redskins and Cowboys, Vikings and Bears, Rams and 49ers. The NFL's Super Bowl was recognized as an unofficial American holiday. Baseball, dormant in the early seventies, was enjoying a surge in popularity thanks to the thrilling 1975 (Red Sox-Reds) World Series, three World Series in New York and a return to real grass and old-fashioned ballparks.

The NBA relied on gate receipts for two-thirds of its revenue, and in the late seventies and early eighties that entire sum was going toward players' salaries. In a seven-year period, NBA salaries had gone up 700 percent. In 1980–1981, seventeen of twenty-three NBA teams lost money. The once-mighty Knicks were playing to only 60 percent capacity in Madison Square Garden. Auerbach, parroting an old Walter Brown line, blamed television, saying, "When revenue increases because local and cable television are up, naturally attendance is down. That's the way it's been with the Knicks, because every one of their games is on television."

Television was a problem. During the years of the Celtic dynasty, ABC's executive producer of sports, Roone Arledge, had fallen in love with NBA basketball, and the network struck a five-year deal in 1965—when the NBA was a nine-team league. ABC followed the five-year deal with a four-year, $22 million contract, but Arledge was concerned about the number of teams in the league. By 1973 there were seventeen teams in the NBA, and the product was diluted. In 1973, several NBA owners, including LA's Jack Kent Cooke, wanted to switch to.CBS. Auerbach didn't think the switch was a good idea. He though ABC was doing a good job and he warned, "You don't really think a man like Roone Arledge is going to take this lying down, do you?"

The switch was made. Later, Arledge sued the NBA and won. He also improved ABC's Saturday afternoon football package to a point where it wiped out the NBA in head-to-head competition. When the NBA switched to Sundays on CBS, Roone's wrath again took a toll. ABC invented "Superstars," better remembered as "TrashSports." NBA ratings on CBS plummeted, and soon the college game was getting better ratings than the NBA. In 1978 the NBA got a four-year, $74 million contract from CBS, but there were a lot of hard feelings on both sides.

The NBA at the turn of the decade was 70 percent black, and 80 percent of the starters were black. The 1980–1981 Knicks did not have any white players, an NBA first. In 1982, twenty-one of twenty-four All-Stars were black. Was the league in danger of becoming too black?

Auerbach admitted at the time, "What happens is that people say, 'You'll draw better if you have white players, or if you don't have too many black players.' Well, that's common sense. I've had black coaches come over to me and say, 'Jeez, I gotta get a white player.' I mean, they're not stupid. It's much more difficult for a white guy to say, 'Hey, I gotta get some white players,' but when a black guy says it, then you know there's a problem."

Image was a problem. Highly publicized long-term, no-cut contracts added to the perception that the players were not trying. The cliché was that you could see everything you needed to in the last two minutes of any NBA game. A couple of drug suspensions further dented the league's image. The NBA was third-rate, owners were losing money and the Celtics were caught in the net with everybody else. Sam Schulman, owner of the Seattle SuperSonics, said, "I see the future as dismal. I think we've had unnecessary setbacks due to lack of leadership within the commissioner's office, as well as with the owners ourselves. If we don't limit our payroll to a plateau where teams can exist, we may all have to fold up."

None of this bothered Auerbach. He'd worked under worse conditions. He'd been to Sheboygan with the Tri-Cities Blackhawks. He'd been in fights with fans in Cincinnati, St. Louis and Syracuse. He'd seen the NBA as Big-Time Wrestling. He'd worked for Walter Brown when Brown couldn't make payroll. He'd worked for carpet-bagging owners who didn't pay phone bills. He'd witnessed his team's total collapse in 1969–1970 and again in 1978–1979. In the fall of 1979, he had much to look forward to. He had a nonmeddling owner in Mangurian—a man cut from the cloth of the great Walter Brown. He had a new, state-of-the-sport coach in Fitch. He had the maneuverability that existed in the presalary cap NBA. He had M. L. Carr, plus a couple of first-round draft picks for 1980. And he had a hotshot rookie who looked as if he might be able to help immediately: Larry Bird.

Bird was rare in every way. In an age of television, marketing and overexposure, he was a highly touted player who came into a sport and proved to be even *better* than his advance billing. Bird was a question mark to some because of his foot speed, his doughy body and his lack of leaping ability. Fans and scouts wondered if he'd be able to get his shot off in the NBA; they remembered Rick Mount, Jack "the Shot" Foley and Bevo Francis as white, 40-points-per-game college scorers who couldn't get open in the NBA. Everybody could see that Bird was a deft passer, but few realized he could also rebound and defend. It seemed obvious that he didn't have the kind of body that would hold up well under the rigors of NBA play.

Late in the summer of 1979, Bird arrived at dumpy Camp Milbrook for the annual Celtic workouts for free agents and rookies. He was accompanied by his wife-to-be Dinah Mattingly, and was greeted in typical Auerbachian fashion: "What's *she* doing here?" Bird wasn't intimidated by the GM's rude greeting. Boston's new star was intent on playing his game and displaying his skills. Auerbach was delighted with what he saw. It had been worth waiting a year to get this player. It had been worth the $650,000 a year he'd received. Bird became an instant All-Star, averaging 21 points and 10 rebounds in his rookie year. Everything else came together. Tiny Archibald, fully recovered from an Achilles tendon injury, made the Celtics run again. Cedric Maxwell blossomed as an offensive force under the basket. Carr was everything he was advertised to be, and Fitch, after nine years of Cleveland purgatory, showed the league what he could do when he had talent on his side. Overnight, Boston was back as an NBA centerfold team. The 1979–1980 Celtics won sixty-one games, an improvement of thirty-two victories over the year before, at that time the greatest single-season improvement in league history. Home attendance improved 46 percent, including thirty sell-outs in thirty-nine Garden games. It was the start of a sellout streak that carried well into the 1990s, years after Bird retired in the summer of 1992.

This cigar was sweet for the Boston boss. He'd done it again, he'd rebuilt his team from ashes for a third time. The national sports media returned to the scene of the dynasty of the 1950s and 1960s. Gloating just a little, Auerbach told the *New York Times,* "I think I'm the same person I've always been—a little older, a little mellower. But I don't live in the past."

This was a pivotal season for the entire league. On the left coast, rookie Magic Johnson, the teen angel with the 150-watt smile, was leading the Lakers to the world championship while Bird brought the Celtics back. Meanwhile, the NBA adopted the popular but gimmicky three-point shot. The trey was a direct ripoff from the ABA and, typically, Auerbach fought it to the end.

"I had a lot of dealing with Red when I was general manager in Chicago," says Red Thorn, now NBA vice president. "Red always had strong opinions, and he'll tell you what he thinks even if it's not popular. I always felt Red was like E. F. Hutton. When Red spoke, people listened. He had tremendous respect from people because of his success and the way he went about his business. He was against the three-point shot for the longest time. He was the last to get on board, and then when it finally got enough votes, Boston was the first team to make a three-point shot [Chris Ford] and they used it to their advantage. He always was very astute at understanding the rules and how you could use them to your advantage."

The 1979–1980 Celtics swept Houston in the first round of the playoffs, then lost to the Philadelphia 76ers in five games. They needed just a little more talent to push them over the top, and Auerbach had the cards in his hand, waiting for draft day. Thanks to Mr. Vitale, he was holding Detroit's first two picks. The Pistons in 1979–1980 finished 16–66, which meant that their top pick was one of the top two selections in the county. Boston also had Detroit's other pick, No. 13 in the land.

Hoop historians know that the Celtics swapped their two picks to Golden State for its first-round pick (No. 3) plus an underachieving center named Robert Parish. Golden State used the No. 1 pick to select Purdue's Joe Barry Carroll, then used the other pick to take Mississippi State's Rickey Brown. With the pick acquired from Golden State, Boston took the player it wanted in the first place: Minnesota's Kevin McHale. In essence, the Celtics got Parish, one of the top ten centers of all time, for nothing.

It almost didn't happen. Auerbach's genius has always been augmented by good fortune, and again in this deal there was a measure of luck. In 1950, he had wanted Andy Phillip or Max Zaslofsky instead of Cousy. Thirty years later, he wanted Ralph Sampson, who would eventually become one of the biggest bowsers in the history of the NBA.

In the spring of 1980, Auerbach went to the office of Commissioner Larry O'Brien for the annual coin flip to determine the top two picks. Utah made the call and called heads. The coin came up tails. Auerbach had the No. 1. Four days after the coin flip, he was on his way to Virginia. He was hoping to use his No. 1 pick on the player he believed was the best in all the land: Virginia's 7-4 freshman Ralph Sampson. In the spring of 1980, Sampson was projected as the next Russell, Chamberlain and Abdul-Jabbar rolled into one. He was a smart, coordinated player from a good program, and he was 7-4. Auerbach loves height. He was never too busy to speak with any youngster tall enough to peek over the transom of the gymnasium door.

Auerbach tried to talk Sampson into leaving college. Sampson was a freshman, but this would be Boston's only chance to get him and Auerbach didn't want to pass up the opportunity. These were the

days of what the NBA termed "hardship players." Any college un-
derclassman who could prove to the league that he had an emergency need to trade in his eligibility for cash could turn pro. The
Celtics never had a "hardship" player. For years, Auerbach had
railed against the hardship rule. Suddenly, it was okay. Always, Red's
ethics were those of convenience. The only time he ever had a conflict of interest was when something conflicted with his own interests.

Sampson was eighteen years old. Playing in the Atlantic Coast
Conference, he was in Auerbach's territory, and Red saw him five
times during his freshman season. On Tuesday, April 8, Auerbach
visited Sampson's home in Harrisonburg, Virginia, in an attempt to
talk Sampson into leaving college for the NBA, for the Celtics. It
was a very transparent effort.

"Too many of them come out who are not ready for the NBA,"
said Auerbach. "They are influenced by unscrupulous agents. They
would be better off staying in school . . . If I didn't believe I was a
hundred percent right, I wouldn't pursue this kid. I see no reason
for him not to turn pro now. What would be the purpose of attend-
ing Virginia one more year, or, at best, two? He would never be
able to make up, in money, experience, later what he would be
passing up right now."

*The Globe*'s Will McDonough went to Virginia with Auerbach.
McDonough remembers the drive home: "We're in the car and it's
raining and he's such a terrible driver and he's smoking the cigar
and the windows are all fogged up. He was pissed. He kept saying,
'We won't get this guy. He didn't show up. I could tell by the mother
and father that this deal is dead.' I'm just hoping he stays awake.
He keeps asking me how far to Washington and it's still like a hundred miles.

"Finally, we got there and we go up from the garage and he's
banging on the door for Dot to let us in; I was staying over at his
place. It was after midnight. Finally, Dot answers the door and she's
in curlers and she's got a cigarette going and he says, 'We're hungry,
make us a couple of sandwiches.' And she says, 'Make 'em yourself.'
It was terrific. It was like being in a TV sitcom. She came into the
kitchen and sat with me and had a cigarette while I had a beer

and Red was over at the counter making the sandwiches, waiting on us. 'How do you want the salami, with mustard on it? Pickles?' And this was at about one in the morning."

Auerbach did not get his man. Sampson elected to stay in school.

Auerbach's response was typical. He said, "Maybe Ralph Sampson and his parents will come to their senses and realize they are being hookwinked by a few glad-handers. I just don't know how they can sleep at night. It's ridiculous. If he were an intellectual genius and was planning on being a surgeon, you could see him wanting to go to school for four, five, six years. Then, I'd buy it. But he has said all along that he would only stay in school for two years. In this situation, how could anyone advise him to stay in school? They are taking away earning potential he'll never get back. And they're forgetting that if he gets hit by a car, it's the end of the line."

In 1980, Dave Gavitt was director of the new Big East Conference. As a coach at Providence, Gavitt had taken the Friars to the Final Four. Gavitt is the man who came on board to take over the Celtics in 1990, and he says, "They kid Red about him trying to get this guy out of school and that guy out of school, but I know of three or four occasions where he talked players into *staying* in school. These were not my players, but when I was in the Big East, a coach would say 'So-and-so is going to leave,' and I'd call Red and he'd tell the player, 'Here's the situation.' He was very fair with them."

Ralph Sampson stayed at Virginia for all four years. He graduated with his class, signed with the Houston Rockets and flopped after a couple of fair seasons in the NBA. He made millions of dollars, and was still being paid long after he stopped playing.

Sampson's staying in school worked out very well for the Celtics. Auerbach lucked out again. Instead of Sampson, he got Parish and McHale.

With Sampson out of the mix, the top three players in the 1980 draft were Carroll, McHale, and Louisville guard Darrell Griffith. There has been much revisionist history regarding the splashdowns of these top three picks. Auerbach has stated that if Boston had not dealt the first pick, he would have opted for Carroll. In the spring of 1980, he made it clear that he liked Griffith very much. And we know how he felt about Sampson. This would make McHale possibly

No. 4 on Auerbach's 1980 depth chart. And yet Red always gets credit for the great Parish/McHale swindle. Reputation has its privileges.

Fitch has always tried to claim that he put the deal together. He'd had his eye on Golden State's Parish for several seasons. He saw the top three in this order: McHale, Griffith, Carroll. Most of America saw Carroll as No. 1, and this is what Fitch counted on when the Celtics talked with Golden State.

Auerbach shakes his head at the view of Fitch-as-mastermind and says, "He was involved to the point of only I would tell him. If you're a general manager, you want your coach to like what you're doing, because he's going to play them. So he agreed with me and we went ahead and did it."

In any event, the trade was made hours before the draft. Boston had Parish and Golden State's No. 3 pick. The Warriors had the first and thirteenth selections. Golden State went ahead and did what everybody knew it would do, selecting Carroll. The Jazz picked next and Fitch held his breath as Frank Layden took Griffith. That was it: McHale belonged to Boston. The player the Celtics most wanted, the player Fitch most wanted, was coming to the Celtics, and Robert Parish was the throw-in. It was a stunning deal for the Boston Celtics.

Smiling, trying not to smirk, Fitch and Auerbach met the press in the early hours after the draft. "What can I tell you?" Fitch said. "Red has done it again."

"The first time I met Red was after the draft," remembers McHale. "I came up from New York. I had no idea that Red had even been to a game at the University of Minnesota, but as soon as I met him, the first thing he said was, 'You got good ice cream up there at your place. Good ice cream.' I had no idea what he was talking about. He said, 'At that Williams Arena. I went up there and watched you and had some great ice cream.' I said, 'How did I do that night?' He said, 'I don't remember. I just remember that they had good ice cream.' That was the first time I met Red. I said to myself, 'Boy, this guy is a piece of work.' "

In March 1981, as the Celtics were fast-breaking toward flag No. 14, sixty-four-year-old Auerbach signed a ten-year contract that was termed a lifetime deal. The agreement called for Auerbach to remain as Celtic GM and president for as long as he lived. He had a window to slide into a consultant position at any time. Mangurian said, "I set it up so he's going to be here as long as he wants to. There won't be any of this business of another contract after this ends."

Auerbach said, "These have been a very happy two years, not only because of the number of games we won, but also because of the way it's being done. We're being appreciated by other teams and fans throughout the country for having risen from the depths of two years ago. I have gotten as much satisfaction from these past two years as I have from some of our championships."

There was another championship to celebrate in May 1981. With a front line of Bird, Parish, Cedric Maxwell, McHale, Carr and Rick Robey, the Celtics beat the Bulls in the first round of the playoffs, rebounded from a 3–1 deficit in the conference finals against Philadelphia to win in seven, then beat the Houston Rockets rather routinely in an anticlimactic, six-game final.

The seven-game conference final with the 76ers had been one for the ages, reminiscent of past showdowns with the Hawks, Lakers and the Chamberlain-led 76ers of the sixties. When the Sixers had gone ahead, three games to one, Auerbach dug into his files for an old-time pep talk, telling Bird and company: "Until they beat you one more time, they can't win a championship. They got to beat you. And if you don't let 'em beat you one more time, you win it."

The Celtics won the title in Houston, and it was on the victory stand there that Bird pulled a cigar from Auerbach's mouth. The Hoosier hotshot put the cigar in his own mouth; puffed and formed his crooked fingers in a "V for victory" sign as Auerbach grinned. Frank O'Brien of *The Globe* snapped a now-famous photograph of the moment, and Bird wrote in his autobiography, "To this day, I love that picture more than any other photo I have."

The Celtics were back. Auerbach was back. Again.

A month later, with flag No. 14 hanging from the rafters, Auerbach went back to the well. At the request of owner Mangurian, he used his second-round draft pick on BYU's Danny Ainge, a Mormon superstar who was at that very moment playing infield for the Toronto Blue Jays at Comiskey Park in Chicago. Thirty players were taken ahead of Ainge, because Ainge had an ironclad, no-basketball agreement in his contract with the baseball team. This didn't faze Auerbach. He'd talked Bill Sharman and Gene Conley into basketball. He took John Havlicek when the Cleveland Browns wanted to make him a wide receiver. K. C. Jones was almost a defensive back with the Los Angeles Rams. Ainge was a big league baseball player. No problem.

Ainge was having trouble hitting the curveball, and when he learned he'd been drafted by the Boston Celtics, the NBA seemed very appealing. He attempted to leave the Blue Jays and there was a bitter court battle over his services. Once again, Auerbach's ethics-of-convenience dominated his thinking. He always preached that one should honor a contract, but he lobbied hard to get Ainge out of his contract with the Toronto baseball team. The Celtics had to pay damages to get Ainge out of his contractual obligation.

When Ainge finally arrived, Auerbach squired him around Boston.

Ainge: "I had just been in town a couple days and he was showing me around and we didn't know each other very well. We were driving around and I told him that I had to pick up my wife, Michelle, at the airport. And he said very delicately—because he didn't know how to put it—he said, 'Now, are you like all the other Mormons or do you just have one wife?' I laughed my head off. Later, when I was on the team, he always would kid me. All the guys would say that I don't smoke or swear, and he used to accuse me of being a closet smoker. He'd say, 'I know Mormons that smoke. I went to a Mormon party with the Marriott family one time. You know, the big Marriott family? All these Mormons. And I went in the bathroom and the whole thing was full of smoke. People in the stalls smoking.' I'd say, 'Shut up Red.' He used to tease me all the time. When I'd play cards with the guys, he'd come in and he'd say, 'Hey, I know for a fact that Mormons are not supposed to gamble.' And I'd come back with, 'Red, be quiet. When I play with these guys, it's not gambling. There's no risk involved.' "

Auerbach was rolling again. He had ended a rare, five-year championship drought. He'd pulled off another draft coup. He was feted on a regular basis. In June of 1981 he was honored by the Touchdown Club of Washington. Senator Edward Kennedy read a Senate resolution and House Speaker Tip O'Neill presented Auerbach with a framed picture of the Capitol Building. Bill Russell attended the Washington testimonial and said, "How great could he be? He coached for twenty-five years and was named Coach of the Year one time." Five months later, there was a huge tribute to Auerbach for the benefit of the Jimmy Fund (cancer research) at the Copley Plaza Hotel.

The plaques and proclamations went on the wall next to the NAACP award for outstanding contributions to the cause of civil rights, the City of Boston Medal for Distinguished Achievement, the 1980 NBA Executive of the Year award and the scroll naming him "Greatest Coach in NBA History." In June of 1982, Auerbach received an honorary doctorate of humanities from the University of Massachusetts at Boston. He was a featured speaker at the Harvard Law School Forum. Boston University made him a Doctor of Humane Letters.

The 1982 NBA Meetings were held in San Antonio, and Dallas GM Norm Sonju came back from them telling a tale of a bored Red Auerbach lighting a napkin on fire and tossing it into the middle of a meeting table. Auerbach scolded Sonju for dousing the napkin with coffee. Clearly, Auerbach felt he was back at the top of his game.

"That's Red," said Sonju. "He's just a tad bigger than the military. Just a tad bigger than the NBA."

Dick Vertlieb, a veteran NBA GM with the Sonics, Warriors and Pacers, told *Sports Illustrated,* "When I came into the league I figured the guy had to be overrated. By the time I left, I wanted him to be commissioner. I started to call him 'Red Stradivarius,' because he played us all like a fiddle."

"Red was always at the league meetings," remembers Washington GM Bob Ferry. "He would get up and make his points. I'd say he was conservative. Some people thought he was old-fashioned, but normally, what he said made sense. He'd be the only guy smoking at the table. Truly great people are at peace with themselves, and his style is exactly Red Auerbach. It wasn't put on. It was him. The only reason I started smoking cigars was because *he* did. That's the truth."

The Celtics didn't repeat in the spring of 1982. They lost the seventh game of the conference finals to the Philadelphia 76ers. There was no disgrace. Tiny Archibald had thrown out his shoulder and Philadelphia was a formidable opponent.

Auerbach's off-season wasn't much. There wasn't much tinkering to be done. These Celtics were growing, flexing their muscles, learning to dominate the NBA. They had a rival in the East—the hated Sixers—and they had the Magic Johnson/Kareem Abdul-Jabbar Lakers winning the West. This is what the decade was going to be like.

Prior to the 1983 season, Auerbach made one deal. In typical fashion, he got something for nothing. Pledging allegiance to a longtime friend, Milwaukee coach Don Nelson, Cowens decided to come out of retirement. He wanted to play for the Bucks, under Nelson. Auerbach, ever consistent, informed Nelson that the Celtics still owned the rights to Cowens (who hadn't played in three years) and would be expecting some compensation. It was agreed that veteran starting guard Quinn Buckner would come to Boston as compensation for Cowens. This was amazing. Cowens was a burnt-out, retired player and Buckner was an established NBA point guard, a player who had an NCAA championship and an Olympic gold medal on his resume. He'd scored as many as forty points in a single NBA game. He was a defensive specialist with the body and aggressiveness of an NFL strong safety. He was an Auerbach-type player. He was schooled in great programs, he was unselfish and he was a winner.

Buckner remembers, "I was a little awestruck by Red, but I was able to get into it because I always felt I should be there. He made me feel comfortable. The Celtic mystique is more Red and how he treats people. He'll come up to you and he knows what to say to you. He understands there's certain guys you've got to kick in the tail. If you've got your head stuck where it doesn't belong, he'll tell you to get it out. If he knows you're one of those guys who needs to be left alone, he'll leave you alone. He never wanted to interfere, but if you went to ask him a question, he'd answer it. He'd handle it without undermining the coach."

With Buckner tossed into the mix, the 1982–1983 Celtics on paper looked like a monster team. Adding one more All-Star, Auerbach early in the season traded forgettable top pick Darren Tillis for shooting guard-forward Scott Wedman. But this unit never jelled.

Fitch was in his fourth year with the same cluster of players, and Parish, Maxwell, McHale and Carr were no longer responding to the clipboard control freak. Fitch's obsession with detail was boundless. He wanted to be coach, physician, GM, traveling secretary, video technician, television commentator, newspaper columnist and bus driver. Folks in the Celtic front office grew uncomfortable with Fitch's intervention.

Auerbach found himself in the middle. He had trained himself to stay out of the way of an occasional meddling owner, but had never had to take a backseat to another Celtic coach, and this started to happen during Fitch's fourth season on the bench. When Auerbach gave bricklayer Charles Bradley some free throw tips—a favorite instruction for the old master—Fitch took Auerbach aside and said, "I wish you wouldn't do that." Ever the team player, Auerbach deferred. Fitch had been granted coaching autonomy. Fitch had won a championship in the new NBA of the eighties. Auerbach didn't like all the video. He didn't like the new breed of coaches who overcoached. But he had hired Fitch, and as long as the results were there, he would stay out of the way.

The 1982–1983 Celtics won a respectable fifty-six games but were no match for the Sixers, who went 65–17. Backboard-eating Moses Malone had been added to the Philadelphia front line, and the long-underachieving 76ers finally appeared ready to win it all. The Celtics once again figured to be Philly's toughest competition in the East, but Boston didn't get that far. The Celts were bounced in four straight games in the conference semifinals by the mediocre Milwaukee Bucks. It marked the first time the Celtics had ever been swept in a four-game playoff series and Auerbach was furious.

The 1982–1983 Bucks were coached by Nelson, one of Auerbach's trusted guys. But everything changed when he pulled an old Auerbach trick out of mothballs during the conference semifinals. One day before the first game in Milwaukee, Nelson went public with a strong complaint against Ainge. He called Ainge a dirty ballplayer. He knew the impact this would have on the obedient Rhinelanders who went to games at the Mecca. Sure enough, every time Ainge touched the basketball, he was booed mercilessly. After the final beating in Milwaukee, Auerbach refused to congratulate the winners and announced that it was the first time he had failed to shake hands with the other team after a playoff defeat.

"I think he was embarrassed as much as anything," Nelson said years later. "The Ainge thing came up and that ticked him off, but it wasn't anything he wouldn't have done. He called me a whore in the paper. I asked for forgiveness, but I'd say it took a couple of years. I wrote some letters. I told him that I didn't mean anything by it and that I learned [that type of thing] from him."

In the summer of 1983, Auerbach announced that he would retire as active everyday general manager at the end of the upcoming season. He would remain as club president and always be "only a phone call away," but he would no longer run the club on a day-to-day basis. After making the announcement, he put the final touches on the last masterpiece team of his career—a team that would appear in four consecutive NBA Finals, winning twice.

Twenty-two days after the final game of the Milwaukee disgrace, Mangurian announced that he was selling the team. Privately, he told Auerbach that he would let him screen potential buyers; neither man wanted a repeat of the John Y. Brown situation. Three days after Mangurian's announcement, Fitch resigned as head coach. Auerbach seized the moment and named assistant coach K. C. Jones the new head coach of the Celtics. Jones, like Nelson before l'affaire Ainge, was one of Red's guys. Fitch-the-outsider had done a fine job and was a pivotal figure in both the development of Bird and the acquisitions of Parish and McHale, but it was time to turn the team over to another family member.

Jones's presence on the bench brought Auerbach back into the process. Auerbach was K. C.'s hoop god, and the new coach would not only encourage intervention, but would solicit help from the mentor. The back page of the June 6, 1983, *Boston Herald* screamed, "Red Is Back!" and Auerbach in the story said, "With Bill as coach, I just didn't feel right about offering input. I saw things I disagreed with, but I believed he deserved coaching autonomy. If he had come to me and asked me to get involved I would have, but he didn't and I wasn't going to ask."

A decade later, Auerbach says, "Bill, he had a theory that he'd sign a three-year contract and after one year, he'd sign an extension.

And I didn't like that, because to me, you sign a contract, finish a contract, then you sit down and talk."

Jones says, "Red's an encyclopedia of basketball. I listen to him and take advantage of his knowledge. The man has such knowledge and sense of this game, hey, why would I shut that out? You can have ego and be dumb or you can have ego and be smart."

The new coach was in place. A few more players had to be gathered.

Auerbach waived Tiny Archibald. The speedy guard had slowed considerably and pouted through most of the 1982–1983 season. With Archibald gone, it was clear that Boston needed a new point guard, but it was unreasonable to think Auerbach would be able to come up with an All-Star player.

Aware that Phoenix was having problems handling Dennis Johnson, Auerbach called his good friend Colangelo. The newest league trend was big guards. Every contending team needed a big guard to contend with Magic Johnson and San Antonio's George Gervin. Was Dennis Johnson available? What would it take to get him?

On the day before the 1983 draft, Boston traded backup center Rick Robey to Phoenix for one of the best defensive guards and big-game players in NBA history. NBA rivals were stunned when they heard the news. Johnson was considered something of a problem child. Phoenix coach John MacLeod was having trouble with Johnson, and Lenny Wilkens, D.J.'s coach at Seattle, had labeled him a "cancer." But there was no doubt about his skills. Every coach in the Western Conference knew that Johnson was the only NBA guard who could at least temporarily smother Magic Johnson.

Colangelo: "John [MacLeod] was very set in his ways, and he had basically said he didn't want D.J. anymore. We had to move him. I had passed up a deal the year before which would have been a very good deal for the Suns—Bill Laimbeer and Kenny Carr, plus another player, for D.J. But as it turned out, when we started shopping D.J., because of the tag that went along, Boston was the only team that showed any interest."

Auerbach says, "As a general manager you've got to avoid your coach being down on certain people."

Dennis Johnson took over as the top Celtic guard for the next five seasons, four of which led to the NBA Finals. Larry Bird termed him "the best player I ever played with," and D.J.'s number was retired in 1991. Robey was out of basketball three years after the trade was made. He averaged fewer than five points per game, playing only 111 games over three seasons. Moreover, the subtraction of Robey from the Celtics in 1983 put Bird over the top as the NBA's premier player. Robey and Bird were late-night running mates during the early years of Bird's career, and Bird himself has admitted that it was no coincidence he won three straight MVP awards after Robey was dealt.

Bob Ferry, a longtime Auerbach friend and admirer and general manager of the Washington Bullets for many years, says, "I don't think I ever made a deal with Red. Other than not winning a championship, the worst thing that could happen would be to see one of your players traded to his team and win one."

Colangelo watched Dennis Johnson win two championships with Auerbach.

"We got some bad merchandise," admits Colangelo. "He [Robey] was hurt. But there are no hard feelings. There aren't any geniuses in this business. When you make a mistake, you cut your losses and don't look back. Nobody did anything to me; I only did it to myself. I take full responsibility for every trade. No hard feelings. I don't think Red and I ever had a cross word with one another."

Dennis Johnson was a seven-year veteran when he came to Boston. He'd broken into the NBA under Seattle coach Bill Russell. He'd heard a few things about Red Auerbach.

Johnson: "He scared you because of his background and his history. I was afraid of him because of all his basketball history. In Seattle, I had Bill out there, and Russ would talk about Red. We'd go through training camp and Russell would tell us about the things they did in training camp and about how Red wouldn't take this. So believe it or not, I came to training camp out of shape, and they were playing shirts and skins. Red said, 'Let him be a skin.' I was five or ten pounds over and I didn't look good. I got dunked on by Charles Bradley and I was awful damn tired. I went over to the bench and he just looked at me and puffed on his cigar. He had to be thinking, 'We traded for you?' But after we got going, I decided

to trim down. And he always liked me. I don't think he likes a whole
bunch of people, but I always felt he liked me."

Auerbach had his new guard, but almost lost his big young forward. Kevin McHale was a free agent in the summer of 1983. The
New York Knicks went after Boston's low-post point machine, and
when the Knicks dangled a five-year, $6.25 million offer sheet, Auer-
bach went ballistic. The Celtics fought back by signing Knick free
agents Marvin Webster, Sly Williams and Rory Sparrow to offer
sheets. NBA teams at this hour were operating under the new, complex restrictions of a salary cap. Auerbach had limited knowledge of
the cap and its flexibilities (that was Volk's job), but Harry Mangurian showed him how he could use it to fight back against the hated
New Yorkers. They knew the Knicks couldn't match the figures
they'd offered New York's free agents and still land McHale. It was
a great counterpunch. Having stopped the Knicks, Auerbach did his
thing: He blasted McHale's agent, John Sandquist.

"You get an agent who wants to get his name in the papers to
enhance his position to get college players," Auerbach reasoned.
"We feel he used the newspapers to get us to increase the amounts
and terms. We've been around too long to have any agent use us
the way this guy has used us."

Auerbach also said McHale was "motivated by greed."

McHale, of course, wound up staying in Boston.

In August, Mangurian found buyers: Don Gaston, Alan Cohen
and Paul Dupee. Cohen was a basketball man, a former chairman
of the board of the New York Nets. Gaston and Dupee were money-
bags. Mangurian subjected these wealthy businessmen to the Red
Auerbach litmus test.

Cohen remembers, "Harry said that we had a deal but that he'd
told Red that it was subject to his approval. I told Don that I didn't
know if we were in trouble or not. I had had a run-in with Red
when we were both on the [NBA] Board of Governors. It was something about changing the backcourt-foul rule. He didn't want to
change it and I did.

"But our meeting turned out all right. The first thing he told me
was, 'I'm so happy to have an owner that I don't have to teach.' "

Gaston says, "Red came to New York and came up to my office

and met with Dupee, Cohen and myself. It was the first time I'd met Red. We just sat there and shot the bull. I didn't realize at the time, but apparently it was an audition of sorts."

Volk says, "The audition is true. And that happened after Red turned down Donald Trump. Trump wanted to buy the club, but Red wouldn't have anything to do with him."

Gaston's first Garden game was an exhibition contest between the Celtics and the defending world champion 76ers. The game was unusually contentious and physical for preseason. It was clear from the outset that the Sixers were flexing their muscle, while the Celtics wanted to establish that the balance of power in the NBA's Eastern Conference had shifted back to Causeway Street. A fight broke out four minutes into the game. When it was announced that Philly's Marc Iavaroni and Boston's Bird had been ejected, the sixty-six-year-old Auerbach bolted from his seat, vaulted over the hockey boards and—as the crowd roared its approval—crossed the fabled parquet floor to have a word with the officials.

Nonunion referees were working the game (NBA officials were on strike) and Auerbach knew he'd seen the Sixers work one of his old tricks: Sacrifice one of your stiffs to get their star thrown out of a game. This was right out of Tri-Cities, circa 1949. He wasn't going to let Philly get away with this in his building. Before this fracas was over, Auerbach found himself in the face of 6-10 behemoth Moses Malone, saying, "Hit me! Hit me! You big son of a bitch!" Sixer coach Billy Cunningham, who had his jacket torn in the fray, was attempting to pull Auerbach away from Malone.

Gaston remembers, "We had virtually just sat down and the game started and this tiff broke out. Next thing I knew, Red was out of his seat and was on the floor. He didn't say anything, he just got up and vaulted out there. I just thought to myself, 'I guess this happens all the time.' "

"Red almost threw me to the ground," says Volk. "I saw him coming. I saw him leap over chairs. We didn't have the cut through the hockey boards that we have now. He had to vault over the boards. I went over to try to calm him down, but he just flung me out of the way."

New coach K. C. Jones says, "In all the years I've seen the Celtics play, I've never seen anything like that. I looked around and here comes Red flying out there like a mad rooster, shouting, the arms flailing. I thing he was having fun. I kept thinking, 'Red is back! Red is back!'"

The NBA fined Auerbach $2,500, and league vice president of operations Scotty Stirling said, "Auerbach's actions were embarrassing and intolerable. A general manager has no place on the court at any time during an NBA game."

Embarrassing and intolerable. Just like the old days.

"If the SOB [Malone] had hit me, I'd have owned him," said Auerbach. "As long as he didn't kill me."

Jake O'Donnell, one of the striking officials, was asked to comment on the situation and said, "The NBA is scared to death of Red."

The NBA of 1983–1984 was polishing its image. Forty-one-year-old league counsel David Stern succeeded retiring commissioner Larry O'Brien, and the league moved ahead of other professional sports with its drug program and innovative salary cap. Fiscal solvency was assured when the players association agreed to make aggregate salaries directly proportionate to league revenue. Showcase stars Magic and Bird were holding up the two most fabled franchises in league history. TV ratings were on the rise. Finally, the NBA was the sport of the future. As part of this new packaging, the annual All-Star Game became the "NBA All-Star Weekend." Instead of a single day of low-intensity basketball, the league would put on a made-for-TV, three-day hoop festival featuring an old-timers' game, a slam dunk contest and a three-point shootout.

The 1984 All-Star Weekend was held in Denver, and Auerbach agreed to coach the East Division old-timer squad. But the East team lost to Alex Hannum's West old-timers, and the game ended with Auerbach swearing in the face of retired referee Norm Drucker.

"These guys came to play, and he worked to make a farce out of this," said the Boston GM. "The guys we're playing got serious, and that bastard was out there globetrotting it."

Drucker calmly said, "Why should anything have changed?"

Auerbach says, "I hate to be a fool. If a guy's out of shape, he shouldn't be out there playing. If he's going to make an ass out of himself, that's his business, but I don't want to be a part of it. If you keep score, you play to win."

"It was the maddest I've seen Red get in a long time," says old-timer Johnny Kerr. "Heinsohn and I were playing against each other and Heinsohn was pulling my pants down and doing the whole thing and Red was so pissed. We couldn't believe it. Tommy and I were laughing. We were going to go out and have a beer afterward."

The NBA's vice president in charge of public relations, Brian McIntyre, remembers, "I was supposed to get both Red and Hannum to go to the interview room. Red didn't want to go. He was screaming about the officials. I got to him and asked him to come with me to the room, and we got into a little argument. Finally he came with me, and when we got there he saw Hannum already at the podium. [Hannum was coach of the only two non-Celtic NBA champions between 1957 and 1969 and Auerbach no doubt was still sensitive about this.] He didn't want to go up and we started yelling at each other again and he said, 'I can have your job!' It got pretty ugly.

"I remember a few weeks later he was in our office in New York. He walked by my door and I got up and went over and told him I was sorry for the *way* I said what I said, but that I wasn't sorry for *what* I said. I put out my hand. He stood there and did nothing for several seconds. Finally, he put out his hand and grunted. 'Okay.' When I told Tod [Rosensweig] about it, he was amazed. He said that was as close to an apology as he'd ever heard coming from Red. We get along okay now. Every once in a while he sends me some stale cigars, the ones he doesn't smoke. I've got a lot of respect for Red, and we get along fine now."

The tone was set, and his team responded the way he hoped it would. The 1983–1984 Celtics were a complete unit, and marched into the playoffs playing terrific basketball. Bird enjoyed the first of his three straight MVP seasons, Dennis Johnson filled the last hole, and Parish, Maxwell, McHale, Danny Ainge and Quinn Buckner—players who'd had trouble producing for Bill Fitch—all prospered under the lenient tutelage of K. C. Jones.

And Auerbach was back. He was at practice. He was in the hotel lobbies at playoff time. He was in the locker room, flicking ashes, kicking butt after wins and handing out selective praise after losses. The Celtics beat the Bullets, Knicks and Bucks to make it back to the finals. Waiting out West were the Los Angeles Lakers. It marked the eighth finals meeting between the Celtics and Lakers, but it was the first time they'd face one another since Russell's last stand in 1969. As they dueled for the NBA championship in 1984, the Celtics and Lakers represented 60 percent (twenty-three of thirty-eight) of all NBA championships. It seemed a fitting finale to Auerbach's long stay as Celtic general manager.

This was the last year of the 2–2–1–1–1 finals playoff format. The NBA today plays the World Series 2–3–2 format, and many believe that something was lost when the extra travel was eliminated.

The Celtics were blown out in two of the first three games, and would have been down 3–0 if not for a steal by Gerald Henderson in the waning seconds of Game 2. Sparked by Kevin McHale's breakaway takedown of Kurt Rambis (a smash-mouth play worthy of Messrs. Brannum and Loscutoff), the Celtics won Game 4 in the Forum and turned the series around.

McHale says, "That was just one of those things I'm sure Red thought needed to be done, and it got done."

They came back to Boston, where Bird destroyed LA in 100-degree Garden heat. It was one of the hottest June days on record in greater Boston, and the Lakers were totally out of sync. LA had an oxygen tank at the end of its bench, and Celtic fans won't soon forget the sight of Kareem Abdul-Jabbar sucking on an oxygen mask while Bird, Mr. White Heat himself, vaporized the mighty Lakers. Josh Rosenfeld was Laker PR director in 1984, and says, "I remember being in the locker room. Byron Scott put his hand down under the bench to pick something up, and he felt heat rushing out from below. They were heating our locker room."

Pat Riley, who coached the Lakers in 1984, developed an obsession with Auerbach and the Celtics. "I don't think he ever helped out our situation," Riley says. "I thought he was the man behind everything. When you're in that situation, it becomes more and more of a hate. I think that's the only way. That was the magic of the rivalry. When they went out and lined up, it wasn't bullshit. It was felt."

In his 1988 book *Showtime,* Riley wrote, "The Boston Mystique isn't leprechauns hiding in the floorboards. It isn't blood and guts. It's a willingness to use any tactic to upset an opponent. Turn up the heat when it's already hot. Shut down the visitor's water heaters. Instigate hard fouls on the court. The general manager chasing officials all the way to the dressing room to try to intimidate them. To hell with dignity. To hell with fair play. The Boston Mystique encourages the lowest common denominator of fan behavior. It grows directly out of the low-rent attitudes of Boston management. They're the Klingons of the NBA. I respect the individual players . . . But the organization and its traditions are out-of-date."

Five years later, Riley and Auerbach were still going after each other. In the spring of 1993, when the Celtics were down and Riley's New York Knicks were in first place, Auerbach went on New York's WFAN radio and ridiculed Riley's candidacy for NBA Coach of the Year. (The trophy, remember, is a statuette of Red Auerbach.) Riley countered, "I kid Red all the time. He's a lot like I am. He hates us. He hates anybody with anything to do with the Lakers or the Knicks. He hates them. I feel the same way about the Celtics. Red still thinks he won in '85, and he didn't. He still thinks they won."

Auerbach came back and said he wanted Riley to win the award. He said it would serve him right: If Riley won, he'd have to look at the image of Auerbach every day.

Magic Johnson remembers, "They did what they had to do to win. Whether Red was behind it or not, who knows? But you've got people telling you that, so you think that's the case. It was all right with me, because I'm the same way: I'll do anything to win. So I learned some tricks from him. When you want to win, you do what it takes, within a legal means. You take it to whatever line you have to. It taught us, as a group, a lot. The rivalry. It made it great for basketball. Look at the ratings. They still can't top them games. I'm about winning, so that's why I respect Red. You don't still continue to win championships unless you know something about basketball. That's the smartest mind in basketball, so you respect that."

The 1984 Celtic-Laker series went the limit, and it was Maxwell who led the charge. In the tradition of Frank Ramsey, who would tell his teammates, "Y'all are playing with mah money," Cedric Maxwell said before Game 7, "Hop on my back, boys." They did, and he carried them to Flag 15. As the champagne sprayed off the grungy locker room walls, Auerbach went on CBS-TV and shouted, "You guys were talking about a dynasty the Lakers had. But what dynasty? Here's the only dynasty right here. This team."

Upstairs, in the Celtic offices on 150 Causeway Street, the brass celebrated deep into the night. Volk today points to a favorite photo on the wall of his new office. The picture shows Auerbach in shirtsleeves, looking totally drained and happy, hoisting a plastic glass of champagne. "It's my favorite picture of Red," Volk says fondly. "I don't remember him ever being so happy."

The Celtics flew to Washington the next morning and were greeted in the Rose Garden by President Ronald Reagan. From Truman to Reagan. Red was home, and so was the NBA championship.

The first weekend of January in 1985 was a Redfest—a celebration of Auerbach's retirement. Auerbach's number (No. 2, in deference to Walter Brown's No. 1) was raised to the rafters on Friday night, moments before the Celtics played the Knicks. Baseball balladeer Terry Cashman performed a song written especially for the Celtic GM—"Light It Up, Red." The NBA announced that its Coach of the Year award was being renamed the Red Auerbach Award, and Auerbach was given a lifetime pass to his favorite Chinese restaurant.

The most emotional moment of Red Auerbach Weekend came when Russell was introduced. The reclusive superstar embraced his former coach and lifted him three feet off the ground, then helped Auerbach pull the rope that raised No. 2 to the Garden ceiling. (Thirteen years earlier, Russell had refused to play a part in any public ceremony to retire his No. 6. At Auerbach's insistence, Russell had eventually, albeit grudgingly, participated in a private flag-raising in an empty Garden.) There was a full house for Auerbach's enshrinement, and Russell said, "I'm here because he's my friend.

Very simply, I don't feel I'd have been nearly as effective with any other man who ever coached a basketball team."

Russell was only one of Auerbach's "guys" who came back for the weekend. There was a "Legends Game" on Saturday, and Auerbach's squad defeated a team coached by Russell, 93–90. Local television sports anchor Mike Lynch served as one of the officials and tried a prank late in the game. Lynch called a foul on Charlie Scott, and when Auerbach stood to protest, the TV anchor whipped a stogie out of his back pocket and said to Auerbach, "Have a cigar."

The crowd loved it. Auerbach's response was, "Shove it up your ass. Be serious, huh? Be serious."

Saturday night there was a Super Bowl–esque bash at the Bayside Exposition Center. The banquet was a $500-per-person event, the money from which was used to establish the Red Auerbach Fund, a $500,000 permanent charity for youth sports in greater Boston.

Auerbach said, "Most guys have to die to get a tribute like that."

The Celtics beat the Knicks on Red Auerbach Weekend. It was Boston's 1,973rd victory since his arrival in 1950.

On September 20, his sixty-eighth birthday, Auerbach's statue was unveiled in Quincy Market. The statue was done by Boston University professor Lloyd Lillie. Auerbach said, "People who are still living don't have statues. Not as rule, anyway. Certainly not sports people."

"I think it's magnificent," says Dorothy. "We went and took pictures one time."

"It's very weird," admits his daughter Nancy. "It's eerie. As proud as I am of it, I find it so sad. I remember when they did the mask for it. He came home with the mask and we said, 'Dad, that doesn't look like you.' And he said, 'How the hell can it not look like me—it's me.'"

The statue rests in the arcade between the Quincy Market Building and the South Market, just a short walk from Faneuil Hall, where the fires of freedom were lit. The bronzed Auerbach has a rolled-up program in his left hand, a cigar in his right. He's sitting on a team bench and there's a single basketball in the rack beneath his seat. He's facing north, in the direction of the Boston Garden. The plaque that accompanies this monument reads, "Arnold 'Red' Auerbach. Inspirational leader of the Boston Celtics as an outstanding coach and general manager. He helped bring 15 championships to Boston. A member of the Hall of Fame, he has exceeded every record for consistent sports achievement. When measured against all standards of success, Red Auerbach stands alone for directing the Boston Celtics to more championships than any other team in sports. He has made the name of Boston synonymous with winning."

With each honor, Auerbach inched away from the day-to-day operation of the team. Jan Volk became the new general manager. Never a whistle-and-sneakers guy, Volk had regal Celtic bloodlines. He was born in Davenport, Iowa—where Red Auerbach coached the Tri-Cities Blackhawks in 1949–1950. In 1960, Volk's father, a friend of Red's, asked Auerbach if the Celtics would like to rent the family-owned camp in Marshfield. Auerbach liked the idea. The Celts didn't have much money, and Camp Milbrook would enable him to mix pro players with college "counselors"—players the Celtics might be interested in signing. Volk was thirteen years old when he first got coffee and did errands for the coach of the NBA champs. When he got his driver's license, he made runs to Logan Airport to pick up ballplayers. Volk went to Colby College in Maine, then Columbia Law School.

"When he went to law school, I figured he might have some brains after all," says Auerbach.

Volk joined the Celtics as director of ticket sales in August 1971. He moved over to travel and equipment purchasing, then business manager and house counsel. In the winter of 1981, he became No. 2 man in the organization.

He quit the Celtics once after a brief blowout with Auerbach. Volk explains, "It was during the 1973–1974 season. Probably January. Ted Kennedy came to a game. It was against the Lakers on national television. Red wanted to get three programs autographed by all the players. He came up to me and asked me this very, very late. I grabbed my brother, Mark, who was assistant trainer. I said, 'Here's three programs; get them autographed.' He told me I'd have to get them at halftime.

"When halftime was over, the team was on the floor and Mark came out with two books, but told me that somebody took the third book. I ran to concessions to get one, but they were sold out. I went to Red and started to tell him what happened. It was in front of [owner] Bob Schmertz. He started to walk across the court to go back to the seats. He walked away, then called me over, and in front of Schmertz he says to me, 'Hey, if you can't do the job, I'll get somebody who can.' He just brought me out to the owner to tell me that. I turned to him and said, 'Then you better get somebody else; I'm leaving.' I turned around and left. I didn't go to work the next day. Two days after it happened, I got a call from Red, and he just said, 'What's up?' I said, 'Well, I quit,' and he said, 'Aww, you didn't quit.' He asked me to come in, so I did, and we talked. I told him that he was the boss and he was entitled to criticize, but don't embarrass me. He said, 'You're right,' and apologized, and it never happened again."

Longtime Celtic employee Rosensweig, another son of one of Auerbach's best friends, says, "It is typical of him to rely on Jan to do silly work like that. He still hasn't figured out that I'm not the media guy [Rosensweig switched from media to marketing in 1982]. He'll still call me and ask me to do something that's totally unrelated to what I do, even though he's well aware there's other people to do things like that."

To this day, GM Volk and Rosensweig still find themselves doing occasional gofer work for Auerbach. They don't mind: It's the loyal thing to do.

Rosensweig admits, "I think Red's a pushover in a lot of ways. My father had a leg amputated maybe six or eight years ago. Red visited him in the hospital every single day and brought him deli sandwiches. He was such a solicitous, sweet friend. If Jan and I fucked up royally, we would probably always have our jobs as long as Red was there. It's that kind of loyalty. He's very loyal and honest and fair with the people he loves, and we're lucky to be in that group."

Volk has always known that Auerbach will get the credit for things that go right, and that when something goes wrong it will fall in the lap of the GM or the CEO, Dave Gavitt. Celtic fans are always most comfortable when they believe Auerbach is behind every move—or every *smart* one, anyway.

Though Volk was officially the GM, it was Auerbach who spoke up when the Celtics had problems signing Maxwell and Henderson after the 1984 championship. Both players went through long and sometimes bitter contract negotiations. The Celtics wound up signing both very late in the preseason, but the hard feelings carried over. Henderson was traded hours after coming to terms. Maxwell lasted one more year in Boston, but he finished his Celtic career deep in Auerbach's doghouse.

The Henderson and Maxwell departures were uncharacteristically harsh and unleashed a series of events and emotions that still haunt the Boston franchise. Maxwell hurt his knee in 1984–1985, and in Auerbach's opinion made little attempt to rehabilitate himself. Max became mud. Suddenly he was overpaid and lazy. A complimentary reference to Maxwell was deleted from Auerbach's new book, and Max was dealt for Bill Walton before the 1985–1986 season. Walton contributed mightily for one glorious season before his cracking feet caused him to retire.

Maxwell never again was an impact player, but his banishment still bothers Bird, Parish, McHale and other longtime Celtic loyalists. Auerbach was petty with Maxwell. The way Max was tossed aside flew in the face of everything Auerbach preached. This was a player who had been a significant contributor, a playoff MVP and a go-to guy who didn't mind playing in the shadows of the superstars. He was everything Auerbach liked—until the final year.

In Harvey Araton and Filip Bondy's controversial 1991 book, *The Selling of the Green,* Maxwell relayed a remark that portrayed Auerbach as racially insensitive. Maxwell claimed that at a 1978 team Christmas party, Auerbach said to him, "You know, Maxwell, you remind me of that old movie guy Stepin Fetchit." Maxwell told the authors, "For a long time, I was waiting for him to say that to me again. I was going to say, 'Yez, suh, massuh.'"

"I don't recall that," says Auerbach. "Max is bitter."

Maxwell doesn't consider Auerbach racist, but he is troubled by the way his career ended in Boston.

"Red is Jewish," says Maxwell. "He understands. How can he be racist? . . . When Red said the things he said after I left, it bothered me. It was like he was trying to hurt me. Red has the greatest basketball mind that there's ever been, but I just don't think he was fair at the end. I don't think the way it was done was the best. After everything I had done, they questioned my desire to win. I was involved with two championships and had a lot to do with winning. And to say I didn't care, and didn't have a desire to come back, was unfair. It was a scornful way of putting me down."

"I really feel sorry with the way Red and Max don't see eye to eye," says Bird. "I really feel bad about that, because I know Red, deep down, really likes Max. He knows how valuable he was to us. I just never could understand that one. It's a shame, because all of us who played with Max absolutely love the guy. I think Max is very bitter toward the organization because of Red's relationship with him. It sort of bothers me, because when I go back ten years from now for something they have, I want Max to be there, because he was a very big part of it."

Bob Costas remembers, "I was master of ceremonies on Larry's big night, and we went into one of those club rooms and did a couple of hours on the radio. We have Larry and Magic and McHale and Havlicek and Red. Here's Red in the afterglow of one of the greatest nights in the history of Boston Garden, and I say how it was great to see the reception that Maxwell got. He said, 'Yeah, yeah, yeah.' Then, like three questions later, I ask Red who was the greatest disappointment, and he says, 'Maxwell. We had a chance to win a championship again and he wouldn't rehab.' I mean, the olive branch was out there, and not only did he not take it, he threw it on the ground and stomped on it."

Auerbach insists, "He had that arthroscopic surgery and he was out for three or four months. Some guys come back in just a few days. He came back and went through the motions. What really, really got me mad—and he was my boy; I discovered him, I drafted him, everything like that—but he got me mad when I wanted him to try his knee in the summertime. His agent said, 'He won't come up, because he just built a house and he wants to enjoy it.' I said, 'How the hell did he build the house? With the money we paid him,

for Christ sake. This is ludicrous.' And I got mad. That's when I
made up my mind. And he was such a great player."

Henderson's departure was more strategic, less spiteful. The
Celtics signed the starting guard just before a preseason game in
Houston. Hours later, as the Celtics took the floor against the Rockets, Henderson was gone. He'd been traded to the Seattle Super-
Sonics for Seattle's 1986 first-round pick. Auerbach couldn't resist a
parting shot and said Henderson was "in horrible shape." Celtic
players laughed at that one: Henderson in the off-season was usually
in better shape than anybody else during the middle of an NBA
campaign.

It was a gamble, but Auerbach was banking on a couple of de-
velopments: He felt Ainge was ready to start. He felt he was over-
paying Henderson. And he felt Seattle might be in for a bad season.
There was a new twist to all of this: the NBA lottery. Before the
lottery, teams would tank games late in the season, in order to finish
as low in the standings—and get as high a draft pick—as possible.
In an effort to stop nonplayoff teams from giving less than their all,
the NBA in 1985 instituted a draft lottery for the nonplayoff teams.
This meant that if the Sonics failed to make the playoffs two years
hence, Auerbach had a chance at the No. 1 pick in the country.
Again, Auerbach was finding ways to exploit the rules.

Without Henderson, and with Maxwell spending most of the year
either injured or out of shape, the 1984–1985 Celtics failed in their
title defense. They won a league-best sixty-three games and made it
all the way to the finals, but lost a six-game rematch with the fast-
breaking Lakers. The Celtics gave up their crown at home, in a
sloppy sixth game, and it was significant that Maxwell, Quinn Buckner, M. L. Carr, Carlos Clark and Ray Williams never got off the
bench in the final game of the championship series. All five were
gone before the start of the next season.

"Just because you lose in the playoffs," Auerbach said after the
1985 finals, "you don't panic and decimate your ball club. That's
what separates the men from the boys. The boys panic."

There was no need to panic. Auerbach made two deals before
the start of the 1985–1986 season: He traded Buckner to Indiana

for shooting guard Jerry Sichting, and he dealt Maxwell to the Clippers for Walton. Sichting was acquired to supplement the starting backcourt of D.J. and Ainge. Walton was added to a front line that already had Bird, Parish, McHale and Scott Wedman. With what Walton had left in 1985–1986, there can be no doubt that for a single season this was the greatest frontcourt in the history of basketball. Not even the USA Olympic Dream Team (Patrick Ewing, Charles Barkley, Karl Malone, David Robinson, Scottie Pippen and a retiring Bird) matches up with the Celtic front line of 1985–1986.

At UCLA, Bill Walton was without question one of the finest college basketball players ever, and in his short NBA career he won an MVP and was considered one of the dominant pivotmen of his generation. Had he not suffered serious foot injuries, he'd be in the pantheon of NBA centers, alongside Russell, Chamberlain and Abdul-Jabbar. The Celtics were the beneficiaries of his final quality performances, and when it was over, Walton wished he'd played his entire career for Boston—for Red Auerbach.

"I was part of two of the greatest basketball families in the history of all sports," says Walton. "I always had a desire to be part of the Boston Celtics. I was a Celtic fan growing up in California. It was my narrow-mindedness that kept me away for so long. I should have barged into Red's office the very first day out of UCLA and said, 'Hey, I gotta be on this team.'

"I give all the credit in the world to Red Auerbach. I can never say enough great things. My feelings for him run so deep. The way he built, and continues to build, the Boston Celtics and the way he makes everybody feel as if they are part of the family. Red, like all great coaches, is a master of psychology. His presence is felt by all, every day. He and [Walton's UCLA coach] John Wooden are like your dad, in that you never want them to know that you're anything other than great. When you let them down because you don't get the job done, nothing feels worse. It's like when you're a teenager and you start to mess up and your dad looks at you in that special way. You have that same feeling with Red Auerbach."

Ainge adds, "Most organizations I've played for look at the stat sheet and say, 'Well, how did you play?' The thing I enjoyed about playing for Red was that he recognized the little things you did to help them win. I remember him coming into the locker room after a game many times, big games, and I would have scored two points and shot one for ten and he'd come over and say, 'You deserve the game ball,' because of how I played against Isiah [Thomas] or how I took a charge at a big moment, or set a pick to get Robert [Parish] open. He recognized the little things and he really appreciated it, and he wanted you to keep doing the little things until you win. I think this was passed down to his coaches as well. The whole organization was like that."

With Walton and Sichting on board to beef up the bench, and everybody else healthy and in their prime, the 1985–1986 Celtics vaporized the NBA. It was one of the best teams in league history. The C's won sixty-seven games and went 40–1 at home. Kevin McHale will tell you today that they could have gone 82–0. Walton will cite all the bunny games that they blew because of a lack of concentration.

While all this was going on in bountiful Boston, Seattle star forward Tom Chambers got hurt and the SuperSonics staggered toward a 31–51 finish. The Celtics were going to be in the finals and Seattle was going to be in the draft lottery. This meant that even though the Celtics had the best team in basketball, they had a chance for the best college player in the country.

In the middle of the 1986 playoffs, Auerbach went to New York to represent Boston in the lottery draw. He blew smoke at everybody. When the Celtics landed the No. 2 pick, Auerbach laughed out loud. Philadelphia got the top pick and Auerbach started the psych job instantly. He leaned over and whispered in the ear of Sixer GM Pat Williams, "If you don't take [North Carolina's Brad] Daugherty, we do."

Williams said, "I'm scared to death of the man. He fleeces everybody in the league. We all start trembling when he picks up the phone."

When the playoffs ended, there was a rally at City Hall, and the Celtic brass prepared for the draft. Things had never looked brighter. Boston had the best team in the league, the best frontcourt in basketball history, a three-time MVP at the height of his game, a string of nonstop sellouts—and now, the No. 2 pick in the entire draft. It was Boston's highest selection since Auerbach traded for the No. 2 pick in 1956—a pick that turned out to be Bill Russell.

Everything was going Auerbach's way. Everything.

# 9

# SEVEN YEARS OF BAD LUCK

*I was in Boston. Lefty Driesell called me early in the morning. Lefty said, 'He died.' And I said, 'There's something wrong, but he'll be all right, won't he?' And he said, 'No, he's dead.' I went* plop. *My belly went* plop. *It couldn't happen.*

AUERBACH, *on the death of Len Bias*

L EN BIAS WAS ONE OF RED'S GUYS. AUERBACH ALWAYS COV-eted players from the D.C. area. He'd been godfather of sorts to Austin Carr, Adrian Dantley, Dave Bing and other kids from the District of Columbia. These were playground players, basketball descendants of the guys he recruited to try out new plays back in the 1940s. He was known on the playgrounds and at the recreation center at Chevy Chase, and on the courts across from the Avalon Theater on Connecticut Avenue. Washington playgrounds were Auerbach's laboratories. He helped recruit for Maryland coach Lefty Driesell, for Georgetown's John Thompson (a former Celtic backup to Bill Russell) and for all those who coached his beloved George Washington Colonials.

Bias's early years were spent in a public housing project in the District of Columbia. The Bias family moved to a brown-shingled, white-trimmed ranch home in Columbia Park, Maryland, and young Len honed his game at the Columbia Park Recreation Center in Prince Georges County on the D.C. line. Auerbach first saw him play when Bias was a junior at Northwestern High School. As Bias and his game got bigger and better, college recruiters started turning up at the home of James and Lonise Bias. Their tall son chose the University of Maryland. It was home. He'd sold ice cream at the Terps' games at Cole Field House. He knew the players.

During his four years at Maryland, Bias's skills and his body developed to NBA proportions. By his senior season he was 6-8, 220 pounds and ran the floor like a Penn Relays quarter-miler. He could bench-press 300 pounds. His vertical leap was 38 inches. He had a soft jumper from 15 feet. You didn't need the trained eye of Red Auerbach to scout Len Bias. Anyone could see he was The Goods.

Auerbach is a close friend of Bias's college coach, Driesell. When Bias thought about entering the NBA draft after his junior season, Auerbach took the young man and his parents to dinner, and told Bias that he probably wouldn't be drafted in the top ten in the spring of 1985. If he waited a year he would be a lottery pick and the Celtics would have a chance to get him. Auerbach was trying to help Bias, but he was also trying to help the Celtics. Had Boston been in position to draft Bias in 1985, Auerbach might have told the young man that another year of school would be a waste of time—the kind of fatherly advice he gave Ralph Sampson. (Bias certainly didn't stay at Maryland for academics; he logged two Fs and two incompletes in his final semester at Maryland and was twenty-one credits shy of graduation at the time of his death.)

Bias was a counselor at Auerbach's camp in Marshfield in the summer of 1985. This was a handy way to scout undergrad ballplayers without breaking NCAA or NBA regulations. The "counselors" competed against professionals and rookie hopefuls, but officially speaking, they were there to work with the kids who paid tuition to attend Auerbach's summer school of hoops. In the summer of 1985, Bias dominated the pro competition at the Marshfield High School gym. Celtic fans tapped one another on the shoulder and said, "Who's that guy?"

Rick Carlisle, a second-year Celtic in the summer of 1985, came to Camp Milbrook to work out with the kids and counselors. Carlisle, a graduate of the University of Virginia, had played against Bias in college. "Lenny Bias is just about the best college player in the country," Carlisle said after one of the Marshfield scrimmages.

Bias had a great senior season and finished his career as Maryland's all-time leading scorer. He was a consensus first-team All-American. After the Celtics learned their place in the 1986 draft lottery, Bias came to Boston for a visit and a physical. He submitted to an illegal drug test and passed. (GM Volk claims the Celtics did not know this was a violation of league rules. The Warriors and Knicks also put Bias through drug tests, and he passed them both.) Bias sat in the stands at the Boston Garden for one of the first games of the Celtic championship series against the Houston Rockets. Before leaving the Celtic offices, he shook Volk's hand vigorously and pleaded, "Please draft me." It was easy to comply. The Philadelphia 76ers had the first pick and were committed to North Carolina's Brad Daugherty. Bias may or may not have enjoyed a better pro career than Daugherty, but there is no question that on June 17, 1986, Bias and Daugherty were the top two available players.

Bias went to New York City for the draft. Almost immediately after Philadelphia selected Daugherty, Auerbach announced that the Celtics had used their lottery pick on Maryland's Len Bias.

"Praise the Lord," said Bias.

Wearing a Celtic baseball cap, Bias posed for a picture with NBA Commissioner David Stern, then told reporters, "I think I could get accustomed to winning. To be able to play for Boston . . . that was a dream within a dream. What do I think of Larry Bird? What do *you* think of him?"

Back in Boston at the Blades and Boards Club in the Garden, Jimmy Rodgers, who in 1986 doubled as Celtic assistant coach and director of player personnel, said, "We feel like Len Bias can make us a better team than we were this year, and that's saying something."

After speaking with reporters in New York, Bias took the shuttle to Boston. He was ushered into the Blades and Boards Club and said, "Every kid wants to play for the Celtics or Lakers. I feel like I have another family up here."

Bias spent the night in Boston. The next day he visited the Celtic offices, spending time with Volk before visiting Reebok's suburban offices with his agent, Lee Fentress, and his father. They attended a reception at the Royal Sonesta Hotel, where Bias ate a hamburger and fries and answered more reporters' questions. Danny Ainge, another Reebock client, was at the reception. Bias excused himself at one point and went to call his mother. He caught an 8:30 P.M. flight out of Logan Airport and returned to Washington at about 10 P.M. He drove his father home, then returned to his Washington Hall dorm at College Park. He was a conquering hero. He walked into his room and emptied a sack of souvenirs onto the bed. There was Celtic and Reebok stuff for everybody.

At Washington Hall, Bias shared a suite with five teammates. Versions vary, and it has not been established how often Bias and his friends partied with cocaine, but it is indisputable that in the hours after midnight on the morning of June 19, Bias ingested enough cocaine to induce cardiac arrest. His party-mates observed him staggering about the suite and advised him to slow down. According to his friends, Len Bias's final words were, "I'm a bad motherfucker."

At 6:33 A.M., Bias's friend Brian Tribble dialed 911 and told the emergency operator, "I'd like to have an ambulance come. It's 1103 Washington Hall. It's an emergency. It's Len Bias, and he just went to Boston and needs some assistance."

Later in the cluttered, panicked conversation, Tribble said, "This is Len Bias. You have to get him back to life. There's no way he can die. Seriously, sir. Please come quick."

Bias was rushed to Leland Memorial Hospital, where he was declared dead of a heart attack at 8:55 A.M.

At his Prudential apartment in Boston, Auerbach got the chilling call from his friend Driesell. Later in the day, the Celtic front office cranked out this release under the headline "Statement of Red":

"The passing of Len Bias is one of the biggest shocks I've ever experienced. The boy achieved one of his goals in life [to be drafted high and by the Celtics]. I had a personal relationship with him which was quite unique. As a matter of fact, we were to meet Tuesday for lunch with Tip O'Neill, Ted Kennedy, John Moakley, John Kerry and Ed Markey and have lunch at the House. We'll always consider him a member of the Celtics family. My heart goes out to his folks, Coach Lefty Driesell, close friend James Brown and all his other friends in their hour of sorrow."

"It's the cruelest thing ever," said Larry Bird.

Five days later, results of an autopsy were made public and the world learned that Bias had died of cocaine intoxication. On the day of this announcement, Auerbach said, "I've always been the strongest advocate of mandatory drug testing, of random spot-testing. People talk about it being a violation of players' civil rights. But what's more important, civil rights or the elimination of a major, pressing problem, one which has now caused the death of a young man? It's still my belief that this was the first time Len tried drugs. They gave him some bad stuff . . . Unfortunately, these kids are convinced they can handle it. They're told by hangers-on, 'Try it one time. You're too smart to get addicted. It's like having a beer.' These hangers-on, they're why I don't like to see strangers in the dressing room. I've let it go on the past three years—but I promise you, there will be no 'friends' coming into the dressing room next year or ever again."

To this day, Auerbach believes Bias was a one-time drug user who paid the ultimate penalty for a single error in judgment. He still blames the "hangers-on."

"I think all rules are made to be broken," Auerbach says. "Anything that happens, there are always exceptions. This was a very unusual thing. I honestly feel that when he knew he was going to be a millionaire, and he fulfilled a dream not only of money, but of being in Boston, where he wanted to go, he got carried away. People forget that he was examined by us and he was clean. It was just one of those crazy things."

Cocaine in 1986 was the drug of choice among wealthy young basketball players bent on self-destruction. Bias paid the steepest price, but fellow 1986 first-round picks William Bedford, Chris Washburn and Roy Tarpley all went through bad times and banishment after "recreational" cocaine use.

At Bias's funeral, Auerbach gave James and Lonise Bias a Celtic jersey (No. 30, last worn by M. L. Carr, and not worn since) and told the crowd that the city of Boston had not been so shaken since the assassination of President John F. Kennedy.

Auerbach began to distance himself from the team immediately after Bias's death. The loss of the No. 2 pick was more than personal, more than personnel; it was a sign that his old ways didn't work in the new world. He had coached and made deals in a time when you worried about a ballplayer being a womanizer, or a boozer. He couldn't fathom that young, superman Len Bias, a kid from such a good family, a kid he knew and endorsed, could forfeit his life in the name of cocaine. Auerbach had made the adjustments to new owners, agents, long-term contracts, a players' union, the death of the dress code, the salary cap, the age of saturation scouting, three officials at every game, overreliance on video, the three-point shot, major marketing and the explosion of staffers (twenty-five plus interns) in the once three-man Celtic front office. This was different. When Bias went down, he took some of Auerbach with him.

Kevin McHale says, "I think after the Lenny Bias incident he had some health problems. I think he lost a little bit of interest. I think the whole thing bothered him a lot more than he'll ever tell anybody."

Owner Alan Cohen adds, "I think it really affected his involvement with the club. Red knew the Bias family. To him, it was like a dream that we were going to get Len Bias. He knew the family and he would have sworn on them, how great they were. When this happened, it was such a tragedy. He wanted to reach out and do so many things that he really couldn't do, and the impact on the team hit him second. But I think he felt tremendously let down. I think [because of] what happened to Red, the next decade of this team had just been torn apart. Those things did not happen in the early days."

Shocked and saddened, Cohen sat down and wrote a letter to GM Volk. The letter was about hubris. Never cease to be humble, he wrote. Just when you think you're invincible, somebody can tear down your house. It was as if Cohen knew the Celts had been too good for too long. The Auerbach Magic was gone. The Celtics were a team with a wealth of history and flags, but they were no longer exempt from the troubles and pains that visited every other NBA team.

The death of Bias unleashed seven years of hard luck, bad news and tragedy for the Boston franchise. It was as if some rowdy reveler had shattered a locker room mirror with a champagne bottle after the 1986 Game 6 clincher against the Houston Rockets. Since winning flag No. 16 in the sunshine of June 1986, the Celtics have been plagued by unwise personnel decisions, coaching instability, injuries, defections, retirements, player incarcerations and sudden death—horribly climaxed by the 1993 heart attack fatality of twenty-seven-year-old captain Reggie Lewis. Lewis, a Baltimore youth, had starred at Northeastern University, located on Huntington Avenue in downtown Boston. Boston drafted Lewis in the first round one year after Bias died. Moments after the draft, Lewis, a shy, quiet young man, was asked, "How are you going to celebrate?"

Bias to Lewis. Heart to heart. Has any team in the history of sports had consecutive No. 1 draft picks die of heart attacks while still in their twenties? Doubtful.

In his autobiography, Bird wrote, "If you believe in omens, the Bias thing was a pretty bad one."

Gerald Henderson chose to see larger forces at work. Henderson was the player coldly traded for the pick that led to Bias. Three years after the death of Bias, Henderson said, "I think everything happens because of the Lord. Maybe it just wasn't right from the very beginning. You never know. Maybe it just wasn't right for everybody involved. At that point [when Henderson was traded] they didn't know who they were going to get. You know. It just wasn't right."

In December 1986, the Green went green. Under a master limited partnership, Gaston, Cohen and Dupee sold 40 percent of the team to the public in 2.6 million shares. Shares started at $18.40 apiece and were traded under "BOS" on the New York Stock Exchange. The shares sold out instantly. A Celtic stock certificate, suitable for framing, was the perfect Christmas gift for the Boston sports fan who had everything.

Suddenly, yahoos who call sports talk radio could boast that they were owners of the team. They gleefully read the annual reports and learned Auerbach's salary. According to Boston Celtics Limited Partnerships, filed with the U.S. Securities and Exchange Commission, Auerbach is under a lifetime contract that paid him $250,000 annually until July 31, 1992, at which time his salary was reduced to $125,000 per year. Upon his death, the agreement calls for Dot Auerbach to receive the same compensation for as long as she lives. Auerbach also receives $21,600 per year from his NBA pension.

In *The Selling of the Green,* former Celtic owner Irv Levin told Harvey Araton and Filip Bondy, "For years, I know Red had plenty of opportunities to own part of the team and never would. They gave Red a contract for $250,000 lifetime, but that team was worth more than $100 million and three owners made a fortune from that public sale. The feeling at the time was that the team was nothing without Red. The stock deal would never have gone through if Red said the word. I was shocked that Red didn't get a piece. I mean, 10 percent and he's got $10 million. If I was closer to him, I would have called him and said, 'You schmuck, why didn't you get in there?' It was all his sweat, and those guys just cashed in."

The three primary owners, who'd bought the team for $17 million in 1983, made more than $44 million when the team went public. And they still had the controlling interest. It was free money.

The Celtics were still defending NBA champs when Green Team stock became a stocking stuffer in December 1986. Despite the Bias setback, the Celts were fat and happy, and it looked as if the string of sellouts and success would go on forever. Bird, Parish, McHale, D.J. and Ainge still were on top of their games, and there was a feeling that the C's might run off another three or four championships in a row. Just like the 1960s. And this time, they had money to go along with their success.

But injuries took a toll on this Boston team. Walton hurt himself riding an exercise bike and played in only six games; it would be the final season of his career. Scott Wedman, another former All-Star, suffered a heel injury and played in only six games. McHale cracked a bone in his foot, although he kept playing. Bias, of course, would have made up for some of these injuries.

During the 1987 NBA playoffs, Driesell said, "I've been watching the Celtics the past few weeks, and it would have been so much different with Leonard. There wouldn't have been two seven-game series if Leonard had been around. The Celtics would have won much easier. Leonard was such a great outside shooter, he would have forced changes in the other teams. It would have been all so different. But that's speculation. We'll never know, will we?"

Auerbach found some of his old feistiness during the smash-mouth playoffs of 1987. In the early rounds he worked as a color commentator for WTBS-TV. Commenting on a Piston-Bullet playoff game, Auerbach said Detroit players Bill Laimbeer and Rick Mahorn were "the dirtiest players in the league." Piston GM Jack McCloskey filed a written protest to the NBA office, saying he didn't believe Auerbach should be allowed to work games while the Celtics were still alive in the playoffs. Auerbach's response was, "The guy is just trying to get some attention for himself by taking potshots at me. The guy is a loser who is just frustrated. This happens to a lot of guys who tried coaching and can't win. They have to find ways to call attention to themselves . . . Hey, who is McCloskey?"

The Celtics beat the Pistons in a thrilling seven-game Eastern Conference final and advanced to the NBA Finals for the fourth time in four years.

For the third time in four years, the championship final was a Boston-LA matchup. When the Celtics lost the fourth game of the finals at home, falling behind three games to one, Auerbach saw something he didn't like and made his way to the officials' room after the game ended.

Veteran NBA official Jake O'Donnell, who was an alternate for the game, remembers, "He wanted to get at Earl [Strom]. He kicked the door. He was screaming at Strom."

NBA Commissioner David Stern says, "I was there when he went and sang a tune to Earl Strom outside the locker room. I said, 'Red, please.'"

In his biography, Strom wrote, "We got to the locker room and here came Red, screaming like a madman. He had chased us through the crowd, cussing us all the way. He was saying that if I had any balls, the Lakers would never have gotten back in the game. He was calling me every dirty-rotten-lowlife name he had called me over the previous thirty years, kicking the same old door."

Strom put his head out the door and said, "Arnold, you're show-ing me all the class I always knew you had."

Rod Thorn, the NBA's fine-master, says, "Red could always con-jure up a hate for any rival. Los Angeles got the ball out-of-bounds

late in the game and Magic threw in a hook in the lane and Red
was not happy. We fined Red for that one."

Auerbach paid the fine and delivered his customary message to
any sitting commissioner: "You have no balls."

Stern laughs and says, "Red starts off by telling you how inade-
quate you are for the job, any job. Red would have been a helluva
coach today, but I'm sure glad he's not, because we've got a bunch
of pussycats compared to Red.

"Other teams always would complain about him and the Celtics.
It was great. The Celtics would call us and complain about how badly
we were treating them, and the rest of the league would call and
complain about the fact that we were favoring the Celtics. It was
wonderful. Red always has an important reason—unrelated to competitive—as to why something should be done, but it always happens
to turn out to be in the best interests of the Celtics. There were
times he misbehaved when he shouldn't have. I don't think anyone
ever confused Red with Winnie-the-Pooh, but in the quiet reflection
he was never too arrogant or important to analyze something and
take a different view than the one he originally had."

The Celtics lost the 1987 finals in six games. Auerbach did not
attend the games in Los Angeles. Instead of flying to LA, he went
to his granddaughter Julie's high school graduation at Bethesda's
Chevy Chase High School. He hadn't been there very often for
Nancy or Randy, and was trying to do more for Julie.

Grandfather Arnold still was feared around the league. NBA executives lived in dread of finding a yellow message slip inscribed,
"Red Auerbach called."

Chicago Bull GM Jerry Krause remembers, "He called me about
an hour before the draft and offered me Sam Vincent for some draft
picks. And I thought, 'Wait a minute, there's something crazy here.
I don't want to deal with Red. He's too good. He's gotten too many
people.' I made some calls about Vincent. In the end, I said, 'No—
Red's gotta know something about this that I don't know and I'm
not going to fool with Red.' When a guy makes a lot of good moves
and does things the right way, you have a tendency to be a little
afraid of him."

In the summer of 1987, Celtic assistant coach and director of player personnel Jimmy Rodgers was offered a job as head coach of the New York Knicks. Auerbach put the kibosh on the deal. Rodgers was still under contract with the Celtics and Auerbach wanted compensation from the Knicks. New York didn't meet Auerbach's demand, and Rodgers was forced to stay. It was harsh treatment for a "family" member, but Auerbach had plans for Rodgers and he didn't want one of his best minds going to the hated Knicks.

Had Rodgers been schooled in Celtic history, he would not have been surprised. In 1969, when Cincinnati Royal coach Cousy wanted to come out of retirement to sell a few tickets and improve his relationship with the Royals' owner, Auerbach demanded compensation. In 1982, when Cowens wanted to come out of retirement to join friend Don Nelson in Milwaukee, Auerbach held out for Quinn Buckner. Compensation was thicker than blood. Rodgers lost out on a golden opportunity and bided his time with the Celtics.

"I don't blame Jimmy for wanting it, but I don't blame us, either," says Auerbach. "We treated him pretty damn good for an assistant coach. He was probably the highest-paid assistant coach in the league, because we were grooming him as the successor. And when you've got all that extra money and stuff invested in a guy, you kind of resent that he would say, 'The hell with you; I'm going.' He was under contract."

Auerbach turned seventy in the fall of 1987. Shortly thereafter, he broke a couple of ribs diving for a ball while playing tennis. He also had prostate surgery, around that time. Auerbach's daughter Randy works with film director Mel Brooks, and Brooks made a telephone call to the basketball legend. Brooks was facing similar surgery. He asked Auerbach what it was like.

"It's no big deal, but it's a deal," said Auerbach.

"Mel loved that," recalls Randy. "He thought that was the greatest thing to say."

Restless on the shelf, Auerbach started thinking about his own mortality.

"I always thought of myself as invincible, sort of an iron man, you know," he told the *Boston Herald*'s Joe Fitzgerald. "I always ate whatever I wanted to eat, whenever I wanted to eat it . . . Then all of a sudden you get older. The body begins to deteriorate a bit and you begin to worry, 'Jeez, this isn't like me, I used to be able to run forever.' And the doc, I guess he must have been reading my mind, because he looked at me and said, 'Hey, Red, even a train must stop sometime.' "

Honors kept coming his way. There were honorary degrees, requests to speak to groups of every kind and more things being named after him. Receiving an honorary degree in humanities from American International College in Springfield, Massachusetts, he missed the climactic seventh game of the 1988 conference semifinals between the Celtics and Hawks. (Boston won, 118–116.) In the fall of 1988, Brandeis University announced plans to build a $25 million athletic/convocation center; today, the Celtics practice in Red Auerbach Arena. When the joint was dedicated, Auerbach said, "We're gonna have a sign in my arena: Cigar Smoking Only."

"There's no smoking allowed in the building, except for Red," says Brandeis athletic director Jeff Cohen.

As always, there was a Chinese food restaurant near the new Celtic facility. It was the same at Hellenic College in Brookline and Camp Milbrook in Marshfield. Suspicious sportswriters wondered if there was perhaps some connection between Celtic practice sites and Chinese eateries.

The aging Auerbach never stopped teaching. Former Celtic center Greg Kite, a backup fixture for five years (and four finals), says, "I always felt that one of his strengths was that he was a teacher in a lot of ways. He'd go up to Larry and D.J. a lot. After practice, he'd make a suggestion to try to help you. With me it was mostly free throws, but I remember K.C. telling me to work on a hook and Red coming out and helping me with that. I think he really realized the importance of different pieces of the puzzle that fit together. It seemed to me he seemed to place a lot of value on good people, people who got along, people who weren't renegades or jerks, people who were willing to work hard."

While Auerbach was enjoying life as legend-in-residence, the Celtics were floundering under the new regime of GM Volk and new coach Jimmy Rodgers. Rodgers had been elevated to the top spot after management urged K. C. Jones to retire from the bench following the six-game 1987–1988 playoff loss to the Pistons. Jones reluctantly took a golden handshake front-office position, and never blasted Auerbach.

Rodgers never had a chance. Bird had double-heel surgery and played only six games of the 1988–1989 season. As a result, the Celtics went 42–40 and were bounced out of the playoffs by Detroit again, this time in three straight games. One round. Over and out.

It got worse for the new coach. In the spring of 1989, the Celtics used their first-round pick to select Brigham Young shooter Michael Smith. One of the players bypassed was Tim Hardaway, who later became an All-Star guard with the Golden State Warriors. Revisionist historians believe that Rodgers wanted to draft Hardaway, but was overruled by Auerbach. Smith was Auerbach's pick—a classic, slow, 1950s player.

Cousy says, "What I do think happened was pure ego. Whoever called him [Auerbach] at the last minute and said, 'Hey, this Smith could be another Bird.' That was what he wanted to hear. Hit one more home run. Because I was told that he was the only one in that room who wanted Smith. He [Auerbach] came in at the last minute. My information is that the only guy who was saying Hardaway was Cohen. Jimmy wanted [B. J.] Armstrong. So they would have taken Armstrong, but Arnold came in at the last minute."

"He was my pick, but he was everybody's pick," says Auerbach. "He was my pick. I saw him and I liked him. But nevertheless, we'll never know how good he would have been. I liked him if I was coaching, but you're not always right. He had all the skills of a professional. His toughness, I think, could have been worked on. His defense could have been worked on. But somehow or other, I always felt that there's certain people that won't teach. They want a finished product, and if they don't get it, they'll trade him to try to get a finished product. They won't teach, and I was predominately a teacher."

This is a not-so-subtle shot at Rodgers, who coached the Celtics during Smith's disappointing rookie year.

Clearly, Auerbach was unhappy with Rodgers. Meanwhile, promising young guard Brian Shaw bolted from the Celtics and went to play for Il Messaggero, in Rome. Yugoslavian Dino Radja, a 6-10 forward who was Boston's second-round pick in 1989, also wound up playing for Il Messaggero. The Celtics looked ridiculous.

After the Smith, Shaw and Radja fiascos, it was obvious that something had to be done in the Celtic front office. Volk was master of law and salary cap complications, but he didn't know courts from torts. Rodgers was on his way out as head coach and Auerbach— forever stung by Bias and in his early seventies—simply was no longer current. On May 6, the Celtics were bumped from the play-offs, losing a fifth and deciding game to the Knicks on the Boston Garden court. It was the second consecutive season in which the Celts were eliminated in the first round of the playoffs. To lose at home to the hated Knicks . . . that meant something had to be done.

Rodgers was fired. The decision was made by Auerbach and own-ers Cohen and Gaston. It was cold. Rodgers had been denied a chance to coach the Knicks, and when he finally got the Celtic job, he was handicapped by the loss of Bird, McHale's broken foot, the Michael Smith draft, and Shaw's defection. Rodgers is a bitter, silent man. Since he was fired by the Celtics he has been hired and fired by the Minnesota Timberwolves. But he has never publicly blasted Auerbach or the Boston franchise.

On May 30, 1990, Dave Gavitt was hired as senior executive vice president of the Boston Celtics. This was the true beginning of the end of Red Auerbach's influence over the franchise. He had "re-tired" once or twice before, but never had there been anybody in any position of power over him in the organization. He had answered to owners and nobody else. Auerbach and Gavitt addressed the press together on the day Gavitt was hired. Auerbach said, "I believe we've landed one of the best basketball minds in the business."

After delivering a brief introduction, Auerbach said, "I'm going to just move the mike over and let Dave answer your questions."

He placed the microphone in front of Gavitt, then pulled a Hoyo de Monterrey cigar from the breast pocket of his blue blazer and lit up as Gavitt started to speak. The torch was passed. A plume of smoke rose over Gavitt's head. One last victory cigar.

Gavitt came to the NBA with a flawless reputation. He was born in Westerly, Rhode Island, grew up in Peterborough, New Hamp-shire, and lettered in baseball and basketball at Dartmouth. He coached at Worcester Academy and Dartmouth before taking over as head coach at Providence College in 1969. He took the Friars to the NCAA Final Four with Marvin Barnes, Ernie DiGregorio and Kevin Stacom. After leaving Providence he invented the Big East Conference, which became the most powerful college basketball league in America in the mid-1980s. He negotiated a billion-dollar NCAA television package. He held a position on the U.S. Olympic Committee and was president of USA Basketball—the official letterhead of America's 1992 Olympic Dream Team in Barcelona.

Celtic fans in the spring of 1990 were buoyed by the addition of his considerable talents, but there was something slightly sad about the ceremony that officially delivered Gavitt to the Celtics. As long as anyone could remember, there had been only one Basketball Guy on Causeway Street.

The press release stated, "Gavitt, 52, will have full and complete authority and responsibility with respect to all phases of the Celtics basketball operation."

Gavitt was sufficiently reverent. He spoke glowingly of Auerbach and likened himself to an apprentice painter "having an opportunity to work with Michelangelo."

But he also said, "I've been given the authority to do the job. There is no issue as far as authority, control or responsibility."

Auerbach said, "Dave's going to come up with suggestions. He'll bounce 'em off me, but he's gonna make the decisions, because you can't hobble a guy. You can't have him come up with ideas, then knock him down. Things aren't really going to change for me. I don't spend as much time with it as I used to, and now I feel more secure because of Gavitt's knowledge of the game. I can tell I'm getting a little older by the way I'm playing racquetball. I'm not as sharp as I used to be in certain veins. It's not that I've lost any of my toughness. I just don't have the energy to get on the phone and call guys and run here and there. I don't have that kind of zing."

The question was posed: What if Gavitt wants to go north and Auerbach wants to go south? What then?

Auerbach shuffled his feet and said, "That's a leading question. We'll approach that. I don't think that that will ever occur. But if it came to that, I'm sure he would explain everything logically to me and I would agree. Or I would explain everything logically to him and he would agree."

Red was reluctant. There was still some fight in him. Gavitt could have the Celtic house, the deed to the land and the mailbox, but Red was still going to hold on to one back-door key.

"Is Dave Gavitt your successor?" Auerbach was asked.

"He's younger," Auerbach said with a wink.

A reporter asked if the selection of Gavitt was Auerbach's way of preparing the Celtics for "life without Red Auerbach."

"I don't talk about life after Red Auerbach," Auerbach said. "I don't talk about that at all. I got a lifetime contract. I don't have any one-year contract, unless you think I'm going to die."

It was 1990. Nobody thought Auerbach was going to die.

Today Gavitt says, "My first memory of Red was me being a kid growing up in New England when he was coaching in the fifties. But I really got to know him more in the sixties, because I was at Worcester Academy for a year and Rudy LaRusso, who played with me at Dartmouth, was playing for the Lakers. So I'd frequently come to games. We became friends during that period of time, and for the next twenty years, we'd talk on the phone or get each other tickets. We always had kind of an unwritten rule: I would never call him for tickets unless they were for me, personally. And he would do the same with me if he wanted to go to the Final Four or the Big East tournament."

Gavitt took on the lofty title of club CEO. There were no CEOs in Red Auerbach's day. The NBA was changing, and the Celtics were merely keeping up with the times. Commissioner Stern had negotiated a four-year, $600 million television package with NBC. The draft was a prime-time television event; the draft *lottery* was a prime-time television event. NBA All-Star Weekend was a festival of self-congratulations. Print journalists were moved away from courtside (not yet in Boston) as owners made room for high-roller fans who didn't mind paying hundreds of dollars for the privilege of literally rubbing elbows with the players. The new NBA was a league with a salary cap, a healthy relationship between players and owners (a six-year collective bargaining agreement had been struck in 1988), lucrative merchandising and successful new franchises in Charlotte,

Miami, Minnesota and Orlando. Stern was the Pete Rozelle of the late eighties and early nineties. The NBA was popular, progressive and profitable. Soon, it would be global. Teams were no longer run like family groceries. Teams had CEOs.

Gavitt was riding a thirty-year winning streak when he came to the Celtics, but things have never been quite right for him since he joined the NBA. As a guru of amateur basketball, he was the best. It has not been easy at the pro level. Gavitt has been unable to have things his way and make it look easy, as he did when he worked at the amateur level.

With Gavitt in charge, the Celtics started their search for a coach, and almost immediately Gavitt and Auerbach clashed. Auerbach wanted to elevate family member Chris Ford, while Gavitt sought the services of Duke head coach Mike Krzyzewski. While Ford twisted in the wind, word got out that Boston wanted to hire Krzyzewski. The Celtics considered it merely an informational interview, but when Krzyzewski's name got into print, Ford looked like second choice.

It was a lesson for Gavitt. He'd been able to control everything when he worked at the amateur level, but in the NBA his work was an open book, even though he'd tried to keep his disagreement with Auerbach private.

Krzyzewski held a press conference announcing that he was not interested in the Celtics. The mighty Celtics had been shot down by a college coach. Ford was hired and Auerbach said, "Chris Ford was our first choice from the get-go." Everybody knew this was not true, but Auerbach always has rewritten history to put himself and the Celtics in the best possible light. It was tough to do this time. Rodgers looked like a scapegoat and Ford a bridesmaid. Auerbach and Gavitt looked like they were feuding. It was not tidy.

After decades of charmed existence, the Celtics suddenly were afflicted with the problems that affected every other sports team in the 1980s. There was coaching instability, player defection, poor drafting and public criticism. Auerbach no longer was the point man, and the franchise was vulnerable to all the traps and critiques that had plagued most organizations at one time or another.

On draft day, 1990, Auerbach ("You can't teach height") promoted 7-1 Dwayne Schintzius. Gavitt scoffed and said, "Only if you can cut him in half and make two point guards out of him." The Celtics drafted point guard Dee Brown.

Gavitt on Auerbach's role in the draft: "He's interested. He's not gonna make the call, but I use him as a great devil's advocate. He's a great insurance policy against making a bad mistake. So I would say his role is a solid one and important. We talk usually every other day, sometime in the morning."

When Ford wanted to hire ex-Clipper coach Don Casey as an assistant coach, Casey had to audition for Auerbach. Auerbach claimed never to have heard of Casey, even though his Clippers had beaten the Celtics in the Garden a year earlier. Auerbach said, "Everybody tells us you're good, but what I want to know is, if you're so goddamned good, why don't you have a job?"

Subtle. Miraculously, Casey was hired.

Not involved with player or coaching decisions, Auerbach was still good for a predictable public blast if any agent threatened the Celtics' interests. When star guard Reggie Lewis retained Jerome Stanley—the same agent who'd shuttled Shaw off to Italy—Auerbach said, "I couldn't believe it when I heard the news. Here is a kid who played ball in college in Boston [Northeastern]. A kid who said he loved to play for the Celtics. He always seemed happy. Then one morning you wake up and his new agent is saying he will never play for the Celtics again after next year . . . You wonder what the hell gets into these kids, and you realize that the dollar is all that counts anymore. Not only with these players, but with some of the clubs in the league, too. The whole thing stinks."

Whether he was commenting on "another money-grubbing agent" or putting his ceremonial stamp of approval on somebody who'd effectively already been hired, it was clear that Auerbach was no longer in charge. Gavitt, meanwhile, went about the task of bringing the Celtics from the fifties to the nineties. He hired a full-time community liaison. He ordered a face-lift for the archaic team practice site at Hellenic College. He bought new exercise equipment, weights, video equipment. He instituted weight training and nutrition programs. A lot of people were hired. A lot of people were working for the Celtics, not all of whom knew each other's names.

While the Celtics were catching up to the rest of the league in the areas of scouting, training, preparation, public relations and bureaucracy, they continued their descent from the top of the standings. The Detroit Pistons were the new champs and the Celtics couldn't beat them anymore. The Chicago Bulls were on the rise and Boston couldn't win in Chicago. In fact, the Celtics couldn't win against any tough opponent on the road.

Bad things continued to happen. In 1991, bench player Charles Smith, who came highly recommended from Georgetown's John Thompson, was sent to jail after a vehicle he was driving killed two Boston University coeds in a late-night driving accident on Commonwealth Avenue. Rookie sensation Dee Brown blew out his knee while simply running the court at the beginning of his second season. HarperCollins in 1991 released *The Selling of the Green,* by New York writers Harvey Araton and Filip Bondy. The book slaughtered the Celtic reputation, concluding, "The Boston Celtics are still for whites." Auerbach, whose picture is on the cover of the book, was portrayed as a sore loser with no ethics who favored whites over blacks (except for superstar-meal ticket Bill Russell) and never lifted a finger to improve the Celtics' relations with the Boston community. There is a copy of the book in Auerbach's den in his Washington apartment. He says he hasn't read it.

The New York press has always been tough on Auerbach. The estimable Peter Vecsey, formerly of the *USA Today* and now the *New York Post*'s hoop guru and NBC analyst, says, "Red and I got into some arguments over the years. At one point I didn't feel like they were doing the right thing with Tiny Archibald, and I let Red know to his face. I just felt they weren't showing respect or loyalty like they would to other guys and he was like, 'Who the fuck do you think you are?' It was a mistake on my part, because it got personal.

"Hey, the man took the league and used everybody and abused 'em as far as trades go. I think it's legitimate that he was way ahead of most of the other club presidents and GMs for many years until it got more sophisticated. He wasn't afraid to take a chance and had street smarts that other guys don't have. But worse than being a sore loser, he was a bad winner. He put it in people's faces. How do you like a guy like that? I got to believe that anybody who ever put on a Laker uniform had no use for him."

Rick Fox was a rookie with the Celtics in 1991–1992.

"My first contact with him was at rookie camp. I didn't have a personal introduction to Red. He walked up to me and looked at me. He had a cigar in his mouth and he was on his way to a row of chairs he was going to sit in. He looked at me. He looked down at my shoes. I had on high-tops. I guess his pet peeve is that he believes you should wear low-tops. He just said, 'You got to cut down,' and then he walked off. Chris Ford came over and I asked him what that comment meant and he told me that it meant Red wants me to wear low-tops. That was my first introduction to the legendary Red Auerbach.

"He exploded on me one day. It was probably the scariest thing I've had happen to me since I've been here. We won a game, but played terrible. I came into the trainer's room and Red had just had his blood pressure checked. The trainer walked out as I was walking in and Red was the only person in there. I said 'How are you doing, Mr. Auerbach?' and he started in on me—'How could you be so fucking dumb? You play so great, and then you do something stupid. And it's not just you, it's the whole team.' He was real fired up, and it caught me off guard."

Rick Carlisle, a Celtic in the mid-1980s and now a coach with the Nets, remembers a similar experience: "I had met him only once, at his camp at Marshfield. I remember being surprised that he knew my name. He just said, 'Hi, Rick,' then drove off in his golf cart. About four days later, I was shooting some free throws and he walked over, looked at me and said, 'How stupid can you be?' He went on to tell me something about my free throw shooting I needed to do differently. It was a simple, but important, thing about the way I was cocking my wrist. He was right. From that point on, I always was very cautious and ready to hear anything from him."

When Auerbach wasn't scaring one of the young Celtics, he often enjoyed a nap, sometimes while he was on the clock.

Gavitt: "Red's not an early-to-bed guy, but he's one of the greatest nappers of all time. He sits at his desk with the cigar going

and he's got the tinted glasses and sometimes you can't tell. He'll
be sitting there like that and he'll be sleeping. It's just for five
minutes. And he has this great ability to come out of it and say
something that'll make you think he never was asleep. A couple of
years ago at the Portsmith Invitational Tournament, he was sitting
under the basket in the first row. He'd make [scouts] Forddy Anderson and Rick Weitzman go three hours early to get a seat. So,
we're sitting there and I know he's taking one of his catnaps. I can
tell, but there's no evidence of it, unless you know him. So he's
taking this catnap and there's a guy with a television camera and
he's filming for a local station. Red's got the tinted glasses on and
he's fast asleep. So we're watching on the late news back at the hotel
and they're talking about the tournament and all the NBA scouts
being on hand. Then they show Red and the narrator says, 'And
here's the keenest eye of them all, Red Auerbach,' and I know that
when the guy filmed the thing, Red was asleep, and so I kid him."

In August 1992, a few weeks after the Dream Team came home
from Barcelona with the gold medal, Larry Bird announced his retirement. He could no longer endure the constant pain in his back.
The announcement was made at a hastily called press conference at
Boston Garden on August 18. It was a sad day for Celtic Nation,
and especially difficult for godfather Auerbach.

"You know how much I care for Cousy and Russell," he said.
"And that I never would say a bad word about them. Never. Not
one word. But this kid . . . Bird. Not putting down any other player
that ever played here, but Bird was the most self-motivated player
ever. He was the best I ever saw getting himself ready for every
game and doing things to get his teammates ready. He was completely into playing, into winning. That's how I remember him."

*Completely into winning.* He might just as well have been talking
about himself.

Bird wore a black and red sweater to his bittersweet retirement
press conference. A large photograph of Bird in the sweater and
Auerbach in one of his brown blazers, walking across the parquet
floor, adorns the wall of Auerbach's den in Washington.

The 1992–1993 Celtics started the season with a 2–8 record, and
Auerbach said, "I think we can make the playoffs, barring further

injury. People forget we prepared for this when we drafted Len Bias. That situation disappeared and that was a huge, bad break. Now, if we had Len Bias, we would be a contender, no question in my mind. And we didn't just lose him—we lost him for ten years."

It was a sad comment. Auerbach was still moaning about a player who'd been dead for six and a half years. And it was not the Celtic way to talk about "making the playoffs." Never before had "making the playoffs" been any kind of Celtic goal. You won the championship, or it was a lost season.

More woes. In January 1993, longtime Celtic broadcaster Johnny Most died. Auerbach told the Celtic fans what they wanted to hear. He said that Most "was part of this whole pride, mystique, Celtic image." Privately, it was known that Auerbach was not a fan of Johnny Most. The announcer had been difficult to handle on the road, and there had been too many bad loans and unpaid bills.

In early February 1993, Bird was feted in a two-and-a-half-hour Larryfest at Boston Garden. Auerbach was a central player in the lengthy tribute. Sharing the stage with master of ceremonies Bob Costas, he got to be Red again.

Auerbach: "He's a man's man. I'm just proud, very proud to call him a friend. And the only regret I have, I've never coached him."

Costas: "Wasn't the deal to get him with the Lakers? Didn't you send Charlie Scott off for that pick?"

Auerbach: "I don't remember."

Everybody laughed. But there was some sad truth to the statement. Auerbach was having more trouble remembering things. Seventy-five years is a long time, and Auerbach had more to remember than most people. He was becoming forgetful. He was mixing up facts in some of his stories. He could still remember how much he was paid for every nickel-and-dime job of his youth, but he was having trouble remembering all of the details of his professional career.

The 1992–1993 Celtic campaign was a sorry season of bad news. Megabuck guard Sherman Douglas took his shoes off while sitting on the bench during a game, then left the team for a few days. A reserve forward named Marcus Webb made unsubstantiated racial charges against local police—charges that embarrassed the Celtic organization. (Webb later went to jail after being charged with rape.) Parish was arrested for marijuana possession. McHale retired.

Auerbach, meanwhile, just kept getting older.

"He hasn't lost any of his sharpness," Gavitt said in the spring of 1993. "His instincts into the game, his insights into the game are every bit as strong as they always were. He's not current, but why should you be current at age seventy-five? He still picks up little things. A couple of times, I think he really helped Reggie. Reggie, sometimes when he's coming off downscreens down low, off to the side, he tends to catch the ball and put in on the floor as a defensive mechanism. Once he does that, he tends to take away a lot of his offensive weaponry—any move he makes has got to be made off the dribble. What he should be doing is coming off the downscreen and catching it and turning and squaring. Now, you've got to respect his shot; you can't crowd him quite as much. Reggie occasionally would fall into this bad habit, and Red picked it up. Red will even pick things up on television. He's a wealth of information, and you'd be crazy not to tap it. If you lay out a scenario to him, he picks up on things I never would. He's not always right, but he's right more often than he isn't."

Shortly after Gavitt made those remarks, Auerbach succumbed to some of the traps of old age. He broke a couple of ribs again, this time while playing racquetball at George Washington with school vice president Bob Chernak.

The Celtics were bounced from the playoffs by the expansion Charlotte Hornets. Boston won the first game, but Lewis collapsed because of a heart malfunction. Lewis never played another game, and the series was over in four. On the evening of May 7, two days after the season ended, Auerbach attended the annual team breakup dinner at the Ritz-Carlton. It would be the last time he would see Reggie Lewis. Auerbach was uncomfortable at the function. He had the sweats and felt a tightness in his chest. When he got back to his apartment at the Prudential, he called his doctor, cardiologist Roman DeSanctis. Then he took a cab to Massachusetts General Hospital. Doctors wanted to do bypass surgery, but Auerbach resisted.

"I think you know Red," said Dr. DeSanctis. "He really didn't want to have an operation, so we decided not to . . . Red is Red. He got someone to sneak him a corned beef sandwich and he pleaded with us to take him somewhere in the hospital where he could smoke a cigar. But he'll have to wait until he's home for that."

*Awww, that clean living. It'll kill you every time.*

Less than a month after his angioplasty procedures, on June 18, 1993, Auerbach was back at Mass. General for a six-hour quintuple heart bypass performed by Dr. Mortimer J. Buckley. Medical center spokesman Martin Bander said, "It wasn't really a significant surprise that he had to return. Only two of the five arteries done by open-heart surgery had blockage treated by angioplasty. There is a high rate of closure, partly due to age."

Auerbach went home to recover. But the summer of 1993 was to be without a doubt the worst off-season in the history of the Boston franchise. Patriarch Red Auerbach almost died. And six months later, there was another bolt of bad news: On July 27, Celtic captain Reggie Lewis collapsed and died on the court of the team practice facility at Brandeis, just one floor above the Red Auerbach Arena. Auerbach was unable to come to Boston for Lewis's funeral.

A month after the funeral, Alan Cohen resigned as vice chairman of Boston Celtics Limited Partnerships. Don Gaston handed the team over to his son, Paul. The younger Gaston said, "We've just had a terrible run of bad luck lately, and I just hope some good things start to happen to us."

Bad luck. Every conversation about the Celtics came back to bad luck.

"It's since the Bias thing," says Cousy. "If you wanted to pick a time—not necessarily to coincide with Arnold's starting to lose touch, but their bad luck, their deals—everything seems to have gone downhill since them. I attribute it more to bad luck than anything."

Ashes to ashes, dust to dust. Bias to Lewis. Seven years of bad luck for Red Auerbach and his Boston Celtics.

# 10

# THE LION IN WINTER

---

*He was a man of his time. His act wouldn't fly today, but it was very effective in those days, and he knew how to get talent. He's way past his time now. I know in my conversations with him now, I've come home thinking, "Wow, he is in another world." He's just not staying up with what the hell's going on. But given his success rate over the years, it's hard to say that he ever lost his eye for talent, or certainly his eye for making a deal. It'll be that way until he dies. I still have people say to me, "Oh, Red will pull something out of the hat."*

BOB COUSY

T HE AUERBACH DAUGHTERS, BY THIS TIME WOMEN IN THEIR forties, remember the strangeness of being in Boston on the eve of their father's heart-bypass surgery in the summer of 1993. In the anxious hours before and after the dangerous procedure, Randy Auerbach and Nancy Collins would have dinner and visit the Quincy Market shops that surround the statue of their famous father.

"It was weird, because we were sitting there at eleven o'clock at night and my father was in the hospital and people were sitting on the statue in his lap and patting his head," says Randy. "It was a very surreal experience. It was kind of weird."

Nancy Collins, Auerbach's oldest child, says, "It was hard to see the statue when he was sick. My sister and I would go down there every day to get our fried dough and we'd see it. It was uncomfortable."

It would be easy to believe that Red Auerbach is the world's worst hospital patient. Dorothy remembers, "One time I brought him the wrong pill and he looked at me and said, 'What are you trying to do, kill me?' "

Auerbach has led a life of control, and one has little control when attached to the apparatus surrounding a hospital bed. One day after the surgery, Randy Auerbach had to call for her dad's doctor.

"When you have surgery there are procedures you must do to protect the patient," says Randy. "And he was not real happy with these things, and it took several people to hold him back. I had to call the doctor very early in the morning and ask him to come over, and the doctor was great. He said, 'Red, I'm the coach here. You're not the coach here. This is my court.' It was perfect, because he was so drugged. It was the morning after his surgery. But he heard it. It was the only thing he could hear. It was so brilliant for the doctor to say that. He listened. After that, there were no problems."

"Every day we had to bring him doughnuts," remembers Nancy. "We were all going crazy. I felt like a Donut Dolly from World War II. Every morning he'd have a Dunkin' Donut. He likes crullers, honey-dipped and chocolate-covered doughnuts."

Dorothy did not fly to Boston for this most serious of surgeries. Ever the homebody, Dorothy stayed at the apartment in Washington and took phone calls from her daughters. "I didn't go on the big deal," she says. "I had gone up for the first one [the angioplasties] and that was bad enough. It was not really hard not to be there. It was a strange hospital. I didn't know the doctors. I just was chicken. I didn't go, and I'm not sorry."

When the Celtic patriarch went home to convalesce and begin rehabilitation, he was weak and depressed. He had to cancel his cameo appearance in William Friedkin's basketball movie, *Blue Chips*. (Auerbach was replaced by Pete Newell.) He was unable to play racquetball. No late-night Chinese food. No (gulp) cigars. There didn't seem to be much purpose.

When Gavitt made the call on Boston's top pick, Acie Earl, it marked the first time since 1949 that Auerbach wasn't present to bark out the name of Boston's top selection. He no longer was a presence. Fans missed him. Even though he hadn't been active in day-to-day operations of the ball club for almost ten years and even though he hadn't necessarily been behind all of the drafts and all of the trades in the late 1980s and early 1990s, there had been the perception that Auerbach was calling the shots. New England sports fans took comfort in this. No more. Auerbach was out of the loop. Totally. He was Marlon Brando as Don Corleone, playing with his grandson in the garden while his progeny carried out the family business.

"I was in a fog during those days," Auerbach says. "I was fighting for my life. You don't realize anything at the time. There are more important things. Dave and I had naturally talked things over before the draft, and it turned out the way it would have if I was there."

Five weeks after the surgery, he told the *Herald*'s Joe Fitzgerald, "You know what really gets to me? Everybody saying, 'Hey, Red, it's no big deal. My neighbor had an operation like that,' or 'My brother-in-law had an operation like that.' All those friggin' guys who had this operation weren't seventy-five years old when it happened . . . I think the best thing you can do for people is shut up and don't talk about it . . . You get down because you want to be well, you want to feel well, and you want it to happen quickly. I mean, who the hell needs this?"

"He was thrown by it," says Randy. "I think we all were."

Then Lewis died. It was the sad, shocking culmination of three months during which Lewis had first collapsed while running his lane in a playoff game, then submitted to numerous medical diagnoses. Lewis's death was the single greatest tragedy visited upon the Celtics, one of the most shocking episodes in the long history of Boston professional sports. There had been ample warning. After his initial collapse during a playoff game against Charlotte in April—an event witnessed by Auerbach and a national television audience—Lewis was examined by a team of twelve prominent cardiologists assembled by the Celtics. The "Dream Team" of cardiology concluded that Lewis had a life-threatening heart condition and should cease his basketball career.

After the findings were made public, Lewis immediately checked himself out of New England Baptist Hospital (where the Celtics had sent him) and transferred to Brigham and Women's Hospital in Boston. At Brigham and Women's, he got a "second" (actually, thirteenth) opinion from cardiologist Dr. Gilbert Mudge. Dr. Mudge concluded that Lewis was afflicted with a relatively minor neurological condition that could be treated with medication, and told the world that Lewis had "a normal athlete's heart."

Gavitt was present at the Mudge press conference and quickly embraced the new findings. He said it was the best news he had heard in a long time. By their own admission, the Celtics never again discussed Lewis's condition with their star player. Meanwhile, team lawyers had advised management to refrain from questioning Dr. Mudge's diagnosis—it would only serve to expose the team to potential legal action if something went wrong.

Less than two months after the Mudge statement, Lewis was dead.

"Dave called me," remembers Auerbach. "I was very sad and very unhappy, because I liked Reggie as a kid. Not only as a player— he was a helluva kid. There are certain things that are no-win situations. If you recommend a doctor and you're ninety-nine percent sure of the doctor—whether it be for an appendectomy or tonsillectomy, or whatever it might be—you can't win, because if the operation is a tremendous success, they accept it, and if it wasn't they blame you, so what do you win? You can't mix in things that you shouldn't mix up in. What bothered me was, somewhere along the line, too many people mixed in, and he didn't get the proper advice."

*Too many people.* It was the new way of the world in the NBA. Privately, Auerbach felt that the Lewis episode would not have ended in tragedy if it had happened on his watch. Things were different in the old days. Walter Brown was not beholden to lawyers and stockholders. The three employees in the Celtic front office in 1950 would have taken a family, hands-on approach with a player whose career was threatened by a heart problem. Had a Celtic physician told Coach Auerbach that a player could never play again, the player would have been told. Face-to-face. Man-to-man.

Was the Lewis death the low point in Auerbach's forty-four years with the Celtics?

"Yeah, that was the lowest, because he was already an established star and a great kid," says Auerbach. "The Lenny Bias thing was something we never had anyway. As great as he would have been, it's all supposition and conjecture. Lewis was just a baby. He had so much strength, so much confidence. I loved watching that guy play. And he was so young. I thought the pain we had with Len Bias was enough for a whole lifetime. This was the worst thing I have ever seen in this business."

Auerbach wasn't in Boston on the hot August Monday when the city laid Lewis to rest. Grieving was public and painful. It was a major event. Lewis's two-hour funeral service at Northeastern's Matthews Arena was telecast live by all three Boston network affiliates. Newspapers devoted special sections to the life and death of the young Celtic captain. As a public event, it was on the same scale as a papal visit or the death of a president. No one could remember anything quite like it.

"I wish I could go, I really do," Auerbach said a few days before the service. "But there's no way. I can only go out for an hour a day and I still have a nurse. I'd like to, but there really is no way."

After the funeral, the Celtics tried to put their house back in order. Gavitt, Volk and other team officials refused to comment on the events that had preceded Lewis's death. The organization said it would attempt to move forward. In Washington, Arnold Auerbach was attempting to do the same thing. There had been days after his surgery when he did not enjoy life, when he thought he was going to die. In midsummer, he started to get back to doing the things that make him happy.

Here's Auerbach explaining his daily routine:

"I get out of bed at around six, six-thirty. Take it easy. Read the paper. *USA Today* and the *Washington Post*. Shave and shower. I don't eat breakfast. I never drank coffee in my life. I've never eaten an egg in my life. I don't know whether that was based on the way it smelled or what. Sometimes now I have a little cold cereal. Years ago, it used to be a doughnut and a Coke.

"Then I go to my Sutton Place office at about eight. The drive

is about one or two minutes. I have a lot of mail and personal business to take care of. I talk to Dave Gavitt and Jan Volk. I stay there
until about ten-thirty and then three days a week I work out at
George Washington. I play a little racquetball. At my age, the hardest part is getting dressed and undressed. I don't play singles anymore. After the surgery, I just started hitting by myself. I still hate
to lose. A lot of it is ego. You don't like to lose to guys you used to
beat the shit out of. After racquetball, I'll schmooze, stay around a
while. Then I'll leave and go to Woodmont [Country Club], have
lunch, sit around and play cards [gin rummy]. I get home around
five and then we get ready for dinner. Sometimes we go out, sometimes we eat in. At night, I sit around and watch TV. I watch basketball games. A couple, usually. I usually turn in anywhere from
around midnight to one."

"He's one of the town's big gin rummy players," says Mo Siegel,
the man who began reporting on Red in 1946. "They play for high
stakes, and Red has no partners. It's a lot of retired guys. You have
to have a great memory to remember what cards have been played.
You have to be very observant. You know that word that's overused
in sports today—'focused'? Those gin games are more fucking focused than the games we watch on television.

"Those cardplayers don't give a shit who he is," says Rosensweig.
"They are well-known people. Seventy-, eighty-year-old men."

"He's an excellent gin player," says Cousy. "He taught me to play.
I'm a pretty good gin player only because I learned from him. He's
completely conservative and defensive."

Gavitt says, "You can't get him in the afternoon, unless you want
to drag him out of the card room at the club."

On a weekend in November 1993, the card game was interrupted
when it was learned that President Bill Clinton was stalking the links
at Woodmont.

"I said, 'Let's go see him,'" recalls Auerbach. "I went out on the
course. The Secret Service men were very unobtrusive. All of a sudden, this guy's riding up driving the cart. He was smiling and all that
stuff. A Secret Service agent came over to me and said, 'Would you
like to meet the president?' I said it would be my honor. So the
president walked from the other end of the green, a big green, all

the way across to come over to me and shake hands. We shook hands and I said, 'You know, you'd look good wearing this cap.' It was a dark green Celtic cap. I gave it to him and he fixed the size and he wore it. Then I walked away. I hate it when people try to be funny and familiar in just ten seconds. I'm not one of these guys who sucks around."

He was getting back to normal: meeting presidents, watching games and smoking two cigars a day—and, on occasion, sneaking a third.

"He's funny," says Larry Bird. "He says to me, 'I get two cigars a day. Should I have one after lunch and one after supper? I always like one in the morning. How in the hell are they gonna know if I have two or three a day?' And I just said, 'Red, you're missing the whole point. They think you should just have two because you shouldn't be smoking. I think if you want to smoke twenty you should smoke twenty. Jesus, you're seventy-six years old.' "

Cards, cigars, exercise, movies, "Jeopardy!": After the heart scare, these pleasures became as important as winning basketball games. Auerbach finally was enjoying his daughters and granddaughter. The slow pace agreed with him. He had beaten death. He was willing to make some concessions to age.

"I never had a heart attack," he says. "Was I scared? Oh sure. Damn right. After it was over, I did nothing. I just wanted to get well. The doctor didn't put me on any diet because my cholesterol is always low anyway. Time is the most important thing. You get to the point where you really don't want to fight crowds. To go to a ball game in Washington and you got to park way the hell away, then you got to walk down the stairs and up the stairs. I don't feel up to it . . . But as long as I've got my marbles pretty good, I'll still have input."

Gavitt: "My own thought is that Red understands very well that when you get older like he is, if you don't stay active like he is, if you don't stay vital, things are going to change fast for you, and that's why he doesn't want to retire. The word 'retire' is not in his vocabulary."

Although not officially retired, he is less involved than ever. When the Celtics convened at Brandeis for their annual Media Day in October, Auerbach admitted, "I don't know who half of these guys in uniform are."

The New York Knicks opened their 1993–1994 season on November 5 at the Boston Garden. It was the beginning of the forty-eighth season of the NBA, and it matched the only 1946 Basketball Association of America franchises still playing in their original cities. The 1993–1994 Knicks were coached by Pat Riley, the former head coach of the Lakers and the man who wrote a book (*Showtime*) that roasted Auerbach and the Celtics. Riley is an X-and-O coach, a tireless worker and one who might be accused of overcoaching. Auerbach, ever the big-picture guy, never liked blackboard coaches or those who kept coaching after the game was won. *Sports Illustrated* recently made Riley coach of its mythical all-time NBA team. In 1996, when the league names its golden anniversary team, Riley will be Auerbach's only competition for all-time coach.

On the weekend of the 1993–1994 NBA opener, the sports section of the national edition of the *New York Times* ran a story headlined, "Tales From Auerbach's Crypt as Season Opens." The story was spiced with delightful episodes of inconveniences endured in Boston by Riley. "I've never shot around at the Garden, not in twelve years," said Riley. "Our floor is always available to them. But don't get me started . . . You could accuse me of being paranoid. But it isn't just me, it's the whole league."

The story, written by Harvey Araton (coauthor of *The Selling of the Green*), concluded, "The Celtics aren't very good. They can't touch Riley anymore. Or can they?"

Auerbach says, "Riley was kissing ass with Harvey Araton, the guy who wrote that horrendous book which I wouldn't read and I don't ever want to read. But it made me wonder—why would a guy like Riley make statements like that when he doesn't know? We don't practice in this building nearly as much as they practice at Madison Square Garden. If we had shot around that day and refused them, then he's got a point. But we weren't there, either. They should know by now. I didn't have a thing to do with it."

The Knicks beat the Celtics by three points in Boston's home opener. It was the first time the Celtics had lost a Garden opener since 1978—the year before Bird came on board. Auerbach watched all the action from his customary seat in Loge 1, but he never once stood to holler at the refs.

After the game, he shuffled across the Garden parquet (shoulders hunched, head down, torso tilted forward) and made his way to the locker room door. He was accompanied by about ten men in suits, including owners Don Gaston and Alan Cohen, chairman of the board Paul Gaston (Don Gaston's son), CEO Dave Gavitt, GM Jan Volk, vice chairman Stephen C. Schram and another three or four well-heeled men who probably could have filled a thimble with their aggregate basketball knowledge. This is what the Celtics had become—a corporation, a lineup of wealthy men who'd attached themselves to the glory that Auerbach built in Boston.

It was somewhat pathetic to see Auerbach forced to schmooze with Paul Gaston, who'd just been anointed chairman of the board. Paul Gaston is young, impeccably dressed and no doubt very bright. But what could he know about the glory of Red Auerbach's time? What could he know about Sheboygan, 1949? What could he have known about the lonesome forward? In the old days, Auerbach had to humor the likes of Marvin Kratter, Bob Schmertz and John Y. Brown. Now he was pretending to exchange ideas with the silver-spooned sons of the owners.

"This happens in all businesses," he says. "I don't have to do much of it anymore. I just do what's best for the ball club. I'll say this: In all honesty they [Gaston, Cohen and Dupee] have been good. The only thing that I object to is too many people involved in decisions and you can't maneuver quick enough. Sure, it stops you from making mistakes and doing things in the heat of passion. But if Seattle wants to make a deal, they got a president and a coach. Here you got to have six people to agree on the talent of this guy. By that time, he's gone, you've lost him. It's like everything else. Football used to have three assistant coaches and they got twelve now. Basically, you lose the point. The object is to take the ball and stick it in a hole. Now how many people have to tell you to do that? Or how?"

After the loss to the Knicks, Auerbach came out of the locker room behind the men in suits, looked over toward a pack of writers who were interviewing coach Chris Ford and said, "Well, at least we tried."

It was very un-Red-like. He'd made a career out of being a poor sport, one who cared only about winning. Now he sounded like he'd been neutered. Had the scare of death made him stop to smell the roses? The old Auerbach never would have shrugged and said, "We tried." But this was not the old Auerbach; it was an Auerbach who'd gotten old. Even in his own building, he was seen as something of a prop, a living, breathing statue—a cardboard cutout in Loge 1.

Nobody expected the Celtics to be very good in their forty-eighth season. Newspaper reviews of the Celts invariably were spiced with the description "once-proud." Around the league, the Boston team was viewed as conservative, unwilling to take risks. It was going to take some rebuilding, but the rules had changed since Auerbach had last rebuilt. New Jersey Net coach Chuck Daly observes, "You can't do it the way the Celtics used to do it. Back then, there were a lot of franchises that weren't being run very well. They could take advantage of other people's mistakes."

Gavitt says, "We do not believe we are a lottery team, and the day we accept that, we are not the Boston Celtics anymore . . . So now people are telling us that we won't be any good this year, but you never know until you play the games."

Auerbach adds, "When you lose a Reggie Lewis, you don't lose him for just a year, you lose him for five or six years. When you lose a Bias, you lost him for ten, twelve years. At the same time, a great player like Kevin McHale retires. And within the space of a year and a half, you lose Larry Bird. At the same time, Robert Parish is a year older. I mean, how unlucky can you be? We've had as many bad breaks as we can possibly have."

Does Auerbach think the Celtics are cursed?

"No," he says. "Sometimes things work in cycles, but when you're in sports, you've got to be philosophical of knowing you're going to have your ups and downs. It happens to everybody if you're in it long enough. Like when Sam Jones and Russell both retired at the same time. I didn't think they were going to retire, but it happened.

"It's just that it's harder to come back now. It's harder from the standpoint of making deals. You can't make deals today. Some are made, but very seldom, because of the cap and other things. Plus the fact that you can't find any sleepers. Everybody's got so many scouts. Right now, I know of a real great player who's going to be great. A high school kid. And they know about him. They got scouts now and coaches that go to Africa. They have tournaments and games in Europe, Australia, everyplace. It's much more difficult to-day than it was when we rebuilt the team after Cowens quit, after Russell quit. It's harder now, I have to admit that."

It's not like picking up the phone and asking Bones McKinney if they have any good players south of the Mason-Dixon line.

In 1993–1994, teams looked forward to beating Boston. The Knicks and Hornets both came into the Garden and won in Novem-ber. The Miami Heat in December beat the Celtics by thirty-one points. In midwinter, Boston lost a team record six straight home games. They went zero for February and lost a team record thirteen straight games. It was the worst Celtic team since the Bob McAdoo–Curtis Rowe edition in 1978–1979. Charlotte's Eddie Johnson, a thirteen-year NBA veteran, says "You never feel sorry for a team that's been successful. With Boston, I always hope they go 0–82. It's not that I dislike their players. But everyone in the league had to live with the fact they beat up on them for so long. They showed no mercy and embarrassed and sent me home every year of my career. I have no sympathy for them at all."

The board of governors seem to feel the same way. Boston was obligated to pay Lewis more than $3 million per year, but the Celtics believed it would be fair if at least a part of Lewis's salary did not count toward the salary cap. The Celtics asked for an exemption. Boston's proposal was shot down with almost no discussion.

Auerbach, clearly starting to feel strong again, says, "After what we've done with the league for so many years, this is their chance to get even. It's 'the heck with the Green, down with the Green,' that type of thing. Whatever we asked for, I didn't think we had a chance. It's jealousy. It's something that they were dreaming about. I think what they should have done was let us use the money we would have paid Reggie to get another player. But they were very cold on the whole thing.

"Years ago, when Walter Brown owned the team, the Knicks were horrible and we gave them another couple of draft choices to bring up the parity of the league. Today, it's a different breed. Many owners, years ago, had the league as the important thing. Today, they don't think that way. All they think about is 'What's good for me?' I told Walter—'God forbid we ever get in that position, nobody will help us, Walter, believe me.' "

The 1993–1994 NBA would have been unrecognizable to Walter Brown. The Hornets signed two-year "veteran" Larry Johnson to a twelve-year, $84 million contract. Draftees who had yet to score a point were signing long-term contracts worth tens of millions of dollars. New Jersey's Derrick Coleman turned down a multiyear offer of $69 million because he figured there would be a better deal if he waited.

Auerbach looks around and says, "It's the most ridiculous thing ever. I've been around professional basketball since the day it started in 1946 and I've never seen anything worse than this. It does not make any sense at all. It's just way out of whack—signing guys for six, eight, ten, twelve years and guaranteeing them sixty million, eighty million. I don't know where it's going. It's crazy. It can't survive if it continues. It can't continue to do what it's doing. The players association thinks short-term. They don't worry about the success of the league. They want more."

At the start of the 1994–1995 season—the final season of the old Boston Garden—Auerbach will be seventy-seven years old. He remains the only survivor from the first days of the league. He says it makes him feel old. There is satisfaction in seeing the prosperity of the league. It affirms the instincts that guided him to quit teaching and go coach the Washington Capitols when he was twenty-eight years old in June 1946.

"I envisioned a definite success because of what was happening in Madison Square Garden with the colleges," he says. "The popularity of the game had to increase, because the game was inexpensive to produce and you have a free minor league system with the colleges. You had a lot of things going for you. I always was of the feeling that the most important thing in running a franchise is the product. Marketing, media, publicity—all that is fine, but the most important thing is who you put on the court, and that's where I was most vitally concerned, and I still am."

No longer the snake oil salesman, no longer hooting on the referees, his presence still counts.

"The players we have now may not know him the way we did, but he still has that effect," says Dennis Johnson, now an assistant coach for the Celtics. "When you're out there practicing, running up and down the floor, all of a sudden the door opens and you smell the cigar. Everything snaps into place. They're like little kids jumping to attention. 'Hut, hut.' That's the type of presence he has. The level of play changes when they smell cigar smoke . . . When someone makes a crack at me like, 'You're a little older now, and we don't do things like that anymore,' I say to them, 'Well, why don't you take a look up there [at the championship banners], because they don't do too many things like that anymore.' "

Former Net coach Chuck Daly says, "His presence is always felt by me. I always know exactly where he is. I usually don't watch anyone in the stands, but he's that kind of figure. I watch him. I'm curious to watch him react to things that happen. I look up there any number of times during our games."

M. L. Carr, who replaced Gavitt as Celtic GM in June 1994, says, "Red has done so many great deals and he's pulled off the fast one so many times. When he's there you feel like, 'Red is still around. The system still works.' Despite the salary cap, free agency and all that, you think he's still going to pull one more big one off before the end of the day. Just seeing him is a comfort. You don't need your dad to do anything other than see him come home from work. You don't need him to fight your battles. But, boy, if he's over there watching you, it really feels good. You feel like everything will be okay if Dad's around."

"Celtic pride" and "Celtic mystique" are sports clichés for two generations of fans. Auerbach is the living, breathing pride. He is the mystique. Cousy, the first Celtic superstar, a man who came to Boston with Auerbach in 1950, says, "I think from time to time when everyone tries to think about what the Celtic mystique is, we should just point to Arnold. He personifies what Celtic mystique means. When he steps down, and ceases to play any part in the organization,

I think the unit will be more susceptible to what happens to other teams."

It is finally happening. As Auerbach fades from the picture, so do the Celtics. Perhaps it is a circumstance of timing, or just the competitiveness of a twenty-seven-team league, but when Auerbach was down with heart problems in 1993—when he missed the first draft since coming to the Celtics—the franchise fell to its most hopeless state since the days before he came to Boston. As it looks ahead to 1994–1995 and the rest of this century, Auerbach and Celtic pride are about the past. Sixteen banners flutter above the famous parquet floor. Eighteen Celtic players have had their numbers retired, and Auerbach's footprint is on the seat of each player's shorts.

Like J. D. Salinger collecting royalties for *The Catcher in the Rye*, Auerbach's forever reaping benefits of deeds done thirty years ago. Every few years, there's another testimonial for an ex-coach who hasn't picked up a technical foul since 1966. The nonstop adulation is almost embarrassing. This is what it's still like for Joe DiMaggio in New York. Auerbach created the legacy, and his star has never dimmed.

When Auerbach was honored with a seventy-fifth birthday bash at the Westin Hotel in downtown Boston on October 3, 1992, Jack Nicholson delivered this video message:

"Well, Red, I guess you're having a great time sitting there listening to what all these people are saying about you, and I agree with 'em. I think you deserve it. The NBA has been our main source of entertainment around here since I was a kid and we couldn't even get it on radio. And I feel close to you, Red. Over those years I think that we have something in common in that in some places we've become the man they love to hate. You talk to people a lot about life with your organization. Celtic pride. Loyalty. And how to peddle snake oil. Red, I think you're on a winning streak. Seventy-five in a row. Light up that cigar. We love ya."

U.S. Senator Bill Bradley, a member of the championship New York Knicks of the early seventies, submitted this salutation: "I was never a Celtic. I hated the Celtics. But I liked John Havlicek and Dave Cowens and Bill Russell and Jo Jo White and Don Chaney

and Don Nelson. I liked the players as people and most of all, Red,
I like you. I really appreciate everything you did for me when I was
in college. You were a true resource. You're a giant in the game of
basketball."

Bird said, "Red always made you feel like you was part of the
family. If you was around here for a period of time, he always made
you feel like you was welcome. He always treated everyone fairly,
and that's what made it so special."

Auerbach was the last to speak:

"In this life, you've got to be lucky. I was lucky first of all in
having the right wife. We've been married for fifty-one years. Anyone that can put up with me for fifty-one years deserves the medal
of honor. I respected her decisions. I think she was more influential
in my staying here than any group of people, even the fans of Boston.
When I talk about luck, I owe it all to these athletes. They're the
guys that did it. I don't remember scoring a point. Bill Russell was
a great, great influence. I could go on and on. Cooz, Heinsohn,
Havlicek, Cowens, Nelson. My only regret is that I never coached
Larry Bird, Chief [Robert Parish] and McHale. I would have liked
that, because I think they got it too easy today. We used to come
to practice with gym bags; today they come to practice with attaché
cases. We had a family. We'd go to movies together. We'd do all
those things. Today, it's a different world. People ask me could I
coach today. I say yes, because people are people. But one thing
I did, and I still do today, I respect the minds of these athletes. I
listen to them. I talk to them. They have good input, especially as
they get older. They're all college people. They've got good minds.
If you don't listen to them you have too much ego, you don't have
humility and you don't get the job done. There's no substitute for
winning. Remember that. That's where it's at. Winning."

# SOURCE LIST

Araton, Harvey, and Filip Bondy. *The Selling of the Green*. New York: HarperCollins, 1991.

Auerbach, Arnold "Red." *Basketball for the Player, the Fan and the Coach*. New York: Simon & Schuster, 1952.

Auerbach, Arnold "Red," and Ken Dooley. *MBA-Management by Auerbach*. New York: Macmillan, 1991.

Auerbach, Arnold "Red," and Joe Fitzgerald. *On & Off the Court*. New York: Macmillan, 1985.

Auerbach, Arnold "Red," and Joe Fitzgerald. *Red Auerbach, an Autobiography*. New York: G. P. Putnam's Sons, 1977.

Auerbach, Arnold "Red," and Paul Sann. *Red Auerbach: Winning the Hard Way*. Boston: Little, Brown, 1966.

Bird, Larry. *Drive*. New York: Doubleday, 1989.

*Boston Globe* newspaper articles, 1950–93.

*Boston Herald* newspaper articles, 1950–93.

*Boston Traveler* newspaper articles, 1950.

Cousy, Bob, and Bob Ryan. *Cousy on the Celtic Mystique*. New York: McGraw-Hill, 1988.

George, Nelson. *Elevating the Game*. New York: HarperCollins, 1992.

Goodman, Irv. "Hothead on the Boston Bench," *Sport*, February 1956.

Goodman, Irv. "The Winning Ways of Red Auerbach," *Sport*, March 1965.

Greenfield, Jeff. *The World's Greatest Team*. New York: Random House, 1976.

Halberstam, David. *The Breaks of the Game*. New York: Alfred A. Knopf, 1981.

Halberstam, David. *The Fifties*. New York: Villard Books, 1993.

Havlicek, John, and Bob Ryan. *Hondo: Celtic Man in Motion*. Englewood Cliffs, New Jersey: Prentice Hall, 1976.

Heinsohn, Tommy, and Joe Fitzgerald. *Give 'Em the Hook*. New York: Prentice Hall, 1988.

May, Peter. *The Big Three*. New York: Simon & Schuster, 1993.

McCallum, Jack. *Unfinished Business*. New York: Summit Books, 1992.

Pluto, Terry. *Tall Tales*. New York: Simon & Schuster, 1992.

Powers, John. *The Short Season*. New York: Harper & Row, 1979.

Riley, Pat. *Showtime*. New York: Warner Books, 1988.

Russell, Bill. *Go Up for Glory*. New York: Medallion Books, 1966.

Russell, Bill, and Taylor Branch. *Second Wind*. New York: Random House, 1979.

Salzberg, Charles. *From Set Shot to Slam Dunk*. New York: E. P. Dutton, 1987.

Shapiro, Leonard. *Big Man on Campus*. New York: Henry Holt, 1991.

Shaughnessy, Dan. *Ever Green*. New York: St. Martin's Press, 1990.

Strom, Earl. *Calling the Shots*. New York: Simon & Schuster, 1990.

Sullivan, George. *The Picture History of the Boston Celtics*. Indianapolis/New York: The Bobbs-Merrill Company, 1981.

# Index